Dmitry Efrosinin

Controlled Queueing Systems with Heterogeneous Servers

Dmitry Efrosinin

Controlled Queueing Systems with Heterogeneous Servers

Dynamic Optimization and Monotonicity
Properties of Optimal Control Policies in
Multiserver Heterogeneous Queues

VDM Verlag Dr. Müller

Imprint

Bibliographic information by the German National Library: The German National Library lists this publication at the German National Bibliography; detailed bibliographic information is available on the Internet at http://dnb.d-nb.de.

Cover image: www.purestockx.com

Publisher:
VDM Verlag Dr. Müller Aktiengesellschaft & Co. KG , Dudweiler Landstr. 125 a, 66123 Saarbrücken, Germany,
Phone +49 681 9100-698, Fax +49 681 9100-988,
Email: info@vdm-verlag.de

Zugl.: Trier, University Trier, Diss., 2004

Produced in USA and UK by:
Lightning Source Inc., La Vergne, Tennessee, USA
Lightning Source UK Ltd., Milton Keynes, UK
BookSurge LLC, 5341 Dorchester Road, Suite 16, North Charleston, SC 29418, USA

ISBN: 978-3-639-02809-6

Contents

Chapter 1

Introduction

1.1 Queues and dynamic control

Many real-life phenomena, such as computer systems, communication networks, manufacturing systems, supermarket checkout lines as well as structural military systems can be represented by means of queueing models. Queueing systems take their origin in the study of design problems for automatic telephone exchange, and were first analyzed by A.K. Erlang in the early 1900s. At that time, in designing telephone systems one main problem with respect to performance criteria was to determine how many lines had to be supplied in order to guarantee a certain grade of service. Similar questions arise in many other cases, e.g. when asking for the maximum number of terminals in a computer system that tolerates keeping the message loss probability below a prespecified level, or when looking at the impact of service speed on waiting lines, and so on. In order to satisfy the people's demands for quality of service (QoS) it is impossible, due to economic aspects, to simply increase resources without limits. In essence, the question that queueing theory faces in practice is how to find a balance between improvement of (QoS) and acceptance economic overhead, i.e. to find the right trade-off between a gain in quality, that is achievable by supplying more resources, and the corresponding economic loss.

By studying mathematical models that reveal the probabilistic nature of real systems, queueing theory has succeeded to obtain many analytical and numerical results for the key-quantities which characterize the *performance behavior of systems*. Such key quantities are, for example, queue length and waiting time distributions, loss probabilities, mean values of sojourn times and throughput, etc.

In classical queueing theory, the corresponding models do not incorporate facilities (controllers) that allow to pursue different strategies, possibly based upon state depending decisions. This is in spite of the fact that man made real systems usually have to be dynamically controlled during operation. Looking at queueing models, a controller may considerably improve the system's performance by reducing queue lengths, or increasing the throughput, or diminishing the overhead, whereas in the absence of a controller the system behavior may get quite erratic, exhibiting periods of high load and long queues followed by periods, during which the servers remain idle. Control is performed by adequate actions that can be described in mathematical terms and can be subjected to the determination of optimal control strategies. Thus, by incorporating such aspects into queueing theory, its field is broadened and may be classified as a branch of optimization theory. As such it forms the area of interest and the subject of the present book.

The theoretical foundations of *controlled queueing systems* are led in the theory of Markov, semi-Markov and semi-regenerative decision processes [31, 39, 49, 57, 58, 61, 64, 70].

Figure 1.1

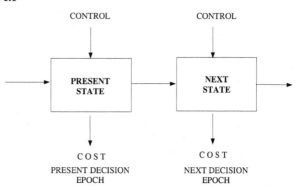

Bellman, in the early 1950s, was one of the first who investigated decision processes and developed computational methods for analyzing sequential deci-

sion processes with finite planning horizon. His ideas have been generalized by
Howard (1960), who used elements from Markov chain theory and dynamic programming to develop a policy-iteration algorithm that provides the solution of
sequential probabilistic decision processes with infinite planning horizon.

A typical sequential decision making model can symbolically be represented
in Figure 1.1. At a specified point of time, which we refer to as *present decision
epoch*, a decision maker or controller observes the state of a system. Based on this
state, the controller chooses a control (performs a decision). The control choice
produces two results: the controller losses an immediate cost, and the system, according to a probability distribution determined by the chosen control, evolves to
a new state at the subsequent point of time, termed the *next decision epoch*. At
the next decision epoch, the controller faces a similar situation. Different states, in
general, determine different sets of possible controls. As such a process evolves in
time, the controller incurs a sequence of costs or, as in sometimes said, a sequence
of *negative rewards*.

The key components of such a *sequential decision model* are the following

- A set of decision epochs

- A set E of system states

- A set A of available controls

- A set of state and control dependent immediate costs

- A set of state and control dependent transition probabilities

All these sets are assumed to be known to the controller at any decision epoch.

Definition 1.2 *A* **strategy** *is a prescription telling the controller out of which
(state depending) set of controls a choice has to be made at any future time epoch.*

Definition 1.3 *A* **policy** *specifies the control to be chosen at a particular point in
time.*

A policy may depend on the present state alone, or on that state and all previous states and controls. A strategy is a sequence of policies. Implementing a
strategy generates a sequence of incurred costs. Thus the control problem consists in the task to choose, prior to the first decision epoch, an "optimal" strategy

that minimizes some certain function of the cost sequence. There are many functions that may be considered suitable for classifying optimum system behaviour. Most common examples are the *expected total discounted cost function* and the *long-run average cost function*. In the present work we confine ourselves to the optimality criterion of minimal *long-run average cost per unit of time*.

Remark 1.4 *The average cost represents an adequate criterion in case that only long-run characteristics of the system are of interest and all short-term effects caused by initial conditions can be neglected.*

In parallel with discounting, computing average cost functions is a natural and popular way of comparing strategies over an infinite horizon. While the aim of discounting is to substitute divergent sequences of total expected costs over finite-horizons for a convergent series, the concept of average cost function consists in measuring and comparing the average speed of growth of those sequences. For most applications of sequential decision models the latter criterion is believed to be more appropriate than the alternative criterion of total expected discounted costs. The average cost criterion is particularly appealing when investigating systems with high transition rates, i.e. those where many state transitions occur within a relatively short time intervals. This is typical, for example, in the case of stochastic control problems in telecommunication applications.

The long-run average cost criterion will be specified in this book for controlled queueing systems. Whereas the foundations of general probabilistic sequential decision making process (also with respect to the average cost criterion) are well known and available in literature [39, 58, 75, 76], controlled queueing systems have been rarely treated and do not, in general, allow a complete mathematical solution.

In present research the dynamic programming analysis are based on the following assumptions:

1. The set of decision epochs is infinite (so called *infinite planning horizon*).

2. The system under consideration is observed at equidistant points in time.

3. The set E of system states is finite.

4. For each system state $x \in E$ a finite set $A(x)$ of controls or decisions is given.

The assumptions of a finite state space is not a strong restriction in case of light traffic models and does not restrict generality at all for models with finite buffer space, that will be considered here.

If the control policies at any state $x \in E$ depend on the total history, the optimization task usually becomes quite complicated. A simplification can consist in trying to limit the search space of possible policies by showing that an optimal policy always belongs to only a small subclass of certain structured policies. Unfortunately, this can be proved rigorously under very restrictive model assumption, only.

A main important goal in the theory of decision processes consist in establishing a Markov property for optimal strategies, for this opens the possibility to construct an optimal strategy using numerical methods. In case of an infinite planning horizon and history-independent policies it is natural to consider so-called *stationary* policies:

A *stationary policy* δ is a rule that always prescribes the same single action $a \in A(x)$ whenever the system stays in state x at the decision epoch.

Optimal stationary policies have been investigated by Lippman [43], who achieved most of the results available so far on the existence of optimal stationary policies for fairly general systems.

Now we introduce a Markov decision model. Let the system is observed continuously. To model the system behaviour consider the process $\{Z(t)\} = \{X(t), U(t)\}$. The observed process $\{X(t)\}_{t \geq 0}$ denotes the system state at time t. As a controlling process consider the process $\{U(t)\}_{t \geq 0}$, where $U(t)$ is a decision which should be taken at the nearest to t control time. Let A be the set of available controls and $A(x)$ be the set of admissible controls when the system state is x. Suppose at a certain instant t, the system state $X(t) = x$. Then the controller chooses an admissible control $U(t) = a \in A(x)$. For each state $x \in E$, a set $A(x)$ of decisions or actions is given. The state space E and the actions $A(x)$ are assumed to be *finite*. The controlled dynamic system is called a *Markov decision model* when the following Markovian property is satisfied. If at a decision epoch the action a is chosen in state x to go to the state y after the time period of duration h, then regardless of the past history of the system, the following happens:

(a) An immediate cost $c(x)h$ is incurred.

(b) At the next decision epoch the system will be in state y with probability

$$\mathbf{P}\{X(t+h) = y | X(t) = x, U(t) = a \in A(x)\} = \begin{cases} 1 + \lambda_{xx}(a)h + o(h), & \text{if } y = x, \\ \lambda_{xy}(a)h + o(h), & \text{if } y \neq x, \end{cases}$$

$\lambda_{xy}(a) \geq 0$, $(y \neq x)$, $\lambda_{xx}(a) = -\sum_{y \in E} \lambda_{xy}(a)$. $\lambda_{xy}(a)$ are the transition intensities of the process $\{Z(t)\}$. Note that the costs $c(x)$ and the transition intensities

λ_{xy} are assumed to be time homogeneous.

Often an optimization problem for controlled queueing systems is easier to handle when formulated as a discrete time problem rather than a continuous time problem, since in that case recursive methods can be applied. In this case a continuous time system is transformed to its discrete equivalent by sampling relevant data — including all relevant arrivals and departures — according to a constant rate Poisson process. The procedure of converting a continuous-time problem into a discrete-time problem is well established and readily available in the literature, see Lippman [42], Rosberg, Varaiya, Walrand [63] and Serfozo [71]. It has been shown, that the corresponding discrete- and continuous-time problems are equivalent in so far as the resulting optimal policies for infinite-horizon cost criteria coincide.

The controlled queueing systems presented in this book can be modelled as Markov decision processes due to appropriate choices for the state spaces and control sets. We focus on the investigation of quantitative and qualitative properties of optimal strategies, determining monotonicity conditions for optimal policies, describing the structure of an optimal control rule, and elaborating algorithmic aspects of numerical analysis.

1.2   Queueing system with heterogeneous servers.

The theory of controlled queueing systems have been developed for optimal control of admission, service, routing and scheduling of jobs in queues, and networks of queues [35, 65, 73, 74, 76]. With respect to the number of servers and their types, the controlled problems can be different. The notion of controlled queueing system allows to discriminate between systems with different controlling mechanism, e.g. the systems with controlled service order, with controlled order of server occupation, with controlled regime of server operation and so on.

In a single-server queueing system a control may consist in varying the service modes (see [18, 56]); examples of corresponding admission control problems are given in ([3, 19]). Controlled multi-server stations for the case of identical servers are further considered in [14, 68].

Here we consider a number of queueing models that have been proved to be useful for analyzing a wide variety of real systems. The discussion is restricted to stations with several heterogeneous servers in front of one common queue, and the control is applied exclusively to the scheduling scheme. Systems of that type are composed of three components: the queue, several heterogeneous servers, and the controller. The controller, at any decision epoch, allocates the customers to the servers according to the observed optimality criterion. We provide a literature review, from time to time, for any of the investigated queueing problems in the relevant sections.

For the description of queueing systems we make use of Kendall's original notation in form of a four-tuple $a/b/c/d$: The first symbol, a, specifies the inter-arrival time distribution, the second symbol, b, specifies the service-time distribution, the third, c, gives the number of servers and the fourth, d, the number of available buffer places. Jobs are assumed to arrive and to be served one by one. Examples are $(K \leq B < \infty)$

1. $M/M/K/B$: Poisson (Markovian) input, *exponential service-time distribution*, K servers and B buffer places.

2. $M/PH/K/B$: Same as above with the exception, that the service time is *phase-type distributed*, i.e. represents a finite sum or a finite mixture of exponentially distributed components, or a combination of both.

3. $MAP/M/K/B$: *Markov additive arrival process*, exponential service time distribution, K servers and B buffer places.

4. $MAP/PH/K/B$: A combination of the previous two models.

In this book we consider system of types $M/M/K/B$ or $MAP/PH/K/B$ and investigate some special cases.

Queueing systems with heterogeneous servers are of increasing importance in many engineering areas, such as telecommunication and computer systems. Considering telecommunication systems, service facilities (e.g. transmission lines) can be switched on and off, or may break down and have to be replaced. Associated with operation of the servers are certain costs, which are determined by the offered speed of service, the duration of holding times, and the number of waiting jobs (messages). Since usually, based on dynamic routing algorithms [30, 34], there exist different choices for alternative links (network paths), the network providers are confronted with control problems of the type that is addressed in this book.

The construction of an optimal control policy, even in the simplest case of Markov model, usually requires a huge amount of work for the computing machinery. Thus, there is an increasing interest in disclosing qualitative properties of control policies that offer the possibility to reduce computing investments and overhead. Monotonicity properties of optimal control functions are characteristics of that type that simpler algorithms to be developed.

In the following subsection we outline the necessary theoretical background for describing monotonicity properties of optimal control policies.

1.3   Monotonicity properties of optimal solutions

In discrete optimization the investigation of monotonicity properties of a solution can be based on the theory of submodular (supermodular) functions [2, 23, 77]. Recent results on that topic (including even more general models) have been presented by Glasserman and Yao [24], and — addressing controlled queueing systems — by Rykov, Stidham and Weber [66, 73, 74]. The special case of hysteretic optimal policies has been discussed in 1984 by Lu and Servozo [44] and in 1988 by Hipp and Holzbaur [26]. We refer to all these previous results when introducing below some notations and essential statements.

Consider a controlled queueing system with heterogeneous servers. The corresponding optimization problem consists in the task to find an optimal control policy such that the state and control depending cost function $b(x; a)$ is minimized for all trajectories:

$$b(x; a) \Rightarrow \min_{a \in A(x)} \text{ for all trajectory values } x \in E. \tag{1.1}$$

$b(x; a)$ is defined on a subset G of the direct product of the state and the control space: $G \subset E \times A$. $x \in E$ and $a \in A$ are discrete variables. The sets $A(x)$ of possible local controls may differ for different states $x \in E$. $A(x)$ represents the partial projection of G to x. The object function $b(x; a)$, which shall be referred to as the *Bellman function*, is defined according to the formulation of the problem, the optimization criterion and other specific properties of the model under study. By virtue of the non-uniqueness of the possible solutions, the problem of discrete minimization consists in determining the family of all optimal control sets $A^*(x)$, $x \in E$, and any of the *control functions* $f(x) \in A^*(x)$, defined by

$$A^*(x) = \{a \in A(x) : b(x; a) = v(x)\},$$
$$f(x) = \mathrm{argmin}\{b(x; a) : a \in A(x)\} \in A^*(x),$$

where

$$v(x) = \min\{b(x; a) : a \in A(x)\}.$$

$v(x)$ is called the *value function*. In order to formulate conditions for monotonicity of a solution $f(x)$ it is necessary to endow the spaces E and A with a partial-order structure. The following is well known.

Definition 1.5 *A set E is called partially ordered iff there is a binary relation "$\leq$" (or "$\geq$") that is*
   (a) reflexive: $x \leq x$;
   (b) antisymmetric: $(x \leq y \wedge y \leq x) \;\Rightarrow\; x = y$;
   (c) transitive: $(x \leq y \wedge y \leq z) \;\Rightarrow\; x \leq z$.

As usual, $x < y$ is written for $(x \leq y \wedge x \neq y)$. Two elements x, $y \in E$ are termed unordered or non-comparable if neither $x \leq y$ nor $y \leq x$. A partial-ordered set is completely ordered if it does not contain any unordered pair of elements.

The controlled queueing systems under consideration are characterized by the fact that the state space E is multidimensional and partially ordered, whereas the finite set A of controls is isomorphic to some subset N_A of the set $I\!N_0$ of non-negative integers and, consequently, can be regarded as completely ordered. To be more precise, we define a bijection $i \,:\, A \rightarrow N_A = \{1, 2, ..., |A|\}$, and identify the order in A with that of N_A. A typical system state may be of the form $x = (q, d_1, \ldots, d_K)$, where q is an integer describing the number of jobs waiting in the queue, and $d_k \in \{0, 1\}$ indicates whether or not server k is occupied or free $(k = 1, \ldots, K)$. In E, a partial ordering is induced with reference to reachability of states upon performing a control action.

The system dynamics, in the majority of cases, can be described in terms of a family of shift operators, denoted by $\{S_\nu\}_{\nu \in I\!N_0}$ and Θ. At some decision epoch T_n the operator S_ν shifts a state $x \in E$ to another state $S_\nu x \in E$ under a control $a(x) \in A(x)$, where ν represents the number $i(a(x))$ of the control $a(x)$. Θ operates on the set A and indicates the change of control actions according to a change of policy.

The shift operators determine individual "directions" within a possible set of paths in the tree structures defined by the ordering (see Figure 1.6).

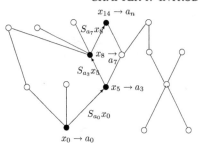

Figure 1.6

Their totality, therefore, constitutes what we call a *cone of order* in G.

Under these assumptions, the problem consists in finding conditions for the function $b(x; a)$ to be satisfied, and properties of its domain G, such that it is possible to determine some *monotonic* solution $f : E \rightarrow A$ (with value $A^*(x)$ at state $x \in E$) of the discrete minimization problem, where monotonicity may be achievable in one or more directions.

In the majority of applications the order on the set of system states admits variations, too. As a consequence, the problem may be re-formulated in more general terms as follows: Determine ordering relationships on E and on A, such that the optimal solution function is monotonic with respect to these orderings. [1]

To provide a connection between the possible orderings in $G = E \times A$ and monotonicity properties of the solutions, we make use of the notation of a *monotonic family of sets* along some fixed direction S.

Definition 1.7 *The family $\mathcal{A}$ of sets $A(x)$, $x \in E$, is called a* **monotonic family, increasing (decreasing) in the direction S** *(S-monotone family), iff for all $a' \in A(x), a'' \in A(Sx)$ the minimum $a' \wedge a''$ belongs to the set $A(x)$ $(A(Sx))$, and the maximum $a' \vee a''$ belongs to the set $A(Sx)$ $(A(x))$.*

The function $f(x)$ is called an **S-monotone increasing (decreasing)**, *if $f(Sx) \geq (\leq) f(x)$ for all $x \in E$.* The monotonicity of $f(x)$ is termed **strict**, if the latter condition holds for strict inequalities.

A **rectangle in direction S** (*S-rectangle*) is a family $\mathcal{A}_S \subset \mathcal{A}$ that does not vary

---

[1]In more general problem settings, ordering may be introduced separately in sets $A(x)$, $x \in E$, such that for an appropriate formulation of monotonicity it is necessary to define proper relationships between sets $A(x)$ in order to be able to discriminate with respect to monotonicity not only between controls inside any $A(x)$ but also between controls in different sets $A(x_1)$ and $A(x_2)$.

in direction S, i.e. $\mathcal{A}_S = \{A(S_n x) : A(S_n x) = A(x),\, n \in I\!N_0,\, x \in E\}$. Any rectangle in direction S is both, S-monotonic increasing and decreasing.

Clearly, there are examples of (non-monotonic) families of sets that do not admit the construction of a monotonic selector. on the other hand, if each of the sets $A(x)$ in an increasing (decreasing) family $\mathcal{A}$ contains only one element such that the mapping $x \mapsto A^*(x)$ is single-valued, then a monotonic selector function $f(x)$ is automatically defined.

A monotonic choice (although possibly not optimal) is always possible if $\mathcal{A} = \{A(x) : x \in E\}$ is monotonic. Indeed,

$$f^*(x) = \max\{a : a \in A^*(x)\} \qquad and \qquad f_*(x) = \min\{a : a \in A^*(x)\}$$

represent monotonic functions in case of an increasing (decreasing) monotonic family. As a consequence, the problem reduces to find those conditions related to the Bellman function $b(x; a)$ and its domain G, which provide monotonicity of the family of sets $\mathcal{A}^* = \{\mathcal{A}^*(x) : x \in E\}$ according to the chosen controls. In what follow we assume that the operators S_i and Θ shift points in the positive direction, i.e. $S_i x \geq x$, $\Theta a \geq a$.

Denote by $b_S(x; a)$, $b_\Theta(x; a)$ and $b_{S\Theta}(x; a)$ the following differences of first and second order:

$$b_S(x; a) = b(Sx; a) - b(x; a), \qquad b_\Theta(x; a) = b(x, \Theta a) - b(x; a),$$
$$b_{S\Theta}(x; a) = b(Sx; \Theta a) - b(Sx; a) - b(x; \Theta a) + b(x; a).$$

Obviously, each the two conditions

$$b_S(x; \Theta a) \leq (\geq) b_S(x; a), \qquad b_\Theta(Sx; a) \leq (\geq) b_\Theta(x; a) \qquad (1.2)$$

is equivalent to

$$b_{S\Theta}(x; a) \leq (\geq) 0. \qquad (1.3)$$

This allows to formulate, in short form, the monotonicity conditions for the solutions in terms of monotonicity conditions for the increments of the Bellman function. Let the boundary ∂G of $G = E \times A$ be defined as the set of those pairs (x, a) for which no successor exists with respect to the ordering. The inner kernel G^o is then defined as $G \setminus \partial G$.

Theorem 1.8 *Let the family of controls constitute an S-rectangle $\mathcal{A}_S$, i.e. $A(Sx) = A(x)$ for all $x \in E$. Then the following holds: Along any monotonic solution $f(x)$ in G^o of the minimization problem $b(x; a) \to$ min, conditions (1.2) and (1.3) are satisfied, either with sign "$\leq$" for an increasing solution or with sign "$\geq$" for a decreasing solution.*

Conversely, if any of the conditions (1.2) and (1.3) for the Bellman function is satisfied everywhere on its domain G, then the family of sets $\{A^*(x) : x \in E\}$, determining the solutions of the minimization problem, is S-monotonic, i.e. increasing, if the conditions are satisfied with sign "$\leq$", or decreasing, if they are satisfied with sign "$\geq$".

A dual assertion exists for the maximization problem.

Proof: To prove necessity, consider the case where the solution of the minimization problem increases: For $f(x) = a \in A(x)$, $f(Sx) = a' \in A(Sx)$, and $a \leq a'$. The controls $a \in A(Sx)$ and $a' \in A(x)$ exist by virtue of the invariance of A under any shift operator S. Due to the complete order induced on A, there is a k such that $a' = \Theta^k a > a$. Thus, the inequalities

$$b(x; a) \leq b(x; \Theta^k a) \qquad \text{and} \qquad b(Sx; \Theta^k a) \leq b(Sx; a)$$

are valid, and

$$b(x; a) - b(x; \Theta^k a) + b(Sx; \Theta^k a) - b(Sx; a) \leq 0.$$

By virtue of monotonicity,

$$0 \geq b(x; a) - b(x; \Theta^k a) + b(Sx; \Theta^k a) - b(Sx, a) = \sum_{0 \leq i \leq k-1} b_{S\Theta}(x; \Theta^i a),$$

and so, there exists $a \in A$ in the neighbourhood of the optimal solution $f(x)$ (i.e. directly reachable under Θ) such that $f(x) \leq a \leq f(Sx)$, and $b_{S\Theta}(x; a) \leq 0$.

Sufficiency follows from Theorem 1.11 and Lemma 1.10 below.
□

On the boundary ∂G of G each shift operator S_i can be defined as the identity operator. We note that in this case conditions (1.2) and (1.3) turn out to be necessary conditions for a minimum (maximum) to be attained on the boundary, but they do not provide the monotonicity of the solution. Rather, for the latter to obtain, it is necessary to impose additional constraints on the family of admissible controls. We call $G = E \times A$ *connected with respect to the set S of shifts S*, if for any pair (x, a_x), $(y, a_y) \in G$ there exists a sequence of shifts $S_\nu \in \mathcal{S}$, such that, when starting in (x, a_x), the successive application of the S_ν, $\nu = 1, 2, \ldots, k$, finally leads to $(S_k x_{k-1}, a_k) = (y, a_y)$.

The above mentioned conditions (1.2) and (1.3) do not "work" if G is not connected with respect to the set of shifts.

To provide monotonicity and connectivity conditions it is convenient to introduce a somewhat more general notation of submodular (supermodular) functions, which is equivalent to condition (1.2) and (1.3) for S-rectangles.

Definition 1.9 *The function $b(x; a)$ is called* **submodular in direction S** *(S - submodular) on an increasing family $\mathcal{A} = \{A(x) : x \in E\}$ iff for any pair $a' \in A(x)$, $a'' \in A(Sx)$ the inequality*

$$b_{S\Theta}(x; a) = b(Sx; a' \vee a'') - b(Sx; a'') - b(x; a') + b(x; a' \wedge a'') \leq 0 \quad (1.4)$$

is satisfied. $b(x; a)$ is called **supermodular in direction S** *(S-supermodular), if (1.4) holds with "$\leq$" replaced by "$\geq$".*

Lemma 1.10 *If the family $\mathcal{A}$ forms an S-rectangle, then conditions (1.2), (1.3) and (1.4) are equivalent.*

Proof: Let any of conditions (1.2) or (1.3) be satisfied. Then, by virtue of the complete ordering of A either $a' \leq a''$ or $a' \geq a''$. In the first case, condition (1.4) is satisfied trivially with the sign "=". In the second case, due to the admissibility of all controls in any state, and due to $A(Sx) = A(x)$, $a' = \Theta^k a''$ for some k. Then inequality (1.4) follows from (1.3) by virtue of

$$b(Sx; \Theta^k; a'') - b(Sx; a'') - b(x; \Theta^k a'') + b(x; a'') = \sum_{1 \leq i \leq k-1} b_{S\Theta}(x; \Theta^i a) \leq 0.$$

To prove the opposite, it suffices to assume that $a' = \Theta a''$, which is possible according to $A(Sx) = A(x)$.
□

The monotonicity of the family $\mathcal{A}$ of control sets $A(x)$ together with submodularity (supermodularity) of the Bellman function are sufficient conditions for existence of a monotone optimal solution of the discrete minimization problem on G. Precisely, the following theorem holds.

Theorem 1.11 *Let the family $\mathcal{A} = \{A(x) : x \in E\}$ be monotonously increasing (decreasing) in direction S, and let the function $b(x; a)$ be S-submodular (S-supermodular). Then the family $\mathcal{A}^*(x) = \{A^*(x) : x \in E\}$ of optimal control sets is monotonously increasing (decreasing), too, in direction (shift S). In that case a monotonic choice can be performed.*
A dual statement holds for the maximization problem.

Proof: Let us consider the minimization problem on the increasing family $\mathcal{A}$ of sets $A(x)$. We have to show that, if the Bellman function $b(x; a)$ is (S, Θ)-submodular, then the family $\mathcal{A}^* = \{A^*(x) : x \in E\}$ of optimal control sets increases as well, implying that there exists a monotone increasing solution. Let $a' \in A^*(x) \subset A(x)$ and $a'' \in A^*(Sx) \subset A(Sx)$. Then,

$$a' \wedge a'' \in A(x) \qquad \text{and} \qquad a' \vee a'' \in A(Sx)$$

since the family $\mathcal{A}$ is increasing, and

$$b(x; a') \le b(x; a' \wedge a'') \qquad \text{and} \qquad b(Sx; a'') \le b(Sx; a' \vee a'')$$

by virtue of optimal choice. Since

$$b(Sx; a' \vee a'') - b(Sx; a'') \le b(x; a') - b(x; a' \wedge a'')$$

according to the (S, Θ)-submodularity of the Bellman function, we obtain from the last three inequalities that

$$0 \le b(Sx; a' \vee a'') - b(Sx; a'') \le b(x; a') - b(x; a' \wedge a'') \le 0,$$

implying equality. Therefore,

$$a' \wedge a'' \in A^*(x), \qquad a' \vee a'' \in A^*(Sx),$$

that is, the family $\mathcal{A}^*(x)$ increases, which offers the possibility of choosing the monotone optimal solution.
$\square$

Remark 1.12 The above theorems extend to the case of monotone conditions for more than one direction (in case of all directions) in the partially ordered set E of states.

Often the Bellman function (1.1) turns out to be constant on the set of trajectory values $x, S_a x, \ldots$, i.e. the Bellman function is representable in the form

$$b(x; a) = v(S_a x), \quad (1.5)$$

where v is the value function, and S_a denotes a monotonic shift in E upon choosing the control a. In what follows we describe monotonicity conditions in terms of the value function (or minimal cost function) v. Strictly speaking, such conditions have to be expressed in terms of the increments of v, and so we re-formulate Definition 1.9 as follows.

Definition 1.13 *The function* $v(x)$ *is called* **submodular in directions S and S_a** *((S, S_a)-submodular) on an increasing family* $\mathcal{A} = \{A(x) : x \in E\}$ *iff for any* $a' \in A(x)$ *and* $a'' \in A(Sx)$ *the inequality*

$$v(S_{\Theta a} S x) - v(S_a S x) - v(S_{\Theta a} x) + v(S_a x) = (1 - S)(S_a - S_{\Theta a}) v(x) \leq 0, \quad (1.6)$$

is satisfied. $v(x)$ *is called* **supermodular in directions S and S_a** *((S, S_a)- supermodular) if the opposite inequality holds.*

Lemma 1.14 *If the family* $\mathcal{A} = \{A(x) : x \in E\}$ *increases (decreases) S-monotonously, the Bellman function of the model is representable as (1.5), and the value function* $v(x)$ *is* (S, S_a)-*submodular* *((S, S_a)-supermodular) everywhere on its domain, then the solution of the minimization problem (1.1) admits an S-monotonously increasing (decreasing) choice*

$$f(Sx) \geq (\leq) f(x).$$

Proof: The proof is obtained by substitution (1.5) in condition (1.3). $\square$

1.4 Numerical methods

In some applications the best choice of design parameters can be determined by simply comparing the results of different alternatives. This, clearly, is feasible only if the number of alternatives is adequately limited. Otherwise, optimization techniques are required to determine a good choice. In case that analytical results are available, a standart deterministic optimization algorithm may suffice. However, for complex — and practically more relevant — cases one has to resort to iterative methods of numerical analysis. This approach requires, at any decision epoch, the calculation of relevant state parameters as, for instance, number of active servers, speeds of the servers, or the number of waiting customers. Since the number of different policies grows exponentially with the number of possible system states, it is clear that simple enumeration procedures for finding an optimal policy are inadequate.

A Markov decision model combines the aspects of a Markov model and a dynamic programming problem. The basic ingredients of dynamic programming are states, optimality criteria and functional equations, and the dynamic programming approach itself may be seen as some sort of a recursion procedure for the calculation of an optimum among the solutions of some functional equation. Recursion for our minimization problem means, that, whatever the initial state and initial decision are, the remaining decisions must constitute an optimal policy again with regard to the state resulting from the first transition.

In order to obtain optimal policies numerically for an infinite horizon problem, the *Howard policy iteration algorithm* [27] can be applied. This algorithm solves the average-cost optimality equation in a finite number of steps by generating a sequence of step-by-step improved policies. Alternatively, a *linear programming formulation* can be performed for the average cost case, with the advantage that this way a powerful generally applicable method is at hand (for detailed descriptions, see for example, [28, 46, 40, 79]). In particular, there are linear programming codes available with additional options of sensitivity analysis. This is not the case for the policy-iteration algorithm. On the other side, the number of iterations required by the simplex method depends heavily on the specific problem under consideration, whereas in most cases the policy-iteration algorithm only needs a very small number of iterations, regardless of the problem size. Viewing this trade-off between two distinct methods, it is interesting to note that the policy-iteration algorithm may itself be interpreted as some modified linear-programming algorithm [65, 75, 76].

Both formulations require to solve, in each iteration step, a system of linear equations of the size of the state space. As a consequence, for large state spaces, there is a significant computational overhead to put up with.

A third approach, avoiding the solution of systems of equations, is a dynamic programming method known as *value iteration algorithm* [58, 75, 76]. It computes recursively a sequence of value functions approximating the minimal average cost per unit of time. The value functions provide lower and upper bounds on the minimal average cost, and under a certain aperiodicity condition these bounds approximate arbitrarily close the minimal cost rate. This value-iteration algorithm represents quite a good computational method for solving large-scale Markov decision problems. Nevertheless, there is a significant shortage to pay attention to: The algorithm is not stable, and the number of necessary iterations, typically, is problem dependent.

Besides the above mentioned methods also simulation-based policy-iteration schemes as well as adaptive aggregation algorithms (as introduced in [25, 82]) can successfully be applied to the analysis of average cost Markov decision processes.

Finally, an interesting and quite different approach for solving the optimization problem is based on *fuzzy logic* [17]. Fuzzy logic, combined with the paradigm of "computing with words", allows the use and manipulation of human knowledge and reasoning in the modeling and control of dynamical systems. The application of fuzzy logic to controlled queueing systems with heterogeneous servers is considered in [83].

In this book, based on *Howard iteration algorithm*, we use Markov decision theory and dynamic programming to propose iteration algorithms, *policy-* and *value-iteration*, which we adapt to the case of controlled queueing systems. One of a modification of these algorithms consists in a transformation of multidimensional into one-dimensional one arrays. This allows successfully solve optimization problems for the systems with a large number of states.

1.5 Outline of the book

In this book, the essential work consists in designing controlled queueing models and investigation of their optimal control properties for the application in the area of the modern telecommunication systems, which should satisfy the growing demands for quality of service (QoS). The following new concepts and results are included. First, for two types of optimization criterion (the model without penalties and with set-up costs), a class of controlled queueing systems is defined. The general case of the queue that forms this class is characterized by a Markov Additive Arrival Process and heterogeneous Phase-Type service time distributions. We show that for these queueing systems, which are the generalizations of a controlled Markovian queue introduced by Rykov [67], the typical properties of optimal control policies, e.g. monotonicity properties and threshold structure, are preserved. Moreover, we show that these systems possess specific properties, e.g. the dependence of optimal policies on the arrival and service statistics.

The importance of these generalizations of simple Markovian queues lies in their ability to be more effective and powerful traffic models, and in turn represent a better approximation of physical systems.

The problem with additional penalties can be divided in subcases. In our work we have shown that in some cases an optimal policy has the same threshold structure as for the model without costs. In other cases there exists another type of threshold policy.

A further new result with respect to controlled queueing models presented in the book consists in the derivation of explicit formulae for the optimal threshold functions under light-traffic system operation. For the general case of phase-type iterarrival and service time distribution the same threshold functions turn out to be suboptimal control rules.

In order to practically use controlled stochastic models, it is necessary to obtain a quick and an effective method to find optimal policies. We present the modified iteration algorithms (based on Howard's iteration algorithm [27]) which can be successfully used to find an optimal solution in case of a large state space.

With increasing system complexity, the amount of attainable theoretical results reduces. The only method to estimate the work of the controlled system is *numerical analysis*. In this book we analyze numerically each mentioned type of queueing systems. For the sake of feasibility we propose a novel approach for observing the course of possible events by use of a representation in the form of control tables and control diagrams.

In Chapter 2 we consider the system $M/M/K$ with allocation control between K heterogeneous servers. At each arrival and service completion epoch the controller can decide which server has to be switched on to serve an arriving or waiting job, or to put an arriving job to the queue. We investigate the system with and without additional penalties. Our goal is to find, for the model without penalties, a scheduling strategy that minimizes the long-run average number of jobs in the system (NJM–problem), and a strategy, for a model with set-up costs, that minimizes the long-run average processing cost of the system (PCM–problem). For both types of optimization problems we formulate a Markov decision model and apply the modified Howard policy-iteration algorithm. Further, for some cases of both, the NJM- and the PCM-problem, we prove the existence of some structured allocation rule, called the threshold function, and investigate the behaviour of that function under variation of the initial system parameters.

In case of the NJM–problem with the servers arranged in decreasing order of service intensities the optimal policy consists in using the fastest available server when a job has to be put to service. The decision whether to put a job into service or to arrange it into the queue is determined according to an optimal threshold policy that in turn is characterized by predetermined threshold levels q_j^*, $j \in \overline{1, K}$, for the servers. In more detail, when the number of jobs in the queue has increased above q_j^*, while the optimal policy so far consisted in sending the job to the queue, a switching on of server j is initiated and, subsequently, the controller continues using server j as long as more than q_j^* jobs are waiting in the queue. The threshold levels are ordered such that $q_1^* \leq q_2^* \leq \cdots \leq q_K^*$. The problem is to find an optimal threshold level q_j^* for each server $j \in \overline{1, K}$. These threshold levels have weak impact on the state[2] of slower servers.

The PCM–model is characterized by assigning costs to server usage (*usage costs* C^U) and to the buffering of jobs in the queue (*holding costs* C^Q). A *mean usage cost* γ_k per server k is defined as the ratio $\frac{C^U(\mu_k)}{\mu_k} =: \frac{c_k}{\mu_k}$ of the assigned usage cost $C^U(\mu_k) = c_k$ to the server's intensity μ_k, and the numbering of servers is done according to increasing mean usage costs:

$$\frac{c_1}{\mu_1} \leq \frac{c_2}{\mu_2} \leq \ldots \leq \frac{c_K}{\mu_K}.$$

With respect to that there exist two possible versions of optimal policy structure. In case of decreasing service intensities with respect to the numbering the optimal policy has the same structure as for the NJM–problem, i. e. the above mentioned threshold sequence $q_1^* \leq q_2^* \leq \cdots \leq q_K^*$ determines the control actions, and the optimal policy is of "threshold type" with threshold levels q_j^*, where the controller always selects the server with the smallest value of mean usage cost (fastest available server). In case that both, the service intensities and the usage costs, are increasing with respect to the above mentioned numbering, namely $\mu_1 < \mu_2 < \ldots < \mu_K$, and $C^U(\mu_1) \leq C^U(\mu_2) \leq \ldots \leq C^U(\mu_K)$, the optimal policy has a more difficult structure, being characterized by *state depending* threshold levels $q_1^*(x) \leq q_2^*(x) \leq \cdots \leq q_K^*(x)$, $x \in E$. To be more precise, the rule in that case says, that server j, in a certain state $x \in E$, is switched on if and only if the queue length $q(x)$ in that state exceeds the threshold q_j^* and stays between the two queue length dependent threshold values $q_j^*(x)$ and $q_{j+1}^*(x)$:

$$q(x) > q_j^* \quad \text{and} \quad q_j^*(x) \leq q(x) < q_{j+1}^*(x).$$

---

[2]A server either is in state "switched on" or in state "switched off", determining whether or not a waiting customer can be put into service.

If $q_j^*(x) = q_{j+1}^*(x)$, then the faster of the servers j and $j + 1$ will be selected, and if server j is the last one[3] being not yet switched on, then it remains in usage also for $q(x) \geq q_{j+1}^*(x)$ $(j = 1, \ldots, K$, where $q_{K+1}^*(x)$ is set to ∞ for every $x \in E)$.

In Chapter 3 we consider queueing systems with more complex arrival streams as, for instance, those with Erlangian and PH-type inter-arrival time distributions or, more generally, with Markovian arrival process (MAP) in the sense of Neuts and Lucantoni. For both problem classes, NJM and PCM, the optimization problem is treated by investigating quantitative and qualitative properties of optimal control rules. In particular, we show that for these systems the properties of optimal control policies as proposed in Chapter 2 are characterized by the same threshold structure as in case of Poisson arrival streams. The only difference is that now the threshold levels depend also on the arrival phases. The determination of these dependencies covers the main part of chapter 3.

In Chapter 4 we study queueing systems with phase-type service time distributions. The control problem in that case turns out to be much more complicated due to the direct dependency between optimal decision making and server characteristics. We consider Erlangian and PH-type service time distributions. A complete theoretical solution of the control problem is not possible here. Therefore, along with some theoretical results, we use plausible reasoning based on numerical test values to formulate the following conjecture concerning an optimal control policy: The optimal policy again is of threshold type, where threshold levels depend on the actual phases of service time.

Chapter 5 is devoted to queueing systems with phase depending inter-arrival time and service time distributions. We consider several examples and propose numerical algorithms to minimize the long-run average cost function, indicating thereby that the optimal control policy once more exhibits a threshold structure with threshold levels depending on the inter-arrival time and service time phases.

---

[3]That is, the server with highest number according to the chosen numbering.

Chapter 2

Controlled $M/M/K$ queue

This chapter considers a queueing system with Poisson input and K heterogeneous servers. The service times of all servers have an exponential distribution with different parameters. The motivation for studying such a system comes from problems of dynamic routing in computer systems or communication networks, where jobs represent messages and the servers represent communication lines with different transmission speeds. The controlled queueing system is described by means of Markov decision process. Activating a server is assumed either to be free of any charge, or to involve a fixed set-up charge (defining the *usage cost*). Similarly, queueing either is free or does cause expenses (defining the *holding costs* for waiting jobs). In case that no costs are charged (no penalties) the problem to minimize the long-run average number of jobs is called the "number of job minimization –" or the NJM–problem. Otherwise, if usage and holding costs are charged, we consider a "processing cost minimization–" or the PCM–problem (see previous chapter).

In both cases we can show that an optimal policy requires that the fastest server is permanently switched on, whereas slower servers are used only when the queue length exceeds certain levels (*threshold values*). *The purpose of this chapter is to develop algorithms for computing optimal threshold values.*

2.1 Literature overview and chapter organization

A simplified version of a controlled queueing model without arrivals (but with K heterogeneous servers) has been considered by Agrawala et al.[1], who showed that an optimal policy requires that, whenever a job is to be assigned to an available server, the job assignment is always done to the fastest server, and further, that the optimal policy is of threshold type. The problem *with arrivals* is much more difficult. Under the assumption of Poisson input the problem of optimal job allocation to two different exponential servers was considered by Larsen in [36] and [37], who also conjectured the optimality of threshold policies and provided a detailed analysis of their performance. Based on dynamic programming arguments, Lin and Kumar [41] considered a similar problem of determining a policy for job allocation to two heterogeneous servers that minimizes the long-run average number of jobs in the system. Again the authors proved that a threshold policy with "fastest server first" - rule is optimal, thereby expressing the conjecture that a generalization of their result to $K \geq 3$ servers would be difficult. Simple proofs of corresponding results have later been given by Koole [33], Walrand [80] and Weber [78]. Luh and Viniotis [45] have studied the problem using a so called *forward induction approach*, that in turn was found to be impracticable for more than two servers.

The threshold structure of an optimal policy minimizing the mean number of jobs in a multi-server system has been established for the first time by Rykov [67]. He also gave evidence for certain monotonicity properties of an optimal policy. Numerical computations for similar problems can be found in [20]. The case of infinitely many servers was proposed by Shenker and Weinrib [72], where an asymptotic analysis of large heterogeneous queueing systems is performed.

Control procedures for queueing systems with penalties (fixed costs) that aim at the minimization of the long-run average total processing cost are notoriously more difficult. Some progress have been made after the appearance of a review paper written by Crabill et al.[16]. Nobel and Tijms [54, 55] studied a model with set-up costs using a hysteretic control rule, thereby stressing the algorithmic aspects of the optimal control structure. The same system has been discussed by Le Ny and Tuffin [38]. These authors proposed a direct method that provides a closed-form expression for the stationary occupancy distribution.

This chapter is further organized as follows. In the following Section 2.2 the $M/M/K$ - model is shortly outlined, whereas in Section 2.3 we present the abstract formulation of the Markov decision problem. As has been mentioned above, for the case of an $M/M/K$ - queueing model, it is formulated in two different versions, named the NJM–problem and the PCM–problem. Section 2.4 is completely devoted to the NJM–problem, and Section 2.5 addresses the PCM–problem.

After defining the NJM–object functional in Section 2.4.1 we introduce, in

Section 2.4.2, the optimality equation that defines the value function with respect to given criteria. This equation is transformed to a convenient form in Section 2.4.3. The transformed form can be used more easily to investigate the quantitative properties of optimal policies. In Section 2.4.4 some monotonicity properties of the optimal solution are established, and in Sections 2.4.5-2.4.7 we discuss the threshold property of an optimal policy for the NJM–problem.

Section 2.5 addresses the control problem with additional penalties. Precisely, the goal of investigation in this section is to determine a control rule that minimizes the long-run average cost per time unit subject to usage and holding costs (PCM-problem). We start from an optimality equation (value function) that is adjusted to allow for the specified cost structure. The object functional and the optimality equation for the PCM-problem are defined in Sections 2.5.1 and 2.5.2.

It is obvious, that different initial system parameters may lead to different optimal policy structures. We investigate the behavior of optimal policies for different relationships between the order of service intensities μ_k and the order of usage costs $C_k^U = c_k$ in comparison with the numbering of servers (that is always done according to increasing order of the *ratios* $\gamma_k = c_k/\mu_k$).

The case of decreasing order of service intensities combined with arbitrary order of usage costs is discussed in Sections 2.5.4-2.5.7. In Subsections 2.5.4 - 2.5.5 we determine its optimal PCM–policy and investigate monotonicity properties, whereas in Subsections 2.5.6 and 2.5.7 we elaborate the corresponding threshold structure. The case of increasing order of service intensities together with increasing order of usage costs is treated in Section 2.5.8.

For other order relationships that cannot be handled analytically the numerical analysis seems to be the only way to determine an optimal policy. In Section 2.6 we provide adequate algorithms for the numerical treatment of the NJM– and the PCM–problem with parameter settings that do not allow an analytical solution.

Section 2.7 is devoted to the discussion of numerical results. In particular, in Section 2.7.1 the dependency between thresholds values and activity status of low-intensity servers is considered, whereas in Sections 2.7.2, and 2.7.3 - 2.7.4, respectively, we provide numerical examples for the NJM– and the PCM–problem. The final Section 2.8 of this chapter contains some concluding remarks.

2.2 Model description

Consider an $M/M/K/B$ ($K \leq B < \infty$) queueing system with K heterogeneous servers of intensities μ_k ($k = \overline{1,K}$), B places in the buffer, and a Poisson input of jobs with intensity λ. The queueing system considered is shown in Figure 2.1.

The restriction to finite buffer sizes does not cause any loss of generality. It is assumed in order to facilitate the numerical treatment. In fact, all equations and theoretical results remain valid also for an infinite buffer size, although in that case the equilibrium condition

$$\lambda < M, \qquad \text{where} \quad M = \mu_1 + \cdots + \mu_K.$$

has to be taken for granted. This shall be the fact throughout this chapter: $\rho = \frac{\lambda}{M} < 1$.

Figure 2.1 Queueing system

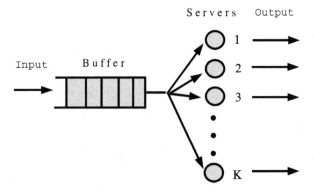

The control times are all arrival and service completion epochs. At an arrival epoch the control consists in sending the arrived job to the queue (if it is not full) or to one of the free servers. At service completion times, when the queue is not empty, the control consists in assigning a waiting job to one of idle servers, or leave the queue as it is. A job arriving to a full buffer is rejected only if i.e. always the total capacity of B is used. Being sent to some server a job can not change it.

2.3   Problem formulation

The controlled queueing system is modelled by a stochastic process $\{Z(t)\} = \{X(t), U(t)\}$, whose structure is depicted in Figure 2.2.

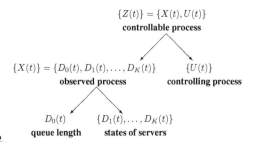

Figure 2.2

Set $\mathbf{N} = \{K, K+1, \ldots, B\}$. The observed vector process $\{X(t)\}_{t \geq 0}$ denotes the system state at time t, $\{X(t)\}$=(queue length, list of active servers)$\in E = \mathbf{N} \times \{0,1\}^K$, with components $D_0(t) =: Q(t), D_1(t), \ldots, D_K(t)$. $Q(t)$ is the r. v. of queue length at time t, and $D_k(t)$ for $k > 0$ describes the state of server k at this time:

$$D_k(t) = \begin{cases} 0, & \text{if the } k\text{-th server is idle at time } t \\ 1, & \text{otherwise} \end{cases}.$$

For each state $x = (d_0, d_1, \ldots, d_K) \in E$, where $d_0 =: q(x)$, let $J_0(x)$ and $J_1(x)$ be the sets of labels assigned to idle and busy servers, respectively, in this state, i.e.

$$J_0(x) = \{j : d_j(x) = 0\}, \qquad J_1(x) = \{j : d_j(x) = 1\}.$$

Further, the summed server intensities for idle and busy servers are termed $M_0(x)$ and $M_1(x)$, resulting in $M = M_0 + M_1$:

$$M_0(x) = \sum_{j \in J_0} \mu_j, \qquad \text{and} \qquad M_1(x) = \sum_{j \in J_1} \mu_j.$$

As a controlling process consider the process $\{U(t)\}_{t \geq 0}$, where $U(t)$ is a decision which should be taken at the nearest to t control time. Let $A = \{0, 1, \ldots, K\}$

be the set of available controls and

$$A(x) = \begin{cases} J_0(x) \cup \{0\} & \text{for } x \text{ with } q(x) < B, \\ J_0(x) & \text{for } x \text{ with } q(x) = B, \end{cases} \tag{2.1}$$

be the set of admissible controls when the system state is x. Soppose at a certain instant t, the system state $X(t) = x$. Then the controller chooses an admissible control $U(t) = a \in A(x)$, where $a = k \geq 1$ has the meaning "switch on server k", and $a = 0$ has the meaning "do not switch on any server".

As has been mentioned already, control actions are performed at arrival or service completion epochs in dependence on the actual system state. To put that in concrete terms, we have to stress the fact that a control action always uses the information about the system state *immediately before a decision epoch*, that is immediately *before* an arrival or immediately *before* a service completion.
Under the considered assumptions, the process $\{Z(t)\} = \{(X(t), U(t))\}$ is a Markov decision process with state space $E = \mathbf{N} \times \{0,1\}^K$ and a control space $A(x) \subset A$ depended on the state $x \in E$.

Consider the shift operators S_0, S_j on the state space E,

$$S_0 x = x + e_0 \mathbf{1}_{\{q(x) < B\}}, \qquad S_j x = x + e_j \mathbf{1}_{\{j \in J_0(x)\}}, \tag{2.2}$$

where we denote by $e_i = (\underbrace{0, \ldots,}_{i} 1, \underbrace{0, \ldots, 0}_{K-i})$ the $K+1$-dimensional vector i-th coordinate of which (beginning from 0-th) is one and all others are zeros, and by $S_j^{-1} x$, $(j = 0, 1, \ldots, K)$ the inverse operators for such points $x \in E$, for which they exist and put $S_j^{-1} x = x$ in another cases, i.e.

$$S_0^{-1} x = x, \quad \text{if} \quad q(x) = 0, \qquad S_j^{-1} x = x, \quad \text{if} \quad j \in J_0(x).$$

Finally, the specification of the Markov decision process is completed by the definition of the transition probabilities. Using the above notations we can represent the transition intensities of the process $\{Z(t)\}$ in the form

$$\lambda_{xy}(a) = \begin{cases} \lambda, & \text{for } y = S_{a_0} x, \\ \mu_j, & \text{for } y = S_{a_j} S_0^{-1} S_j^{-1} x, \quad j \in J_1(x), \\ 0, & \text{otherwise}, \end{cases}$$

where $a = a_0 \in A(x)$ denotes the control which has to be chosen in the case of an arrival to the state x, $a = a_j \in A(S_j^{-1} S_0^{-1} x)$ denotes the control in the case of a service completion on the j-th server. It is taken into account as well that $y = S_{a_j} S_0^{-1} S_j^{-1} x = x$ for $j \in J_0(x)$.

In the case of arrivals to some state $x = (q, d_1, \ldots, d_K)$ with j-th idle server $d_j(x) = 0$, and in the case of service completion on the j-th server in some state $x = (q, d_1, \ldots, d_K)$, $d_j(x) = 1$, transitions are illustrated in the Figure 2.3 (a) and (b), respectively,

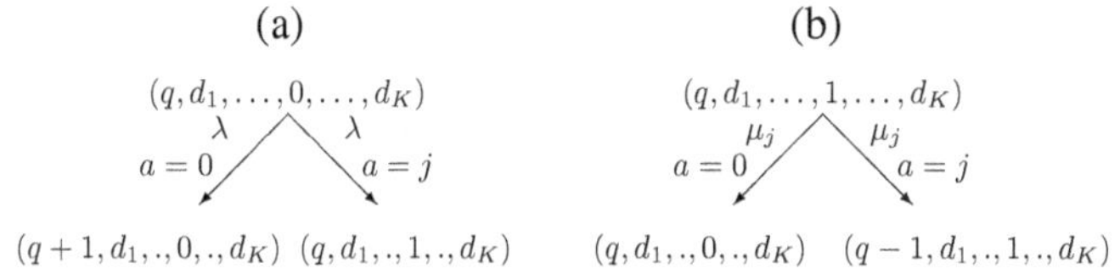

(a)	(b)

$$(q, d_1, \ldots, 0, \ldots, d_K) \qquad\qquad (q, d_1, \ldots, 1, \ldots, d_K)$$

$$a = 0 \quad\nearrow^{\lambda} \quad^{\lambda}\searrow \quad a = j \qquad\qquad a = 0 \quad\nearrow^{\mu_j} \quad^{\mu_j}\searrow \quad a = j$$

$$(q+1, d_1, \ldots, 0, \ldots, d_K) \quad (q, d_1, \ldots, 1, \ldots, d_K) \qquad (q, d_1, \ldots, 0, \ldots, d_K) \quad (q-1, d_1, \ldots, 1, \ldots, d_K)$$

Figure 2.3

Now we can formulate cost criterion which is used to solve optimization problem. In the next section we consider a cost criterion with respect to minimizing the mean number of jobs in the system.

2.4 Number of jobs minimization (NJM–problem)

2.4.1 Quantity functional

In the present section we consider the "mean number of jobs in the system minimization problem" (NJM–problem). The total number of jobs in the system equals the sum of jobs waiting in the queue and being under service. Thus, by Little's theorem [32], this problem is equivalent to minimizing the mean sojourn time of customers in the system.

Denote by $L(t) = D_0(t) + \sum_{1 \leq k \leq K} D_k(t)$ the random process of number of jobs in the system, where $D_0(t) = Q(t)$.

For the NJM–problem, the quantity functional underlying the minimization problem takes the form

$$Y(t) = \int_0^t L(u)\, du, \qquad\qquad (2.3)$$

or, using the definition of the process $L(t)$

$$Y(t) = \int_0^t \left(Q(u) + \sum_{1 \leq k \leq K} D_k(u) \right) du.$$

Let

$$l(x) = q(x) + \sum_{1 \leq k \leq K} d_k(x) \tag{2.4}$$

denote the number of jobs in state x (which does not depend on the control a). This number represents the sum of jobs in the queue plus the number of busy servers.

As is common in Markov decision theory (see [31, 58, 75]), we define a strategy δ, and the probability distribution $\mathbf{P}_{x_0}^\delta$ which is a measure on the set of the *trajectories* (the sequence of states and controls during the observation period) of the process $\{Z(t)\}$, given an initial state x_0 and a strategy δ, the expectation $\mathbf{E}_{x_0}^\delta$ shall denote the expectation with respect to this distribution. Then the problem of minimizing the the long-run average number of jobs in the system can be represented as follows: Minimize

$$g(x_0; \delta) = \lim_{t \to \infty} \frac{1}{t} \mathbf{E}_{x_0}^\delta Y(t) \tag{2.5}$$

with respect to all admissible strategies. $g(x_0; \delta)$ is the object function.

2.4.2 Optimality equation

Our dynamic decision process is associated with a Markov process that operates on one ergodic class. The rates and costs are assumed to be time homogeneous and uniformly bounded in the states. From this fact it is known (e.g. [31, 61, 64]) that the following *optimality principle* is valid.

(i) the gain $\inf_\delta g(x_0; \delta)$ exists and is independent of the initial ("starting") state x_0; that is, $\inf_\delta g(x_0; \delta) = g$;

(ii) there exists a function $v : E \to \mathbb{R}$, called the *value function*, that allows to determine, at any state $x \in E$, an optimal decision $a^*(x) \in A(x)$ with respect to the total future development of the process, that is,

$$v(x) = \min_{a \in A(x)} b(x, a), \qquad x \in E;$$

(iii) an optimal strategy can be chosen as a stationary Markov strategy, i.e. it is determined by the optimal policy $f = \{f(x) : x \in E\}$ with

$$f(x) = \operatorname*{argmin}_{a \in A(x)} b(x, a), \qquad x \in E,$$

minimizing the function $b(x, a)$.

Thus the function $b : E \times A \to \mathbb{R}$ is a right hand side of optimality equation (in fact, also depends on the function $v(x)$) and plays the role of the so called *Bellman function* in Markov decision theory.

In [75] it has been proved that the average cost per unit time and the value function can be calculated simultaneously by solving a system of linear equations. To specify this system, and represent the optimality equation for the model, let us denote by

$$V(x, t) = \inf_{\delta} \mathbf{E}_x^{\delta} Y(t)$$

minimal total operating cost of the system during time t.

For some small time interval of length h the following equation can be obtained according to common Markov process arguing:

$$
\begin{aligned}
V(x, t+h) \;=\; & l(x)\,h + (1 - (\lambda + M_1(x))\,h)\,V(x, t) \\
+ \;& \lambda h \min_{a_0 \in A(x)} V(S_{a_0} x, t) \\
+ \;& 1_{\{q(x)=0\}} \sum_{j \in J_1(x)} \mu_j\, hV(S_j^{-1} x, t) \\
+ \;& 1_{\{q(x)>0\}} \sum_{j \in J_1(x)} \mu_j\, h \min_{a_j \in A(S_j^{-1} S_0^{-1} x)} V((S_{a_j} S_j^{-1} S_0^{-1} x, t).
\end{aligned}
$$

In this equation the first term in the right side represents the number of customers resident in the system during a time interval of duration h, the second term represents the total processing cost of all customers being in the system during the subsequent time interval of duration t in case that there are no arrivals and no departures, and the remaining two terms, respectively, represent the total processing cost of all customers being in the system during t in the case of an arrival before the next service completion, and in the case of a departure before the next arrival.

After some elementary manipulation, and and passing to the limit when $h \to 0$, the above equations leads to

$$\frac{\partial V(x, t,)}{\partial t} = - (\lambda + M_1(x))V(x, t) + l(x)$$
$$+ \min_a \left[\lambda V(S_{a_0}x, t) + \sum_{j \in J_1(x)} \mu_j V(S_{a_j} S_j^{-1} S_0^{-1} x, t) \right].$$

This differential equation describes the behaviour of the minimal operating cost of the system till the time t. The obvious relation is

$$\lim_{t \to \infty} \frac{1}{t} V(x, t) = \inf_\delta \lim_{t \to \infty} \frac{1}{t} \mathbf{E}_x^\delta Y(t) = g(\delta^*) = g$$

for all x. This relation motivates the heuristic result concerning asymptotic behavior of $V(x, t)$ for $t \to \infty$ [75], with an assumption that values $v(x)$, $x \in E$, exist such that, for each $x \in E$,

$$V(x, t) \approx tg + v(x) \quad \text{for large } t. \tag{2.6}$$

The value function $v(x)$ indicate the transient effect of the starting states on the expected costs under the given strategy. Note that $v(x) - v(y) \approx V(x, t) - V(y, t)$ for t large, so that $v(x) - v(y)$ measures the difference in total expected costs when starting in state x rather than in state y, given that the optimal strategy δ^* is followed. Next by substituting the above asymptotic expansion in the recursion equation, we find, after cancelling out common terms, that the average cost g and the value function $v(x), x \in E$, satisfy a simultaneous system of linear equations, which will refer to as an *optimality equation*

$$v(x) = \frac{1}{\lambda + M_1(x)} \min_a \left[l(x) - g + \lambda v(S_{a_0}x) \right. \tag{2.7}$$
$$\left. + \mathbf{1}_{\{q(x)>0\}} \sum_{j \in J_1(x)} \mu_j v(S_{a_j} S_j^{-1} S_0^{-1} x) + \mathbf{1}_{\{q(x)=0\}} \sum_{j \in J_1(x)} \mu_j v(S_j^{-1} x) \right],$$

where $a = a_0 \in A(x)$ and $a = a_j \in A(S_j^{-1} S_0^{-1} x)$. Based on (2.7) we shall investigate the qualitative and quantitative properties of an optimal policy. It is convenient to transform, for that purpose, equation (2.7) to some more feasible form, which will be done in the next section.

2.4.3 Transformation of Optimality Equation

Now we assume the stability of system states which are included into the optimality equations.

Definition 2.4 The state x is called stable with respect to the function $v(x)$ if it does not prescribe to send the job from the queue to server immediately, which can be presented formally as

$$v(x) = \min_{k \in A(x)} v(S_0^{-1}S_k x).$$

In order to simplify equation (2.7) we multiply it by $\lambda + M_1$ and add to both of sides the sum $\sum_{j \in J_0(x)} \mu_j v(x)$ (putting $v(S_{a_j}S_j^{-1}S_0^{-1}x) = v(x)$, for $j \in J_0(x)$, and $M = \sum_j \mu_j$ for $j \in J_0(x) \cup J_1(x)$. By dividing both sides by $(\lambda + M)$ one obtains

$$v(x) = \frac{1}{\lambda + M} \min_a \left[l(x) + \lambda v(S_{a_0}x) + \sum_j \mu_j \, v(S_{a_j}S_j^{-1}S_0^{-1}x) - g \right] \quad (2.8)$$

Introducing the operators T_0 and T_j by

$$T_0 v(x) = v(S_0 x) = \min_{k \in A(x)} v(S_k x), \quad (2.9)$$

$$T_j v(x) = \begin{cases} v(S_j^{-1}x) = T_0 v(S_j^{-1}S_0^{-1}x) & \text{for } j \in J_1(x), \quad q(x) > 0, \\ v(S_j^{-1}x) & \text{for } j \in J_1(x), \quad q(x) = 0, \\ v(x) & \text{for } j \in J_0(x). \end{cases}$$

(2.8) can be rewritten as

$$v(x) = \frac{1}{\lambda + M} \left[l(x) + \lambda T_0 \, v(x) + \sum_j \mu_j T_j \, v(x) - g \right] = Bv(x), \quad (2.10)$$

where B is termed the *dynamic programming operator*.

Theorem 2.5 *Equations (2.7), (2.8) and (2.10) are equivalent in so far as their solutions and value functions coincide.*

Proof: Let $\hat{v} = \{\hat{v}(x), x \in E\}$, $\hat{g}$, $\hat{a} = \{\hat{a}(x), x \in E\}$ solution of the equation (2.7). Then for any $a \in A$

$$\frac{1}{\lambda + M_1(x)}[l(x) + \lambda\hat{v}(S_{\hat{a}_0}x) + \sum_{j \in J_1(x)} \mu_j\hat{v}(S_{\hat{a}_j}S_j^{-1}S_0^{-1}x) - \hat{g}]$$

$$\leq \frac{1}{\lambda + M_1(x)}[l(x) + \lambda v(S_{a_0}x) + \sum_{j \in J_1(x)} \mu_j v(S_{a_j}S_j^{-1}S_0^{-1}x) - g].$$

Then, using the same steps as at the beginning of the present section, one obtains

$$[l(x) + \lambda\hat{v}(S_{\hat{a}_0}x) + \sum_j \mu_j\hat{v}(S_{\hat{a}_j}S_j^{-1}S_0^{-1}x) - \hat{g}]$$

$$\leq [l(x) + \lambda v(S_{a_0}x) + \sum_j \mu_j v(S_{a_j}S_j^{-1}S_0^{-1}x) - g].$$

Thus $\hat{v} = \{\hat{v}(x), x \in E\}$, $\hat{g}$, $\hat{a} = \{\hat{a}(x), x \in E\}$ is a solution of (2.8). The inverse proposition can be proofed analogously. The equivalence of the equations (2.8) and (2.10) with respect to *coincidence of value functions* follows from the independence of the chosen decisions at arrival and service completion epochs (equation (2.8) is minimized over the same independent parameters a_j, that leads to the equation (2.10).
□

From the optimality equation (2.10), one can obtain some useful results, as is shown below.

Theorem 2.6 *Any optimal policy* $f = \{f_j(x) : j \in \{0\} \cup J_1(x),\ x \in E\}$ *has the form*

$$f_0(x) = \operatorname{argmin}\{v(S_kx) : k \in A(x)\},$$
$$f_j(x) = \operatorname{argmin}\{v(S_kS_0^{-1}S_j^{-1}x) : k \in A(S_0^{-1}S_j^{-1}x)\} = f_0(S_0^{-1}S_j^{-1}x).$$

Proof: The statement of the theorem follows from the optimality principle and the independence of the decisions at the arrival and the service completion points of time.
□

Theorem 2.6 shows that it is only necessary to investigate the component $f_0(.)$. Additionally, the last assertion shows that the optimal policy is completely defined by the function
$$b(x,\,k) = v(S_kx), \qquad k \in A(x), \tag{2.11}$$

which depends rather simply on the value function $v(x)$ of the model and can be used here as its *Bellman function*. Thus, the optimal policy $f = \{f(x) : x \in E\}$ with respect to $b(x, k)$ takes the form

$$f(x) = \operatorname{argmin}\left[b(x, a) : a \in A(x)\right]. \qquad (2.12)$$

and all qualitative properties of an optimal policy depend on the properties of the value function of the model.

A similar transformation of the underlying optimality equation can be carried out for many controlled queueing systems, where control consists in sending the jobs to the queue or allocating jobs to servers upon state changes.

2.4.4   Monotonicity properties of optimal policies

In this section we apply the results of Section 1.3 to the system $M/M/K/B$ and represent results of Rykov in [67].

To study the monotonicity properties of optimal policies we exploit a partial ordering of the state space E, and the complete ordering of the set A of controls. For that purpose the servers are arranged in order of decreasing service intensities (increasing mean service times)

$$0 \leq \mu_1^{-1} \leq \mu_2^{-1} \leq \cdots \leq \mu_K^{-1} \qquad (2.13)$$

and the components of the vector $d = (d_1, \ldots, d_K)$ are numbered accordingly. Assume, that the operators S_0 and S_i shift the points of E in positive direction, that is,

$$S_0 x \geq x \quad \text{and} \quad S_i x \geq x, \quad i \in J_0(x). \qquad (2.14)$$

Then, these shifts determine a partial ordering "$\rightarrow$" in E according to $x \rightarrow y$ iff $y = S_\nu x$. Shifted points are ordered with respect to increasing mean service times, i.e.

$$S_i x \geq S_j x, \quad \text{iff } i \geq j, \quad i, j \in J_0(x) \quad (\text{that is } \mu_i^{-1} \geq \mu_j^{-1}). \qquad (2.15)$$

Points $S_0 x$ and $S_j x$, $(j \neq 0)$ are not comparable.

In the set A of controls a complete ordering is given according to the numbering $1 < 2 < \cdots < K$ (with respect to servers $1, \ldots, K$). Clearly, this induces the corresponding ordering in any subset $A(x)$.

We are going to show that for the NJM–problem (2.3) the value function increases monotonically relative to the introduced ordering. We need to prove a general property of the operator Before considering the corresponding theorem we need to proof a general property of the operator (2.9). Note that the proposed properties hold only for the defined ahead stable states.

Lemma 2.7 *The operator T_0 retains the property of nondecreasing functions relative to the partial ordering of E, i.e.*

1. $v(S_i x) \geq v(x)$, $i \in A(x)$,
2. $v(S_i x) \geq v(S_j x)$, $i, j \in A(x)$, $i \geq j$, $\mu_j \geq \mu_i$,
3. $v(S_0 x) \geq v(S_1 x)$.

Proof: Let the function $v(x)$ be nondecreasing with respect to the introduced ordering, namely

$$v(S_i x) \geq v(x),\ i \in A(x);\ v(S_i x) \geq v(S_j x),\ i, j \in A(x),\ v(S_0 x) \geq v(S_1 x).$$

To prove the inequalities 1–3 it has to be shown that $T_0 v(x)$ does not decrease:

$$T_0 v(S_i x) \geq T_0 v(x),\ i \in A(x),\ T_0 v(S_i x) \geq T_0 v(S_j x),\ i, j \in A(x),$$
$$T_0 v(S_0 x) \geq T_0 v(S_1 x).$$

For the inequality 1 we have for $i \in A(x)$

$$T_0 v(S_i x) = \min_{k \in A(S_i x)} v(S_k S_i x) \geq \min_{k \in A(S_i x)} v(S_k x) \geq \min_{k \in A(x)} v(S_k x) = T_0 v(x),$$

where the first item follows from assumption that the function $v(x)$ is nondecreasing and the second item follows from relation $A(S_i x) \subset A(x)$ together with the fact that the minimum does not increase upon expanding the minimization set.

For the inequality 2 we prove that upon passing from S_j to S_i, $i, j \in A(x)$, $i \geq j$, the operator T_0 preserves the property to be nondecreasing. Let $i, j \in A(x)$. Then the set $A(x)$ can be represented as $A(x) = M(x) \cup \{i\} \cup \{j\}$ with some $M(x)$ so that $A(S_i x) = M(x) \cup \{j\}$, $A(S_j x) = M(x) \cup \{i\}$ and the relations

$$T_0 v(S_i x) = \min_{k \in A(S_i x)} v(S_k S_i x)$$

$$= \min \left\{ \min_{k \in M(x)} v(S_k S_i x), v(S_i S_j x) \right\}$$

$$\geq \min \left\{ \min_{k \in M(x)} v(S_k S_j x), v(S_i S_j x) \right\} = T_0 v(S_j x)$$

are valid by virtue of inequality $v(S_i x) \geq v(S_j x)$.

Finally, for the inequality 3 we have two possible subcases

(a) $\quad T_0 v(S_0 x) = \min\limits_{k \in A(S_0 x)} v(S_k S_0 x) = v(S_0^2 x)$

$\qquad \geq v(S_0 S_1 x) \geq \min\limits_{k \in A(S_1 x)} v(S_k S_1 x) = T_0 v(S_1 x)$

(b) $\quad T_0 v(S_0 x) = \min\limits_{k \in A(S_0 x)} v(S_k S_0 x) = v(S_1 S_0 x)$

$\qquad \geq \min\limits_{k \in A(S_1 x)} v(S_k S_1 x) = T_0 v(S_1 x)$

by taking the property 3 of the function $v(x)$.

□

Due to the fact that the optimality equation holds only for the stable states, i.e. $v(x) = \min\limits_{k} v(S_0^{-1} S_k x) = T_0 v(S_0^{-1} x)$ and the definition of operators T_j by the formula (2.9) they are also preserve the property of functions to be monotonically nondecreasing. We only have to specify the inequality $T_j v(S_j x) \geq T_j v(x)$. The function $v(x)$ in equation (2.10) is defined after the decision that has been made in state x. This means that this function satisfies the condition

$$v(x) = \min\limits_{k \in A(x)} v(S_k S_0^{-1} x) = T_0 v(S_0^{-1} x).$$

Further according to this condition we get for $j \in J_0(x)$

$$T_j v(S_j x) = T_0 v(S_0^{-1} x) = v(x) = T_j v(x).$$

2.4.5 Assignment to the fastest available server

By virtue of results from Lemma 2.7 the following statement holds.

Theorem 2.8 *The value function $v(x)$ increases monotonously relative to the ordering introduced in E, i.e. the dynamic programming operator B preserves the inequalities 1–3 of the lemma 2.7*

Proof: By virtue of the monotonicity of $l(x)$ with respect to the shift operators S_i, $i \in A(x)$, and linearity of the operator B (defined by (2.10)), this operator B in turn preserves monotonicity relative to these shifts.

To prove the monotonicity upon passing from $S_i x$ to x, $i \in A(x)$ we write down the optimality equation for the inequality 1

$$Bv(S_i x) - Bv(x) = [l(S_i x) - l(x)] + \lambda[T_0 v(S_i x) - T_0 v(x)]$$
$$+ \sum_{l \neq i} \mu_l [T_l v(S_i x) - T_l v(x)]$$
$$+ \mu_i [T_i v(S_i x) - T_i v(x)] \geq 0$$

that follows from the above properties of the value function and shift operators T_0 and T_i.

Now we prove that it also retains monotonicity upon passing from $S_j x$ to $S_i x$, $i, j \in A(x)$, $i \geq j$ in the inequality 2. Let the function $v(x)$ be nondecreasing as in Lemma 2.7. Then, for any i, $j \in A(x)$ such that $i \geq j$ we get

$$Bv(S_i x) - Bv(S_j x) = [l(S_i x) - l(S_j x)] + \lambda[T_0 v(S_i x) - T_0 v(S_j x)]$$
$$+ \sum_{l \neq i, j} \mu_l [T_l v(S_i x) - T_l v(S_j x)]$$
$$+ \mu_j [T_j v(S_i x) - T_j v(S_j x)] - \mu_i [T_i v(S_j x) - T_i v(S_i x)] \geq 0,$$

where the first three items in the right–hand side are nonnegative by virtue of the constancy of the function $l(x)$ upon passing from $S_j x$ to $S_i x$, $i, j \in A(x)$, $i \geq j$ and the fact that operators T_0 and T_j retain the monotonicity of the functions.

For the last two items by virtue of the operators T_j properties and definition (2.9)

$$T_i v(S_i x) = v(x), q(x) = 0,$$
$$T_i v(S_i x) = T_0 v(S_0^{-1} x) = v(x), q(x) > 0,$$
$$T_i v(S_j x) = v(S_j x),$$
$$T_j v(S_i x) = v(S_i x),$$

we obtain

$$\mu_j [T_j v(S_i x) - T_j v(S_j x)] - \mu_i [T_i v(S_j x) - T_i v(S_i x)]$$
$$= \mu_j [v(S_i x) - v(x)] - \mu_i [v(S_j x) - v(x)]$$
$$= \mu_i \mu_j \left[\frac{v(S_i x) - v(x)}{\mu_i} - \frac{v(S_j x) - v(x)}{\mu_j} \right] \geq 0,$$

since

$$v(S_i x) - v(x) \geq v(S_j x) - v(x) \geq 0$$

and $\mu_i \leq \mu_j$, owing to the monotonicity assumption.

At last for the inequality 3 we get

$$Bv(S_0 x) - Bv(S_1 x) = [l(S_0 x) - l(S_1 x)] + \lambda[T_0 v(S_0 x) - T_0 v(S_1 x)]$$
$$+ \sum_{l \neq 1} \mu_l [T_l v(S_0 x) - T_l v(S_1 x)]$$
$$+ \mu_1 [T_1 v(S_0 x) - T_1 v(S_1 x)] \geq 0,$$

by virtue of the above properties of the value function and shift operators T_0 and T_i.

Finally, in spite of the operator B not being a constraction operator for the long-run average problem, if we put one of the values of the value function to zero, for example $v(0) = 0$, the sequence $\{B^n l(0)\}_{n \in \mathbb{N}_0}$ converges monotonously to the gain g^* of the model,

$$g^* = \lim_{n \to \infty} B^n l(0),$$

as was shown in Howard [27] and Lippman [42]. But, for any given value of the gain g^*, the operator B preserves inequalities in the sense that, if $v_1(.) \geq v_2(.)$, then $Bv_1(.) \geq Bv_2(.)$, and so the assertion follows from

$$v(x) = \lim_{n \to \infty} B^n l(x)$$

and the fact, that the function $l(x)$ is constant relative to shifts from S_i to S_j.
□

Using Theorem 2.8 we immediately obtain the following statement.

Theorem 2.9 *The optimal control policy consists in activating the available fastest server, if necessary. The first server should always be used.*

Proof: The proof follows from the fact that owing to the monotonicity of the model value function with respect to the shifts from the point $S_j x$ to the point $S_i x$, $i, j \in A(x)$, $i \geq j$, the minimal value of the function $v(S_k x)$ of k is attained for the minimal admissible value of $k \in A(x)$, that is, on a free maximal-intensity server.
□

2.4.6   Supermodularity of the value function

We note that since the points $S_k x$ ($k \in A(S_1 x)$) and $S_0 x$ are incomparable, this assertion does not allow us to determine whether a server must be activated. Now we show that an optimal policy features monotonicity relative to the queue length increasing. Since for the shift S_0 the family of controls does not vary, this suffices to prove the monotonicity of the increments of the Bellman function everywhere on the domain. By virtue of the fact that the Bellman function satisfies the condition $b(x; a) = v(S_a x)$, it suffices that the value function of the model $v = \{v(x) : x \in E\}$ has increments $v(S_k x) - v(S_0 x)$ that are monotone in S_0 or feature the property of (S_0, S_k)-supermodularity (1.6), which assumes here the form

$$(1 - S_0)(S_0 - S_k)v(x) \leq 0. \tag{2.16}$$

To prove this inequality for the operator B we have to introduce some additional supermodularity properties, namely

$$(1 - S_0)(S_k - 1)v(x) \leq 0, \tag{2.17}$$

$$(1 - S_k)(S_l - 1)v(x) \leq 0, \tag{2.18}$$

$$(1 - S_0)(S_0 - 1)v(x) \leq 0. \tag{2.19}$$

Note that summing (2.16) and (2.17) yields (2.19).

Theorem 2.10 *The value function $v(x)$ is supermodular, i.e. it has monotone increments (2.16)–(2.19) with respect to the partial order introduced in E.*

Proof: According to Theorem 2.9 only two solutions are possible in each state x: $f_0(x) = 0$ (not to serve the job) or $f_0(x) = k$ (to use the fastest free server), that is $\mu_k = \max\limits_{l \in A(x)} \mu_l$, so that here the family $A(x)$ of controls is independent on the shift S_0.

We set out to prove that the operator T_0 retains the supermodular nature (1.6) of the functions. Thus it is necessary to check whether the inequalities (2.16)–(2.19) are satisfied for the function $\hat{v}(x) = T_0 v(x)$ if it is satisfied for some function $v(x)$. We are able to give an exact proof for the system with $K = 3$ servers. According to (2.16) we have to prove

$$(1 - S_0)(S_0 - S_k)\hat{v}(x) = \hat{v}(S_0 x) - \hat{v}(S_k x) - \hat{v}(S_0^2 x) + \hat{v}(S_0 S_k x)$$
$$= \min\{v(S_l S_0 x) : l \in J_0(x)\} - \min\{v(S_l S_k x) : l \in J_0(S_k x)\}$$
$$- \min\{v(S_l S_0^2 x) : l \in J_0(x)\} + \min\{v(S_l S_0 S_k x) : l \in J_0(S_k x)\} \leq 0.$$

To prove this assertion for each point $x \in E$ we divide it into several cases

1. First we consider the case when the optimal solutions coincide at the points $S_k x$ and $S_0^2 x$ (where $\hat{v}(x)$ is involved in inequality with negative sign), and $f(S_k x) = f(S_0^2 x) = f$. Obviously, by replacing the optimal solution at the rest of the points by f, we obtain that

$$
\begin{aligned}
(1 - S_0)(S_0 - S_k)\hat{v}(x) &= \hat{v}(S_0 x) - \hat{v}(S_k x) - \hat{v}(S_0^2 x) + \hat{v}(S_0 S_k x) \\
&= \hat{v}(S_0 x) - v(S_f S_k x) - v(S_f S_0^2 x) + \hat{v}(S_0 S_k x) \\
&\leq v(S_f S_0 x) - v(S_f S_k x) - v(S_f S_0^2 x) + v(S_f S_0 S_k x) \\
&= (1 - S_0)(S_0 - S_k)v(S_f x) \leq 0.
\end{aligned}
$$

2. The case of different optimal solutions at the points $S_k x$ and $S_0^2 x$ (where $\hat{v}(x)$ is involved in inequality with negative sign) should be divided into two subcases: $f_0(S_0^2 x) = 0$, $f_0(S_k x) = l \neq 0$, where l is the index such that $\mu_l = \max\limits_{j \in J_0(S_k x)} \{\mu_j\}$, and $f_0(S_0^2 x) = k \neq 0$, $f_0(S_k x) = 0$.
In the first subcase, by summing the inequalities (2.16) at the points $S_k x$ and $S_0 x$, respectively,

$$
v(S_0 S_k x) - v(S_l S_k x) - v(S_0^2 S_k x) + v(S_0 S_l S_k x) \leq 0,
$$

and

$$
v(S_0^2 x) - v(S_0 S_k x) - v(S_0^3 x) + v(S_0^2 S_k x) \leq 0,
$$

we get the inequality

$$
v(S_0^2 x) - v(S_k S_l x) - v(S_0^3 x) + v(S_k S_l S_0 x) \leq 0,
$$

which shows that the inequality $(1 - S_0)(S_0 - S_k)\hat{v}(x) \leq 0$ is satisfied for the function $\hat{v}(x)$ at the point x by virtue of the inequality

$$
\begin{aligned}
(1 - S_0)(S_0 - S_k)\hat{v}(x) &= \hat{v}(S_0 x) - \hat{v}(S_k x) - \hat{v}(S_0^2 x) + \hat{v}(S_k S_0 x) \\
&= v(S_0^2 x) - v(S_k S_l x) - v(S_0^3 x) + v(S_k S_l S_0 x) \leq 0.
\end{aligned}
$$

In the second subcase, the relation has the form

$$
\begin{aligned}
(1 - S_0)(S_0 - S_k)\hat{v}(x) &= \hat{v}(S_0 x) - \hat{v}(S_k x) - \hat{v}(S_0^2 x) + \hat{v}(S_0 S_k x) \\
&= \hat{v}(S_0^2 x) - v(S_0 S_k x) - v(S_k S_0^2 x) + \hat{v}(S_0 S_k x) \\
&\leq v(S_k S_0 x) - v(S_0 S_k x) - v(S_k S_0^2 x) + v(S_0 S_0 S_k x) = 0.
\end{aligned}
$$

For the inequality (2.17) we have to show that

$$(1 - S_0)(S_k - 1)\hat{v}(x) = \hat{v}(S_0 x) - \hat{v}(x) - \hat{v}(S_k S_0 x) + \hat{v}(S_k x)$$
$$= \min_{l \in A(x)} v(S_l S_0 x) - \min_{l \in A(x)} v(S_l x)$$
$$- \min_{l \in A(S_k S_0 x)} v(S_l S_k S_0 x) + \min_{l \in A(S_k x)} v(S_l S_k x) \leq 0.$$

To prove this assertion we also distinguish three possible cases
1. $f(x) = f(S_0 S_k x) = f.$

$$\min_{l \in A(x)} v(S_l S_0 x) - v(S_f x) - v(S_f S_k S_0 x) + \min_{l \in A(S_k x)} v(S_l S_k x)$$
$$\leq v(S_f S_0 x) - v(S_f x) - v(S_f S_k S_0 x) + v(S_f S_k x) \leq 0$$

assuming the inequality (2.17) for the state $S_f x.$
2. $f(x) = k$ and $f(S_0 S_k x) = 0.$

$$\min_{l \in A(x)} v(S_l S_0 x) - v(S_k x) - v(S_k S_0^2 x) + \min_{l \in A(S_k x)} v(S_l S_k x)$$
$$\leq v(S_k S_0 x) - v(S_k x) - v(S_k S_0^2 x) + v(S_0 S_k x)$$
$$= 2v(S_k S_0 x) - v(S_k x) - v(S_k S_0^2 x) \leq 0,$$

due to the convexity property (2.19).
3. $f(x) = 0$ and $f(S_0 S_k x) = l.$

$$\min_{l \in A(x)} v(S_l S_0 x) - v(S_0 x) - v(S_l S_k S_0 x) + \min_{l \in A(S_k x)} v(S_l S_k x)$$
$$\leq v(S_k S_0 x) - v(S_0 x) - v(S_l S_k S_0 x) + v(S_0 S_l x) \leq 0$$

applying the inequality (2.18) for the state $S_0 x.$

Since we consider the case with three servers, the policy in state $S_k S_l x$ can take only one possible value, $f(S_k S_l x) = 0$. Thus the inequality (2.18)

$$(1 - S_k)(S_l - 1)\hat{v}(x) = \hat{v}(S_k x) - \hat{v}(x) - \hat{v}(S_k S_l x) + \hat{v}(S_l x)$$
$$= \min_{l \in A(S_k x)} v(S_l S_k x) - \min_{l \in A(x)} v(S_l x)$$
$$- \min_{i \in A(S_k S_l x)} v(S_l S_k S_l x) + \min_{k \in A(S_l x)} v(S_k S_l x) \leq 0$$

assumes the following relations

1. $f(x) = f(S_k S_l x) = 0$.

$$\min_{l \in A(S_k x)} v(S_l S_k x) - v(S_0 x) - v(S_k S_l S_0 x) + \min_{k \in A(S_l x)} v(S_k S_l x)$$
$$\leq v(S_k S_0 x) - v(S_0 x) - v(S_k S_l S_0 x) + v(S_l S_0 x) \leq 0$$

that satisfies the inequality (2.18) for the state $S_0 x$.

2. $f(x) = k$ and $f(S_k S_l x) = 0$.

$$\min_{l \in A(S_k x)} v(S_l S_k x) - v(S_k x) - v(S_k S_l S_0 x) + \min_{k \in A(S_l x)} v(S_k S_l x)$$
$$\leq v(S_k S_0 x) - v(S_k x) - v(S_k S_l S_0 x) + v(S_k S_l x) \leq 0$$

according to the inequality (2.17) for the state $S_k x$.

For the boundary points $q(x) = B$, $J_0(x) = \emptyset$, the inequalities (2.16)–(2.19) also hold since the shift operators are defined by (2.2).

The operators T_j, $j \neq k$ also retain the (S_0, S_k)-supermodularity of the functions by virtue of (2.9). To show the inequality for the operator T_k denote by $\hat{v}(x) = T_k v(x)$. Then we have

$$(1 - S_0)(S_0 - S_k)\hat{v}(x) = \hat{v}(S_0 x) - \hat{v}(S_k x) - \hat{v}(S_0^2 x) + \hat{v}(S_0 S_k x)$$
$$= v(S_0 x) - v(x) - v(S_0^2 x) + v(S_0 x) = 2v(S_0 x) - v(x) - v(S_0^2 x) \leq 0$$

by virtue of the inequality (2.19). Finally, applying the operators T_k and T_l to (2.17) and (2.18) we get the equalities.

Now it is possible to prove that the value function $v = \{v(x) : x \in E\}$ is (S_0, S_k)-supermodular. This assertion follows from the fact that property of (S_0, S_k)-supermodularity is retained for linear operations defining the operator B as defined by (2.10), the function $l(x)$ is (S_0, S_k)-supermodular and the successive approximations $B^n l(x)$ converge monotonously to the value function $v(x)$.
□

2.4.7 Threshold phenomenon of optimal policy. Threshold function for NJM–problem

From the previous section, (see Theorem 2.10) it follows that the optimal policy is of a threshold type. Although we can exactly prove this structural result for the system with $K = 3$ servers, we conjecture the correctness of the following statement in general case.

Theorem 2.11 *The optimal policy for the queueing system $M/M/K/B$ in the NJM–problem is of a threshold type, i.e. for each state x, there exists some level of the queue length $q^*(x)$ (depending on the collection of busy servers $J_1(x)$) such that it is necessary to switch on the fastest j among the idle servers only if $q(x) > q_j^*(x)$. If in some state x the optimal decision is to allocate a customer to the queue, then this decision is optimal for all y with $q(y) \leq q(x)$ and the same collection of busy servers $J_1(y) = J_1(x)$*

Proof: The proof follows from the reasoning of the previous section.
□

The theorem states that the threshold depends on the state of the servers in such manner that if it is not optimal to assign a job to processor j then it is not optimal to make an assignment to processor j until such time as there is at least one more arrival. That is, the state cannot change to one in which it becomes optimal to assign a job to the server j simply by the departure of the jobs.

It is obvious that, if the buffer is nonempty and the first server with service intensity $\mu_1 = \max\limits_{k \in J_0(x)} \{\mu_k\}$ is available (idle), then the idleness of the fastest server is never optimal, i.e. the threshold level for the first server $q_1^* = 0$.

We note that for the NJM–problem the threshold level for the j-th server $q_j^*(x)$ depends on the state x, that is it can depend on the states of other slower servers. Such influence arises only in the case of a large arrival intensity that will be investigated in Section 2.7.1.

Further in this section we consider the special type of the system operation, i.e. so called *light traffic* regime ($\lambda < \mu_K$). We shall show that in this case the threshold level for the j-th server is independent of the slower servers and obtain the explicit form of the threshold functions. We will use the denotation of the thresholds independently on the state x, that is, for j-th server the threshold level is q_j^*.

As it was shown in [62], the threshold policy which is optimal for the system without future arrivals, i.e., $\lambda = 0$ is also optimal for small enough values of the arrival rate λ. Thus, there exists some value $\lambda_0 > 0$ with the property that every optimal policy for the system with arrival rate λ in $(0, \lambda_0]$ is contained in this class of simple threshold policies and every such threshold policy is optimal when $\lambda = 0$. This light traffic result is established also independently by Reiman [59], whose approach is based on the light traffic theory developed by Reiman and Simon [60].

For the system under consideration it is clear that $\lim_{\lambda \to 0} g(\lambda; \delta) = 0$. This statement with respect to the formula (2.7) when $\lambda = 0$ leads to the optimality equation determined by

$$v(x) = \frac{l(x)}{M_1} + \sum_{j \in J_1(x)} \frac{\mu_j}{M_1} T_j v(x). \tag{2.20}$$

Now using the equation (2.20) we just want to clear a system which already contains some amount of customers. If the threshold levels for the servers $2, \ldots j - 1$ are $q_2^*, \ldots, q_{j-1}^*$, respectively, then we can find the threshold q_j^* for the j-th server, recursively solving the optimality equation (2.20). The solution for the state $x = (0, \ldots, 0)$

$$v(x) = 0;$$
$$v(S_1 x) = \frac{1}{\mu_1};$$
$$v(S_0 S_1 x) = \frac{2}{\mu_1} + v(S_1 x);$$
$$v(S_0^2 S_1 x) = \frac{3}{\mu_1} + v(S_0 S_1 x);$$
$$\cdots\cdots\cdots$$

yield

$$v(S_0^{q_2^*-1} S_1 x) = \frac{q_2^*(q_2^* + 1)}{2\mu_1}.$$

Let the number of the customers in the queue reaches the value q_2^*, that is the controller has to use the second server. Thus, for the state $S_0^{q_2^*-1} S_1 S_2 x$ we have

$$v(S_0^{q_2^*-1} S_1 S_2 x) = \frac{q_2^* + 1}{\mu_1 + \mu_2} + \frac{\mu_1}{\mu_1 + \mu_2} v(S_0^{q_2^*-2} S_1 S_2 x) + \frac{\mu_2}{\mu_1 + \mu_2} v(S_0^{q_2^*-1} S_1 x),$$

or recursively we get

$$v(S_0^{q_2^*-1}S_1S_2x) = \sum_{i=0}^{q_2^*-1} \frac{q_2^*+1-i}{(\mu_1+\mu_2)^{i+1}} + \left(\frac{\mu_1}{\mu_1+\mu_2}\right)^{q_2^*}\frac{1}{\mu_2}$$

$$+ \sum_{i=0}^{q_2^*-1} \frac{\mu_1^{q_2^*-1-i}\mu_2}{(\mu_1+\mu_2)^{q_2^*-i}}\sum_{j=1}^{i+1}\frac{i}{\mu_1}$$

$$= \frac{1}{\mu_2} + \frac{q_2^*(q_2^*+1)}{2\mu_1}\frac{1}{\mu_1} = \frac{1}{\mu_2} + v(S_0^{q_2^*-1}S_1x).$$

Further we analogously obtain

$$v(S_0^{q_2^*}S_1S_2x) = \frac{q_2^*+2}{\mu_1+\mu_2} + v(S_0^{q_2^*-1}S_1S_2x);$$

$$\cdots\cdots\cdots\cdots$$

$$v(S_0^{q_3^*-1}S_1S_2x) = \frac{(q_3^*-q_2^*)(q_3^*+q_2^*+3)}{2(\mu_1+\mu_2)} + v(S_0^{q_2^*-1}S_1S_2x).$$

Again using the threshold structure of an optimal policy we have

$$v(S_0^{q_3^*-1}S_1S_2S_3x) = \frac{1}{\mu_3} + \frac{(q_3^*-q_2^*)(q_3^*+q_2^*+3)}{2(\mu_1+\mu_2)} + v(S_0^{q_2^*-1}S_1S_2x).$$

Under further increasing of the queue length, it is possible to obtain the value function in state x, where $q(x) = q_j^*$

$$v(S_0^{q_j^*-1}S_1S_2\dots S_{j-1}x) = \frac{(q_j^*-q_{j-1}^*)(q_j^*+q_{j-1}^*+2j-3)}{2\sum_{k=1}^{j-1}\mu_k}$$

$$+ v(S_0^{q_{j-1}^*-1}S_1S_2\dots S_{j-1}x).$$

Analogously, when the total number of jobs in the queue is $\geq q_j^* - 1$, then

$$v(S_0^{q_j^*-1}S_1S_2\dots S_{j-1}S_jx) = \frac{1}{\mu_j} + v(S_0^{q_{j-1}^*-1}S_1S_2\dots S_{j-1}x)$$

$$= \frac{1}{\mu_j} + \frac{(q_j^*-q_{j-1}^*)(q_j^*+q_{j-1}^*+2j-3)}{2\sum_{k=1}^{j-1}\mu_k} + v(S_0^{q_{j-1}^*-1}S_1S_2\dots S_{j-1}x).$$

Since q_j^* is an optimal queue length to switch on the j-th server, it is necessary to require the following condition: The value function in the state, in which the controller begins to use the j-th server, i.e. $q(x) = q_j^*$, with respect to the optimal policy must be less or equal to the value function in the state, in which the controller does not use the server j, that is

$$\frac{1}{\mu_j} + \frac{(q_j^* - q_{j-1}^*)(q_j^* + q_{j-1}^* + 2j - 3)}{2 \sum_{k=1}^{j-1} \mu_k} + v(S_0^{q_{j-1}^* - 1} S_1 S_2 \ldots S_{j-1} x)$$
$$< \frac{(q_j^* - q_{j-1}^* + 1)(q_j^* + q_{j-1}^* + 2j - 2)}{2 \sum_{k=1}^{j-1} \mu_k} + v(S_0^{q_{j-1}^* - 1} S_1 S_2 \ldots S_{j-1} x).$$

Now the threshold level for the j-th server can be obtained by the formula which will refer to as the *NJM threshold formula*

$$q_j^* = \frac{1}{\mu_j} \sum_{k=1}^{j-1} \mu_k - (j - 1). \tag{2.21}$$

This formula means the following. Let j be the fastest idle server when q jobs are waiting in the queue. If $q > q_j^*$, then one job from the queue is dispatched to server j. If $q = q_j^*$, then a customer may or may not be dispatched to server j. If $q < q_j^*$, then no jobs is dispatched to any of the idle servers.

The optimality of the policy determined by (2.21) will be proved in the next section in Section 2.5.7 in analogous theorem for the PCM–problem. According to the obtained result for the system without future arrival it follows that if for some state $x = (q, d_1, \ldots, d_K)$ there exists some threshold q_j^* for any idle server d_j, then no job waiting in x will be scheduled on any server d_i, $i > j$ before d_j becomes busy. Thus, all the jobs waiting in x will be scheduled only on processors d_i, $i \leq j$. This states that the threshold function is an increasing function of j.

Corollary 2.12 *Let $x = (q, d_1, \ldots, d_K)$ be an arbitrary state. A server d_i idle in x is left idle while $q(x) \leq q_i^*$ if $q(x) = 0$ or if $i > j$, where d_j is the lowest indexed idle processor in x. A waiting job in x is assigned to d_j if inequality (2.21) is true.*

Proof: The proof is follows from above explanation.
□

As expected, if $\mu_1 \geq \cdots \geq \mu_j \geq \cdots \geq \mu_K$ it implies the following Corollary

Corollary 2.13 *The threshold function defining in (2.21) is an increasing function of j.*

It follows from this observation that

Proof: Indeed, for $j < i \leq K$ according to (2.21) we have

$$\frac{\mu_1 + \cdots + \mu_{i-1}}{\mu_i} - (i-1)$$

$$\geq \frac{\mu_1 + \cdots + \mu_{j-1}}{\mu_j} + \frac{\mu_j + \cdots + \mu_{i-1}}{\mu_i} - (i-1)$$

$$\geq \frac{\mu_1 + \cdots + \mu_{j-1}}{\mu_j} + (i-j) - (i-1)$$

$$= \frac{\mu_1 + \cdots + \mu_{j-1}}{\mu_j} - (j-1),$$

that is required.

□

Also it follows that in the problem without arrivals the value function for the state x with respect to the threshold function on $d_{j+1}, \ldots, d_K$ are independent of those on $d_1, \ldots, d_j$ and we can write

$$v(x) = \sum_{\substack{k \in J_1(x) \\ k > j}} \frac{1}{\mu_k} + v(y), \tag{2.22}$$

where y has the same number of waiting jobs as x, but d_i is active in y only if $i \in J_1(x)$ and $i \leq j$.

The general problem (when an arrival intensity is large) is much more difficult, especially in multi-server case, in order to obtain estimation for the thresholds relatively to the arrival intensity λ. As it was shown by Larsen and Agrawala in [37] for two-server system it is possible to consider probabilistic control policy which will be suboptimal for NJM–problem with threshold for the second server

$$q_2^* = \frac{\mu_1 - \lambda + \sqrt{4\mu_2\lambda + (\mu_1 - \lambda)^2}}{2\mu_2}$$

In multi-server case we conjecture that the optimal threshold decreases when the arrival intensity increases. Moreover, if there are future arrivals, they see a shorter queue, thus there is an extra reduction in cost. Therefore, the upper bound on the thresholds approximately can be applied to all λ. In the case of future arrival with some arrival intensity the problem of optimal threshold behavior investigation can be considered successfully in the framework of numerical analysis. Numerical results will be proposed in the Sections 2.7.

2.5 Processing cost minimization (PCM–problem)

2.5.1 Quantity functional

Unlike the NJM–problem, to analyze the problem of average processing cost of the system minimization (PCM–problem) we introduce an additional cost structure. We define $C^Q(q)$ as the cost for q customers holding in the queue and $C^U(\mu_k)$ as the *usage cost* of the k-th server (with intensity μ_k) per unit of time.

The functions $C^Q(q)$ and $C^U(\mu_k)$ are assumed to be non-decreasing while the function $C^Q(q)$ assumed to be convex. In this section we consider the case of fixed set-up costs, that is $C^Q(q) = c_0 q$ with *waiting cost* $c_0 \geq 0$ and $C^U(\mu_k) = c_k$.

In accordance with the given cost structure, the quantity (cost) functional to be minimized has the form

$$Y(t) = \int_0^t \left(c_0 Q(u) + \sum_{1 \leq k \leq K} c_k D_k(u) \right) du. \tag{2.23}$$

Let

$$c(x) = c_0 q + \sum_{j \in J_1(x)} c_j \tag{2.24}$$

denote the *loss rate* at the state x (which does not depend on the control a).

We note that the NJM–problem is a particular case of the PCM–problem, i.e. one has to put $c(x) = l(x)$, where $l(x) = q(x) + d(x)$ is the number of jobs in the system, and $d(x) = \sum_{1 \leq k \leq K} d_k$ is the number of busy servers.

Similar to the NJM–problem (2.5), the problem of minimizing the long-run system average processing cost is presented as follows: Minimize

$$g(x_0; \delta) = \lim_{t \to \infty} \frac{1}{t} \mathbf{E}_{x_0}^{\delta} Y(t)$$

with respect to all admissible strategies.

2.5.2 Optimality equation

Exactly as in previous case, for Markov decision problem with respect to the long-run average criterion the optimality principle is valid. Moreover, with exception of the first term in the right-hand side, the optimality equation has the same form as for the NJM–problem. Therefore, the optimality equation for the PCM–problem is determined by

$$v(x) = \frac{1}{\lambda + M_1} \min_a \left[c(x) + \lambda v(S_{a_0} x) + \sum_{j \in J_1(x)} \mu_j \; v(S_{a_j} S_j^{-1} S_0^{-1} x) - g \right]. \quad (2.25)$$

To consider the monotonicity properties of an optimal solution in the representation of an optimality equation, it is more convenient to use the introduced in 2.9 operators T_0 and T_k, and after the transformation we get

$$v(x) = \frac{1}{\lambda + M} \left[c(x) + \lambda T_0 \, v(x) + \sum_{1 \leq k \leq K} \mu_k T_k \, v(x) - g \right] = B v(x). \quad (2.26)$$

We note that all the theorems and results with respect to the transformation of the optimality equation and the definition of an optimal policy are also hold for this type of optimization problem.

Numerical investigations lead to some conjectures about the structure of an overall average cost optimality policy that will be the topic of the next sections.

2.5.3   Monotonicity properties of optimal policies. Two types of optimal policy structure for PCM–problem

In this section we consider the monotonicity conditions of the PCM–problem. For this problem we the servers will be arranged in order of their quotient value γ_k increasing

$$\gamma_k = \frac{\text{server usage cost}}{\text{server service rate}} = \frac{c_k}{\mu_k}, \quad (2.27)$$

such that

$$0 < \frac{c_1}{\mu_1} \leq \frac{c_2}{\mu_2} \leq \cdots \leq \frac{c_K}{\mu_K}. \quad (2.28)$$

The value γ_k we call *mean usage cost*.

If all the costs $c_0, c_1, c_2, \ldots, c_K$ are equal to one, we obtain the NJM-rule (2.13), that is the servers will be arranged in order their service rates decreasing.

The partial ordering of the state space E is determined by the inequalities (2.14) and (2.15).

It is interesting to investigate the properties of an optimal policy for the PCM–problem and estimate the influence of the initial parameters, in particular γ_k, on the stamp of this policy. Numerical results for the PCM–problem motivated the consideration of different groups of initial parameters, such as service intensities and usage costs. It turned out, that these parameters can be divided into two groups, and that to each of the group there corresponds a certain optimal policy structure. In more detail, under the condition (2.28) we shall distinguish two groups of mentioned parameters, the first group corresponding to expressions (2.29) and (2.30) below, the second corresponding to expression (2.31):

- $\quad 0 \leq \mu_1^{-1} \leq \mu_2^{-1} \leq \cdots \leq \mu_K^{-1}, \quad c_1 \leq c_2 \leq \cdots \leq c_K;$ \hfill (2.29)
- $\quad 0 \leq \mu_1^{-1} \leq \mu_2^{-1} \leq \cdots \leq \mu_K^{-1}, \quad c_1 > c_2 > \cdots > c_K;$ \hfill (2.30)
- $\quad 0 < \mu_K^{-1} < \cdots < \mu_2^{-1} < \mu_1^{-1}, \quad c_1 \leq c_2 \leq \cdots \leq c_K.$ \hfill (2.31)

We note that the third case with $c_1 > c_2 > \cdots > c_K$ is impossible with respect to the introduced condition (2.28).

The PCM–problem under the conditions (2.28)-(2.30) is discussed in Sections 2.5.4-2.5.7. We expect that the optimal policy in these cases is of a threshold type as for the NJM–problem and consists in using the server with smallest mean usage cost or, with respect to introduced servers' order, the fastest available server.

The PCM–problem under the conditions (2.28) and (2.31) we consider in Section 2.5.8. An optimal policy for such values of system parameters has a more complex structure than in previous cases, i.e. there exists two-level threshold optimal policy which implies the using of some server j according to some rule. This server may not be necessary the fastest or the cheapest available, or even can be with larger ratio γ_j, but this server is used by the controller only if the current queue length is between two prespecified levels. Moreover, all other available is some state servers are switched on in order of the servers' index increasing (order of the mean usage costs γ_k increasing).

2.5.4 Assignment to the server with the lowest mean usage cost

The numerical results motivate us to make the following conjecture about the quantitative properties of an optimal control for the PCM–problem under the conditions (2.28)-(2.30).

Conjecture 2.14 *The optimal control policy consists in activating the available server with the lowest mean usage cost (fastest server), if necessary.*

There is, at least, one thing that can be proved for the PCM–problem. It is the part of Conjecture 2.14, as can be reasserted in the following theorem.

Theorem 2.15 *The value function of the model $v = \{v(x) :, x \in E\}$ increases monotonously relative to the order introduced in E if conditions (2.28) and (2.29) hold.*

Proof: According to the condition (2.29) the function $c(x)$ is nondecreasing with respect to the shifts from the point $S_j x$ to $S_i x$, $i, j \in J_0(x)$, $i \geq j$ $(c_i \geq c_j)$, i.e. $c(S_i x) - c(S_j x) = c_i + q(x)c_0 - c_j - q(x)c_0 = c_i - c_j \geq 0$. Now using the same steps as in Theorem 2.8, taking into account that $\mu_i \leq \mu_j$, we obtain that for some nondecreasing function $v(x)$ the operator B, introduced in (2.26), retains the monotonicity property.

Now the theorem follows from the fact that the value function of the model $v = \{v(x) : x \in E\}$ is a fixed point of the operator B, i.e.

$$\lim_{n \to \infty} B^n c(S_i x) - B^n c(S_j x) = v(S_i x) - v(S_j x) \geq 0,$$

where $c(S_i x) \geq c(S_j x)$ for any state $x \in E$ and $i, j \in J_0(x)$, $i \geq j$.
□

For the PCM–problem under the conditions (2.28) and (2.30) the statement above is confirmed by the numerical results. We note that for simplified system in the case without arrivals, when only two servers present in the system, theoretical results are fully carried over the problem with condition (2.30). Indeed, in this case we have

$$v(S_i x) - v(S_j x) = \left[\frac{c_i}{\mu_i} - \frac{c_j}{\mu_j} \right] + c_0 q(x) \left[\frac{1}{\mu_i} - \frac{1}{\mu_j} \right] \geq 0,$$

for any $q(x) \geq 0$.

2.5.5   Supermodularity of the value function

As before, in order to determine whether a server must be activated, we have to show that the optimal policy features monotonicity property with respect to the queue length increasing. Using the statement of Conjecture 2.14, the following theorem can be formulated.

Theorem 2.16 *The inequalities (2.16)–(2.19) for the monotone increments with respect to the partial ordering of E hold for the PCM–problem under the conditions (2.28)-(2.31)*

Proof: To prove the statement it is necessary to show that the operator T_0 preserves the properties (2.16)-(2.19) of the functions to have the monotone increments. This theorem can be proved using the same arguments as for the NJM–problem in Theorem 2.10 of Section 2.4.6.
□

The results for the NJM–problem can be generalized for the PCM–problem with the convex function $C^Q(q)$.

Theorem 2.17 *If the function $C^Q(q)$ is convex, and service intensities μ_k with usage costs c_k satisfy the conditions (2.28) and (2.29), then the value function of the model $v = \{v(x) : x \in E\}$ has the monotone increments (2.16)–(2.19).*

Proof: The proof follows from the successive approximation method because the value function of the model is a fixed point of the operator B, determined by (2.10), if it preserves the properties (2.16)–(2.19). Indeed, the convexity of the function $C^Q(q)$ implies

$$(I - S_0)(S_0 - S_k)c(x) = c(S_0 x) - c(S_0^2 x) - c(S_k x) + c(S_k S_0 x)$$
$$= [C^Q(q(x) + 1) + \sum_{j \in J_1(x)} C^U(\mu_j)]$$
$$- [C^Q(q(x) + 2) + \sum_{j \in J_1(x)} C^U(\mu_j)]$$
$$- [C^Q(q(x) + \sum_{j \in J_1(x)} C^U(\mu_j) + C^U(\mu_k)]$$
$$+ [C^Q(q(x) + 1) + \sum_{j \in J_1(x)} C^U(\mu_j) + C^U(\mu_k)]$$
$$= -[C^Q(q + 2) - 2C^Q(q + 1) + C^Q(q)] \leq 0.$$

The inequality (2.16)–(2.19) keep the linear operations. Therefore, the statement of the theorem follows from the fact that the operators T_0 and T_j preserve the properties given in Theorem 2.10.
□

2.5.6 Threshold function for PCM–problem

From the previous section it follows that the optimal policy is of threshold type.

Theorem 2.18 *The optimal policy in the PCM–problem with additional condition (2.29) and (2.30) (for the last condition we require Conjecture 2.14) is of threshold type, i.e. for each server j, there exists some level of the queue length q_j^* (depending on the collection of busy servers $J_1(x)$ with smaller indexes) such that it is necessary to switch on the server with lowest mean usage cost γ_j (or the fastest) among the idle servers only if $q > q_j^*$.*
If in some state x the optimal decision is allocate a customer to the queue, then this decision is optimal for all y with $q(y) \leq q(x)$ and the same collection of busy servers $J_1(y) = J_1(x)$

Proof: The proof follows from the reasoning of the previous section.
$\square$

It is evident, that the idleness of the fastest server is never optimal, i.e. $q_1^* = 0$.

As for the previous model we consider the case without future arrivals (*light traffic* regime), when we want to clear a system which already contains the customers. Taking into account that in this case $\lambda = g = 0$ the optimality equation can be written as follows

$$v(x) = \frac{c(x)}{M_1} + \sum_{j \in J_1(x)} \frac{\mu_j T_j(x)}{M_1}, \qquad (2.32)$$

where according to the definitions M_1 is a total intensity of busy servers in the state x $M_1 = \sum_{j \in J_1} \mu_j$ and operator $T_j(x) = T_0(S_0^{-1} S_j^{-1} x)$.
We obtain the form of threshold function in similar way as it was done for the NJM–problem. With respect to our assumption about threshold structure of the optimal policy recursively solving the optimality equation (2.32) using thresholds $q_2^*, \ldots, q_{j-1}^*$ we obtain the threshold q_j^*. For the state $x = (0, \ldots, 0)$ we have

$$v(x) = 0$$
$$v(S_1 x) = \frac{c_1}{\mu_1},$$
$$v(S_0 S_1 x) = \frac{c_0 + c_1}{\mu 1} + v(S_1 x),$$
$$v(S_0^2 S_1 x) = \frac{c_1 + 2c_0}{\mu_1} + v(S_0 S_1 x)$$

$$\cdots\cdots\cdots$$
$$v(S_0^{q_2^*-1}S_1x) = \frac{q_2^*(q_2^*-1)c_0}{2\mu_1} + \frac{q_2^*c_1}{\mu_1}.$$

When the queue length has reached the threshold level for the second server q_2^*, the controller has to use this server. Then using the equation (2.32) we have

$$v(S_0^{q_2^*-1}S_1S_2x) = \frac{c_2}{\mu_2} + \frac{q_2^*(q_2^*-1)c_0}{2\mu_1} + \frac{q_2^*c_1}{\mu_1}$$

Repeating the procedure up to the threshold for the j-th server q_j^* one can obtain

$$v(S_0^{q_j^*-1}S_1S_2\ldots S_{j-1}x) = \frac{(q_j^*-q_{j-1}^*)\sum_{k=1}^{j-1}c_k}{\sum_{k=1}^{j-1}\mu_k} + \frac{(q_j^*-q_{j-1}^*)(q_{j-1}^*+q_j^*-1)c_0}{2\sum_{k=1}^{j-1}\mu_k}.$$

Again, since q_j^* is optimal threshold the condition

$$v(S_0^{q_j^*-1}S_1S_2\ldots S_{j-1}S_jx) = \frac{c_j}{\mu_j}+v(S_0^{q_j^*-1}S_1S_2\ldots S_{j-1}x) < v(S_0^{q_j^*}S_1S_2\ldots S_{j-1}x)$$

implies

$$\frac{c_j}{\mu_j} + \frac{(q_j^*-q_{j-1}^*)\sum_{k=1}^{j-1}c_k}{\sum_{k=1}^{j-1}\mu_k} + \frac{(q_j^*-q_{j-1}^*)(q_{j-1}^*+q_j^*-1)c_0}{2\sum_{k=1}^{j-1}\mu_k}$$
$$< \frac{(q_j^*-q_{j-1}^*+1)\sum_{k=1}^{j-1}c_k}{\sum_{k=1}^{j-1}\mu_k} + \frac{(q_j^*-q_{j-1}^*+1)(q_{j-1}^*+q_j^*)c_0}{2\sum_{k=1}^{j-1}\mu_k}.$$

From the last inequality we get the *PCM threshold formula*

$$q_j^* = \frac{1}{c_0}\left[\frac{c_j}{\mu_j}\sum_{k=1}^{j-1}\mu_k - \sum_{k=1}^{j-1}c_k\right]. \qquad (2.33)$$

The last equation defines the threshold scheduling function. The server d_j which is idle in x is left idle in $S_0^{q_j^*-1}x$. A waiting job in x is assigned to d_j if and only if the inequality (2.33) holds.

We note that $\frac{c_i}{\mu_i} \geq \frac{c_j}{\mu_j}$ with $i \geq j$ implies the following corollary.

Corollary 2.19 *The threshold function defining by (2.33) is an increasing function of server's index j.*

Proof: Indeed, if $\frac{c_1}{\mu_1} \leq \cdots \leq \frac{c_j}{\mu_j} \leq \cdots \leq \frac{c_K}{\mu_K}$ for $j < i \leq K$ we have

$$\frac{1}{c_0}\left[(\mu_1 + \cdots + \mu_{i-1})\frac{c_i}{\mu_i} - (c_1 + \cdots + c_{i-1})\right]$$

$$\geq \frac{1}{c_0}\left[(\mu_1 + \cdots + \mu_{j-1})\frac{c_j}{\mu_j} + (\mu_j + \cdots + \mu_{i-1})\frac{c_i}{\mu_i} - (c_1 + \cdots + c_{i-1})\right]$$

$$\geq \frac{1}{c_0}\left[(\mu_1 + \cdots + \mu_{j-1})\frac{c_j}{\mu_j} + (c_j + \cdots + c_{i-1}) - (c_1 + \cdots + c_{i-1})\right]$$

$$= \frac{1}{c_0}\left[(\mu_1 + \cdots + \mu_{j-1})\frac{c_j}{\mu_j} - (c_1 + \cdots + c_{j-1})\right].$$

□

It follows that if

$$q(x) \leq q_{j+1}^* = \frac{1}{c_0}\left[\frac{c_{j+1}}{\mu_{j+1}}\sum_{k=1}^{j}\mu_k - \sum_{k=1}^{j}c_k\right]$$

for some state $x = (q, d_1, \ldots, d_K)$, then no job waiting in x will be scheduled on any server d_i, $i > j$. Similar to the NJM–problem, since every subsequent state will have at most q_j^* waiting jobs, all jobs waiting in x will be scheduled only on processors d_i, $i \leq j$. It follows, that the value function for the state x with respect to the threshold function on $d_{j+1}, \ldots, d_K$ are independent of those on $d_1, \ldots, d_j$ and we can write

$$v(x) = \sum_{\substack{k \in J_1(x) \\ k > j}} \frac{c_k}{\mu_k} + v(y), \tag{2.34}$$

where y has the same number of waiting jobs as x, but d_i is active in y only if $i \in J_1(x)$ and $i \leq j$. This equation will be used for the next theorem.

2.5.7   Optimality of threshold function

In this section we generalize the result obtained first by Agrawala et al. [1] for the minimization of expected total flow time, and it will be shown that the introduced threshold policy (2.33) for the PCM–problem is optimal.

Theorem 2.20 *The threshold policy introduced in (2.33) for PCM–problem in the case without arrivals and with conditions (2.28) and (2.29) is optimal.*

Proof: Let the number of servers is K with ordered ration of the type $\frac{c_1}{\mu_1} \leq \frac{c_2}{\mu_2} \leq \cdots \leq \frac{c_K}{\mu_K}$. As it was denoted in Section 2.3 any system state x belongs to the E, which is a set of possible system states with partial order introduced on it in (2.14) and (2.15). According to the definition of optimal policy (2.33) we consider two types of optimal policies (2.12), namely $f(x)$ is arbitrary scheduling policy and $t(x)$ is proposed by (2.33) threshold policy. Without loss of generality we may restrict attention to $f(x)$ that satisfy the property, that for any state $x = (q, d_1, \ldots, d_K)$ either $f(x) = 0$ or $f(x) = k$, where k is an idle server with lowest index. In other words, we assume that $f(x)$ represents the optimal server in increasing order of index (increasing order of the ratio γ_k).

quad We will prove the theorem by means of induction with respect to the states $x = (q, d_1 \ldots d_K)$ and will show that $v^t(x) \leq v^f(x)$ that is the value function with using of threshold policy is less or equal to one with arbitrary scheduling. We have the desired result for any state x with $q(x) = 0$, because there are no waiting jobs and as consequence there no scheduling decisions to be made. Therefore, $x = 0$ provides the basis for induction. Soppose, that the results holds for all states x where $q(x) \leq I$. With induction we add one more assumption, that $f(x) = t(x)$ for all states x where $q(x) < I$. In order to show that $v^t(x) \leq v^f(x)$ we divide the problem into cases.

1. Let after service completion in state x on the k-th server $f(S_0^{-1} S_k^{-1} x) = 0$ and $t(S_0^{-1} S_k^{-1} x) = 0$, that is the optimal control for both of cases is to keep a job in the queue. In this case by the inductive hypothesis f and t are identical for any state obtained from a job completion on some server which is active in x. Thus, $v^f(x) = v^t(x)$.

2. Let $f(S_0^{-1} S_k^{-1} x) = i$ and $t(S_0^{-1} S_k^{-1} x) = j$. If $i = j$ then the equality $v^f(x) = v^t(x)$ follows from the previous case. Therefore, we suppose that $i \neq j$. According to the property (2.33) of threshold policy t which assigns the job to the server with the least ratio γ_k with lowest indexed server, it is necessary, that $j < i$. By virtue of the assumption about policy $f(x)$, any newly activated server in $f(S_0^{-2} S_l^{-1} S_k^{-1} S_i x) = m$ must have an index exceeding $m > i > j$. Therefore, the server d_j must be idle in $S_0^{-2} S_l^{-1} S_k^{-1} S_i S_m x$. But since the state $S_0^{-1} S_k^{-1} S_i x$ has less waiting jobs than x the inductive hypothesis implies that f and t is identical at the state $S_0^{-1} S_k^{-1} S_i x$. Thus, since d_j is idle in $S_0^{-1} S_k^{-1} S_i x$, the policies f and t cannot activate the server with index greater than j. It follows, that $f(S_0^{-2} S_l^{-1} S_k^{-1} S_i x) = t(S_0^{-2} S_l^{-1} S_k^{-1} S_i x) = 0$. Since $t(S_0^{-2} S_l^{-1} S_k^{-1} S_i x) = 0$ and the server d_j is idle in this state, the definition

of the threshold policy implies

$$q_j^* - 1 \leq \frac{1}{c_0}\left[\frac{c_j}{\mu_j}(\mu_1 + \cdots + \mu_{j-1}) - (c_1 + \cdots + c_{j-1})\right].$$

But if $r > j$ according to the property of the threshold policy we have

$$\frac{1}{c_0}\left[\frac{c_r}{\mu_r}(\mu_1 + \cdots + \mu_{r-1}) - (c_1 + \cdots + c_{r-1})\right]$$
$$\geq \frac{1}{c_0}\left[\frac{c_j}{\mu_j}(\mu_1 + \cdots + \mu_{j-1}) - (c_1 + \cdots + c_{j-1})\right].$$

Thus, no idle servers d_r, $r > j$, can be newly activated by t in $S_0^{-1}S_k^{-1}S_j x$. Therefore, $t(S_0^{-2}S_l^{-1}S_k^{-1}S_j x) = 0$.
Consequently, both of scheduling policies f and t allocate between the servers only one job in state x. Since all subsequent states in either case have at most $q_j^* - 1$ waiting jobs, the threshold policy t and policy f will schedule waiting jobs only on servers in the set $\{d_1, \ldots, d_{j-1}\}$.

Now consider the states $y = \{q_j^*-1, d_1, \ldots, d_K\}$ with active servers $d_1, \ldots, d_{j-1}$ and idle servers $d_j, \ldots, d_K$. Since none of the $q_j^* - 1$ waiting jobs will be allocate between the servers $d_j, \ldots, d_K$ using t or f we can write as in (2.34)

$$v^t(x) = v^t(S_0^{-1}S_k^{-1}S_j x) = \sum_{\substack{r \in J_1(S_0^{-1}S_k^{-1}S_j x) \\ r \geq j}} \frac{c_r}{\mu_r} + v^t(y),$$

and hence

$$v^t(x) = \frac{c_j}{\mu_j} + \sum_{\substack{r \in J_1(x) \\ r \geq j}} \frac{c_r}{\mu_r} + v^t(y).$$

For the policy $f(x)$ we have

$$v^f(x) = \frac{c_i}{\mu_i} + \sum_{\substack{r \in J_1(x) \\ r \geq j}} \frac{c_r}{\mu_r} + v^f(y).$$

Note, that the states y have less number of jobs waiting in the queue, thus by virtue of inductive hypothesis $v^f(x) = v^t(x)$. After the subtraction of the previous expressions we get

$$v^t(x) - v^f(x) = \frac{c_j}{\mu_j} - \frac{c_i}{\mu_i} \leq 0,$$

because of $\frac{c_j}{\mu_j} \leq \frac{c_i}{\mu_i}$ for $j \leq i$.

3. If $f(S_0^{-1}S_k^{-1}x) = i \neq 0$ and $t(S_0^{-1}S_k^{-1}x) = 0$. If l is the largest index satisfying

$$q_l > \frac{\sum_{k=1}^{l-1} \mu_k}{\mu_l} - (l - 1).$$

It follows that all jobs waiting in x have to be subsequently sent to servers in the set $\{d_1, \ldots, d_l\}$. But $t(S_0^{-1}S_k^{-1}x) = 0$, therefore all of the servers $\{d_1, \ldots, d_l\}$ must be occupied in x. Now we can write as before

$$v^t(x) = \sum_{\substack{r \in J_1(x) \\ r > l}} \frac{c_r}{\mu_r} + v^t(y),$$

where $y = \{q_l, d_1, \ldots, d_K\}$ with active servers $d_k = 1$ if $k = \overline{1, l}$. According to the definition (2.32) of the value function $v(x)$ we have

$$v^t(x) = \sum_{\substack{r \in J_1(x) \\ r > l}} \frac{c_r}{\mu_r} + \frac{c(y)}{\sum_{k=1}^{l} \mu_k} + \frac{\sum_{k=1}^{l} \mu_k T_0 v^t(S_0^{-1}S_k^{-1}y)}{\sum_{k=1}^{l} \mu_k}.$$

But with respect to the condition for the threshold policy $t(S_0^{-1}S_k^{-1}y) = 0, k = \overline{1, l}$, that is after service completions in the state y controller has to send a new job to a server $d_k, k \leq l$. Now expressing $c(y)$ as $c(y) = c_0 q_l + \sum_{k=1}^{l} c_k$ we can write

$$v^t(x) = \sum_{\substack{r \in J_1(x) \\ r > l}} \frac{c_r}{\mu_r} + \frac{c_0 q_l + \sum_{k=1}^{l} c_k}{\sum_{k=1}^{l} \mu_k} + v^t(S_0^{-1}y). \qquad (2.35)$$

Let us consider $v^f(x)$. For the case under consideration we assumed that $f(S_0^{-1}S_k^{-1}x) = i \neq 0$. With respect to the above choice l, we have $i > l$. By the definition of l and the inductive hypothesis $f(S_0^{-2}S_l^{-1}S_k^{-1}S_ix) = t(S_0^{-2}S_l^{-1}S_k^{-1}S_ix) = 0$. Thus no job waiting in $S_0^{-1}S_k^{-1}S_ix$ will be scheduled by policy f on a server with index exceeding l and we get

$$v^f(x) = v^f(S_0^{-1}S_k^{-1}S_ix) = \sum_{\substack{r \in J_1(S_0^{-1}S_k^{-1}S_ix) \\ r > l}} \frac{c_r}{\mu_r} + v^f(S_0^{-1}y).$$

By virtue of the fact that the states x and $S_0^{-1}S_k^{-1}S_ix$ is differ only through the active server d_i, we have

$$v^f(x) = \frac{c_i}{\mu_i} + \sum_{\substack{r \in J_1(x) \\ r > l}} \frac{c_r}{\mu_r} + v^f(S_0^{-1}y). \qquad (2.36)$$

Now by subtracting the last expression (2.36) for the functions $v^t(x)$ from expression for $v^f(x)$ (2.35) we get

$$v^t(x) - v^f(x) = \frac{\sum_{k=1}^l c_k + c_0 q_l}{\sum_{k=1}^l \mu_k} - \frac{c_i}{\mu_i}$$

$$\leq \frac{c_0 q_l + \sum_{k=1}^l c_k}{\sum_{k=1}^l \mu_k} - \frac{c_{l+1}}{\mu_{l+1}},$$

by virtue of the fact that $i \geq l+1$ and $\frac{c_{l+1}}{\mu_{l+1}} \leq \frac{c_i}{\mu_i}$. The threshold for the l-th server has the form

$$q_l \leq \frac{1}{c_0} \left[\frac{c_{l+1}}{\mu_{l+1}} \sum_{k=1}^l \mu_k - \sum_{k=1}^l c_k \right]$$

and after some transformations

$$\frac{c_0 q_l + \sum_{k=1}^l c_k}{\sum_{k=1}^l \mu_k} \leq \frac{c_{l+1}}{\mu_{l+1}}.$$

From this the required result $v^t(x) \leq v^f(x)$ follows.

4. If $f(S_0^{-1} S_k^{-1} x) = 0$ and $t(S_0^{-1} S_k^{-1} x) = j$. For the policy $f(x)$ due to the inductive hypothesis and (2.32) we can write

$$v^f(x) = \frac{c(x)}{\sum_{k \in J_1(x)} \mu_k} + \frac{\sum_{k \in J_1(x)} \mu_k T_0 v^f(S_0^{-1} S_k^{-1} x)}{\sum_{k \in J_1(x)} \mu_k}, \qquad (2.37)$$

where $T_0 v^f(S_0^{-1} S_k^{-1} x) = v^f(S_k^{-1} x)$ under condition of this case. We assume that under the threshold policy t controller assigns $m \geq 1$ waiting jobs to idle servers in x and the system moves to the state z. Let us assume that l is the largest index which satisfies

$$q_l - m > \frac{1}{c_0} \left[\frac{c_l}{\mu_l} \sum_{k=1}^{l-1} \mu_k - \sum_{k=1}^{l-1} c_k \right].$$

Thus, policy t subsequently schedules jobs waiting in z only on the servers in the set $\{d_1, \ldots, d_l\}$. Here, two subcases are possible, based on the largest index i such that d_i is idle in x but active in z.

In the first subcase $j \leq l$. By the choice of l we can write as before

$$v^t(x) = v^t(z) = \sum_{\substack{r \in J_1(z) \\ r > l}} \frac{c_r}{\mu_r} + v^t(S_0^{-m} x), \qquad (2.38)$$

where the state $S_0^{-m}x$ in which the servers d_k, $k = \overline{1,l}$ are busy. As in previous case we can get for $v^t(S_0^{-m}x)$,

$$v^t(x) = \sum_{\substack{r \in J_1(z) \\ r>l}} \frac{c_r}{\mu_r} + \frac{c(S_0^{-m}x)}{\sum_{k=1}^{l} \mu_k} + v^t(S_0^{k-m-1}x). \tag{2.39}$$

Now consider the state $S_k^{-1}z$ under assumption $j \leq l$. In the state $S_k^{-1}z$ m jobs waiting in $S_k^{-1}x$ will be assigned by t and f to those servers newly activated in z. One more will be assigned to the server d_k only if $k \leq l$. Therefore, with respect to the inductive hypothesis

$$v^f(S_k^{-1}x) = v^f(S_k^{-1}z) = v^t(S_k^{-1}z) = \sum_{\substack{r \in J_1(S_k^{-1}z) \\ r>l}} \frac{c_r}{\mu_r} + v^t(S_0^{-m}x), \qquad k > l.$$

Taking into account that the states z and $S_k^{-1}z$ differ only in the server d_k which is busy in z and idle in $S_k^{-1}z$ if $k > l$, we get

$$v^f(S_k^{-1}x) = \sum_{\substack{r \in J_1(z) \\ r>l}} \frac{c_r}{\mu_r} - \frac{c_k}{\mu_k} + v^t(S_0^{-m}x), \qquad k > l. \tag{2.40}$$

But if $k \leq l$ then $m + 1$ waiting jobs are assigned and

$$v^f(S_k^{-1}x) = \sum_{\substack{r \in J_1(S_k^{-1}z) \\ r>l}} \frac{c_r}{\mu_r} + v^t(S_0^{k-m-1}x), \qquad k \leq l.$$

By virtue of the equality $J_1(S_k^{-1}z) = J_1(z)$ if $k \leq l$, we have

$$v^f(S_k^{-1}x) = \sum_{\substack{r \in J_1(z) \\ r>l}} \frac{c_r}{\mu_r} + v^t(S_0^{k-m-1}x), \qquad k \leq l. \tag{2.41}$$

Substituting into (2.40) and (2.41) for $v^t(S_0^{-m}x)$ and $v^t(S_0^{k-m-1}x)$ from (2.38) and (2.39), respectively, we obtain

$$v^f(S_k^{-1}x) = \begin{cases} v^t(x) - \frac{c_k}{\mu_k}, & k > l \\ v^t(x) - \frac{c(S_0^{-m}x)}{\sum_{i=1}^{l} \mu_i}, & k \leq l \end{cases}$$

Now substitute these expressions into (2.37)

$$v^f(x) = \frac{c(x)}{\sum_{i \in J_1(x)} \mu_i} + \sum_{\substack{k \in J_1(x) \\ k \le l}} \left[v^t(x) - \frac{c(S_0^{-m}x)}{\sum_{i=1}^l \mu_i} \right] \frac{\mu_k}{\sum_{i \in J_1(x)} \mu_i}$$
$$+ \sum_{\substack{k \in J_1(x) \\ k > l}} \left[v^t(x) - \frac{c_k}{\mu_k} \right] \frac{\mu_k}{\sum_{i \in J_1(x)} \mu_i},$$

by means of which one can get

$$v^f(x) - v^t(x) = \frac{1}{\sum_{i \in J_1(x)} \mu_i} \left[c(x) - \sum_{\substack{k \in J_1(x) \\ k > l}} c_k - \frac{c(S_0^{-m}x)}{\sum_{i=1}^l \mu_i} \sum_{\substack{k \in J_1(x) \\ k \le l}} \mu_k \right].$$

Since $j \le l$ there are m servers among $\{d_1, \ldots, d_l\}$ which are idle in x but active in $S_0^{-m}x$. But since no server with index higher than l is active in $S_0^{-m}x$ we can obtain $\sum_{\substack{k \in J_1(x) \\ k > l}} c_k = c(x) - c(S_0^{-m}x)$, or

$$v^f(x) - v^t(x) = \frac{c(S_0^{-m}x)}{\sum_{i \in J_1(x)} \mu_i} \left[1 - \frac{1}{\sum_{i=1}^l \mu_i} \sum_{\substack{k \in J_1(x) \\ k \le l}} \mu_k \right].$$

But $\sum_{i=1}^l \mu_i \ge \sum_{\substack{k \in J_1(x) \\ k \le l}} \mu_k$, and hence we obtain the required result $v^t(x) \le v^f(x)$.

In the second subcase $j > l$. Analogously to (2.38) we have

$$v^t(x) = \sum_{\substack{r \in J_1(x) \\ r > j}} \frac{c_r}{\mu_r} + v^t(S_0^{-m}y), \qquad (2.42)$$

where the state $y = \{q_l - m, d_1, \ldots, d_K\}$ with active servers from the set $\{d_1, \ldots, d_j\}$. For the function $v^f(S_k^{-1}x) = v^t(S_k^{-1}x) = v^t(S_k^{-1}z)$ we consider the case $k > j$. In this case no job is assigned to the server d_k by f and t in the state $S_k^{-1}x$. But m waiting jobs are assigned to the servers which are newly activated in z. Therefore,

$$v^f(S_k^{-1}x) = v^t(S_k^{-1}z) = \sum_{\substack{r \in J_1(S_k^{-1}z) \\ r > j}} \frac{c_r}{\mu_r} + v^t(S_0^{-m}y), \qquad k > j.$$

From (2.42) by virtue of the fact that the state $S_k^{-1}z$ and z are the same with exception of the server k which is active in z we get

$$v^f(S_k^{-1}x) = \sum_{\substack{r \in J_1(x) \\ r>j}} \frac{c_r}{\mu_r} - \frac{c_k}{\mu_k} + v^t(S_0^{-m}y), \qquad k > j. \tag{2.43}$$

The equality $k = j$ is impossible since $d_j(x) = 0$. But if $1 \le k < j$, then there will be exactly $m + 1$ idle servers in the set $\{d_1, d_2, \ldots, d_l\}$ in state $S_k^{-1}x$, that is m servers in z and one more newly idled server d_k. Since $j > l$ and d_j is idle in $S_k^{-1}x$ and $S_k^{-1}z$ the policies f and t will assign waiting jobs in this states to the same m servers as in z, except that d_k will be busy and d_j will be left idle. Therefore,

$$v^f(S_k^{-1}x) = \sum_{\substack{r \in J_1(S_k^{-1}z) \\ r>j}} \frac{c_r}{\mu_r} + v^t(S_0^{-m}y^{'}), \qquad 1 \le k < j$$

where $S_0^{-m}y^{'}$ represents the state with active servers $\{d_1, \ldots, d_j - 1\}$. But since $j > l$ no job waiting in $S_0^{-m}y$ will subsequently be scheduled by t on d_j and $v^t(S_0^{-m}y) = v^t(S_0^{-m}y^{'}) + \frac{c_j}{\mu_j}$. Thus, since $S_k^{-1}z$ and z are the same with exception that d_j is active in z but not in $S_k^{-1}z$ we have from (2.42)

$$v^f(S_k^{-1}x) = \sum_{\substack{r \in J_1(S_k^{-1}z) \\ r>j}} \frac{c_r}{\mu_r} + v^t(S_0^{-m}y) - \frac{c_j}{\mu_j} = v^t(x) - \frac{c_j}{\mu_j}, \quad 1 \le k < j.$$

$$\tag{2.44}$$

Substituting (2.43) and (2.44) into (2.37) we get

$$v^f(x) = \frac{c(x)}{\sum_{i \in J_1(x)} \mu_i} + \sum_{\substack{k \in J_1(x) \\ k<j}} \left[v^t(x) - \frac{c_j}{\mu_j} \right] \frac{\mu_k}{\sum_{i \in J_1(x)} \mu_i}$$

$$+ \sum_{\substack{k \in J_1(x) \\ k>j}} \left[v^t(x) - \frac{c_k}{\mu_k} \right] \frac{\mu_k}{\sum_{i \in J_1(x)} \mu_i},$$

which can be simplified to the following

$$v^f(x) - v^t(x) = \frac{1}{\sum_{i \in J_1(x)} \mu_i} \left[c(x) - \sum_{\substack{k \in J_1(x) \\ k>j}} c_k - \frac{c_j}{\mu_j} \sum_{\substack{k \in J_1(x) \\ k<j}} \mu_k \right],$$

where $c(x) = c_0 q(x) + \sum_{k \in J_1(x)} c_k$. By virtue of the threshold function definition

$$q(x) > \frac{1}{c_0} \left[\frac{c_j}{\mu_j} \sum_{\substack{k \in J_1(x) \\ k < j}} \mu_k - \sum_{\substack{k \in J_1(x) \\ k < j}} c_k \right]$$

we can get the following sequence of inequalities

$$c_0 q(x) + \sum_{k \in J_1(x)} c_k - \sum_{\substack{k \in J_1(x) \\ k > j}} c_k - \frac{c_j}{\mu_j} \sum_{\substack{k \in J_1(x) \\ k < j}} \mu_k$$

$$\geq \frac{c_j}{\mu_j} \sum_{\substack{k \in J_1(x) \\ k < j}} \mu_k - \sum_{\substack{k \in J_1(x) \\ k < j}} c_k + \sum_{k \in J_1(x)} c_k - \sum_{\substack{k \in J_1(x) \\ k > j}} c_k - \frac{c_j}{\mu_j} \sum_{\substack{k \in J_1(x) \\ k < j}} \mu_k = c_j > 0.$$

Thus, $v^f(x) - v^t(x) \geq 0$.

We have that in all cases $v^t(x) \leq v^f(x)$ for all states x and hence the threshold rule t is optimal.

$\square$

2.5.8   Two-level threshold function for PCM–problem

If additionally to the usage and holding costs some fixed switching cost for changing the servers will be introduced, we receive the model (see, [55]) for which the class of two-level hysteretic (q_*, q^*) optimal control rules exists, where $0 \leq q_* < q^*$. Under these rules the slower server is switched on only when at an arrival epoch the number of jobs present in the system increases up to or above q^* and the slower server is switched off when at a service completion epoch of the slower server the number of jobs left behind in the system is smaller or equal to q_*. But while the first steps in the numerical analysis of hysteretic optimal control rules have been done and despite the empirical evidence of the optimality of such rules, theoretical proof of this optimality is still lacking. Mentioned above hysteretic control rules are very similar to that we want to consider in this section for the PCM–problem without switching cost but with conditions (2.28) and (2.31). In view of the fixed set-up costs and these conditions, we can no longer restrict ourselves to the threshold policies with a single threshold level for the turning the slower server on, as in previous model.

As we have already mentioned numerical investigation lead to conjecture that if the servers are arranged as in (2.28) and condition (2.31) holds, the optimal control rule is characterized by threshold sequence depending on the system state x. With respect to this rule some server is used only if the current queue length is between the low and upper bounds. Moreover, it is not optimal at all to use always the fastest available server, i.e. Theorem (2.15) does not hold for the PCM–problem under condition (2.31). This can be easily shown by means of a simple system without arrivals ($\lambda = 0$) and with two servers i, j, $i > j$, where

$$\frac{c_i}{\mu_i} > \frac{c_j}{\mu_j}, \quad c_i \geq c_j \quad \text{and} \quad \mu_i > \mu_j.$$

For the value function $v(x)$ in the points $S_i x$ and $S_j x$ we get

$$v(S_i x) - v(S_j x) = \left[\frac{c_i}{\mu_i} - \frac{c_j}{\mu_j}\right] + c_0 q(x) \left[\frac{1}{\mu_i} - \frac{1}{\mu_j}\right].$$

the last expression is nonnegative only if the queue length satisfies an inequality

$$q(x) \leq \frac{1}{c_0} \left[\frac{1}{\mu_j} - \frac{1}{\mu_i}\right]^{-1} \left[\frac{c_i}{\mu_i} - \frac{c_j}{\mu_j}\right],$$

where the expression in the right–hand side is greater than zero.

It is still an open problem to prove the theoretical optimality of this control rule. Nevertheless, the proposed numerical analysis confirms the assumptions which can be formulated as a following conjecture.

Conjecture 2.21 *An optimal policy in the PCM–problem for the system with servers arrangement (2.28) under condition (2.31) has such a structure, that at any state for idle server there exists two–level threshold switching rule that turns the faster but more expensive server on when the number of jobs in the system exceeds some prespecified upper level and turns such a server off when upon service completion by this server the number of jobs is below some prespecified lower level. Thus, some available in state x server j is used if $q_j^*(x) \leq q(x) < q_{j+1}^*$.*

We can rewrite Conjecture 2.21 in terms of the value function, i.e. we expect

$$v(S_0 S_j x) \leq v(S_0 S_i x) \Rightarrow v(S_j x) \leq v(S_i x) \quad \text{for all } j, i \in J_0(x), j \leq i$$

or using the representation by means of the operators

$$(1 - S_0)(S_j - S_i) v(x) \leq 0 \qquad \text{for all } i, j \in J_0(x), j \leq i. \tag{2.45}$$

Now we have to determine whether a server must be activated, that is we have to check the inequality (2.16). According to the optimal policy when the values of initial system parameters satisfy the conditions (2.28) and (2.31), the controller may use any of available server in some state, i.e. there exist no common rule to choose a server in each state as it was in previous cases. Therefore, the inequality (2.16) we can prove successfully only for the system with two servers and generalization mainly follows from intuitive assumptions and numerical results. As before, it is necessary to show that if some function $v(x)$ satisfies the condition (2.16) then the operator T_0 preserves this property.

Lemma 2.22 *In the system with two servers the operator T_0 preserves the property (2.16) of the monotonicity increments of the function.*

Proof: To prove that the operator T_0 preserves the property (2.16) we have to prove that if this property holds for some function $v(x)$ it holds also for the function $\hat{v}(x) = T_0 v(x)$.
Note, that for each point x it is possible to make only two decisions, namely, to send a job to the queue or to switch on some server. The last action depends on the queue length.

Using the definition (2.9) of the operator T_0 it is necessary to check the inequality

$$
\begin{aligned}
(1 - S_0)(S_0 - S_k)\hat{v}(x) &= \hat{v}(S_0 x) - \hat{v}(S_k x) - \hat{v}(S_0^2 x) + \hat{v}(S_0 S_k x) \\
&= \min\{v(S_l S_0 x) : l \in J_0(x)\} - \min\{v(S_l S_k x) : l \in J_0(S_k x)\} \\
&\quad - \min\{v(S_l S_0^2 x) : l \in J_0(x)\} + \min\{v(S_l S_0 S_k x) : l \in J_0(S_k x)\} \leq 0,
\end{aligned}
$$

where for the system with two servers $k = \{1, 2\}$. As usual, we prove the result for any point $x \in E$ and divide it into several cases.

1. For the case when the optimal policies at the points $S_k x$ and $S_0^2 x$ (where $\hat{v}(x)$ is involved with the negative sign) are equal, i.e. $f(S_k x) = f(S_0^2 x) = f$ we have

$$
\begin{aligned}
(1 - S_0)(S_0 - S_k)\hat{v}(x) &= \hat{v}(S_0 x) - \hat{v}(S_k x) - \hat{v}(S_0^2 x) + \hat{v}(S_0 S_k x) \\
&= \hat{v}(S_0 x) - v(S_f S_k x) - v(S_f S_0^2 x) + \hat{v}(S_0 S_k x) \\
&\leq v(S_f S_0 x) - v(S_f S_k x) - v(S_f S_0^2 x) + v(S_f S_0 S_k x) \\
&= (1 - S_0)(S_0 - S_k)v(S_f x) \leq 0.
\end{aligned}
$$

2. For the case, when $f(S_k x) = 0$ and $f(S_0^2 x) = k$ we get the inequality

$$(1 - S_0)(S_0 - S_k)\hat{v}(x) = \hat{v}(S_0 x) - \hat{v}(S_k x) - \hat{v}(S_0^2 x) + \hat{v}(S_0 S_k x)$$
$$= \hat{v}(S_0 x) - v(S_0 S_k x) - v(S_0^2 S_k x) + \hat{v}(S_0 S_k x)$$
$$\le v(S_0 S_k x) - v(S_0 S_k x) - v(S_0^2 S_k x) + v(S_0^2 S_k x) = 0.$$

3. If $f(S_k x) = 0$ and $f(S_0^2 x) = l \ne k$, the chain of relations is the following

$$(1 - S_0)(S_0 - S_k)\hat{v}(x) = \hat{v}(S_0 x) - \hat{v}(S_k x) - \hat{v}(S_0^2 x) + \hat{v}(S_0 S_k x)$$
$$= \hat{v}(S_0 x) - v(S_0 S_k x) - v(S_0^2 S_l x) + \hat{v}(S_0 S_k x)$$
$$\le v(S_0 S_l x) - v(S_0 S_k x) - v(S_0^2 S_l x) + v(S_0^2 S_k x) =$$
$$(1 - S_0)(S_l - S_k)v(S_0 x) \le 0,$$

by virtue of the property (2.45).

4. If $f(S_k x) = l \ne 0$ and $f(S_0^2 x) = 0$, the result will be the following

$$(1 - S_0)(S_0 - S_k)\hat{v}(x) = \hat{v}(S_0 x) - \hat{v}(S_k x) - \hat{v}(S_0^2 x) + \hat{v}(S_0 S_k x)$$
$$= \hat{v}(S_0 x) - v(S_l S_k x) - v(S_0^3 x) + \hat{v}(S_0 S_k x).$$

To determine the sign of the last expression we take the operator under consideration at the points $S_k x$ and $S_0 x$, that is

$$(1 - S_0)(S_0 - S_l)v(S_k x) = v(S_0 S_k x) - v(S_l S_k x) - v(S_0^2 S_k x) + v(S_0 S_k S_l x) \le 0,$$
$$(1 - S_0)(S_0 - S_k)v(S_0 x) = v(S_0^2 x) - v(S_0 S_k x) - v(S_0^3 x) + v(S_0^2 S_k x) \le 0,$$

respectively. Now summing these inequalities we get

$$v(S_0^2 x) - v(S_l S_k x) - v(S_0^3 x) + v(S_0 S_k S_l x) \le 0.$$

Using the last inequality we can prove the statement for this case, namely,

$$\hat{v}(S_0 x) - v(S_l S_k x) - v(S_0^3 x) + \hat{v}(S_0 S_k x)$$
$$\le v(S_0^2 x) - v(S_l S_k x) - v(S_0^3 x) + v(S_0 S_k S_l x) \le 0.$$

5. Finally in the case when $f(S_k x) = l \ne 0$ and $f(S_0^2 x) = k$ we have

$$(1 - S_0)(S_0 - S_k)\hat{v}(x) = \hat{v}(S_0 x) - \hat{v}(S_k x) - \hat{v}(S_0^2 x) + \hat{v}(S_0 S_k x)$$
$$= \hat{v}(S_0 x) - v(S_l S_k x) - v(S_0^2 S_k x) + \hat{v}(S_0 S_k x)$$
$$\le v(S_0 S_k x) - v(S_k S_l x) - v(S_0^2 S_k x) + v(S_0 S_k S_l x) = (1 - S_0)(S_0 - S_l)v(S_k x) \le 0.$$

For the boundary points $q(x) = B$ and $J_0(x) = \emptyset$, the inequality (2.16) is also satisfied because the shift operators do not drive the point x outside the admissible set of states. Finally, the operators T_j also retain the (S_0, S_k)-supermodularity of the functions by virtue of the fact that they are defined by (2.9).

Now we can prove that the value function of the model $v = \{v(x) : x \in E\}$ is (S_0, S_k)-supermodular. This assertion follows from the fact that the property of (S_0, S_k)-supermodularity is retained for linear operations defining the operator B as in (2.5.2), the function $c(x)$ is (S_0, S_k)-supermodular and successive approximations $B^n c(x)$ converge monotonously to the value function $v(x)$.

$\square$

2.6 Algorithm

In this section we propose an algorithm and a routine for the optimal policies calculating. The following algorithm is based on Howard policy-iteration [27] and value-iteration [75] algorithms but with modifications according to specific properties of the problem. The algorithm consists of two general steps: Policy Evaluation, and Policy Improvement. At the first step the optimality equation for given policy is solved. It is necessary to remind that only relative value function $v = \{v(x) : x \in E\}$ can be found from the optimality equation, that means that one of $v(x)$ has to be fixed as zero, for example. In the algorithm bellow we put $v(0) = 0$. At the second step a new improved policy have to be found, which minimizes the Bellman function of the model (2.12). Because of the high dimensionality of the problem in the first step of the algorithm we also use an iterative method to solve the equations with the given accuracy ϵ. The algorithm stops when two successive approximations of policies coincide. The algorithm is represented below.

The realization of this algorithm with respect to the multidimensional system states is quite complex and require a lot of processing time to obtain the results. Therefore, for description of system states changing at the control epochs we consider the one-to-one correspondence between the multidimensional representation of the system state x and the index of such a state. Namely,

$$\#(x) = q(x) \cdot 2^K + \sum_{j=1}^{K} d_j(x) 2^{j-1} \equiv x, \qquad x = \overline{0, I - 1} \qquad (2.46)$$

with $I = (B - K) \cdot 2^K$. Here, the first item represents the queue length in state x, and the second one represents the binary number depending on the number of busy servers in the sate x.

Now, if $S_j x$ is the state after possible transition from the j-th coordinate it can be obtained with respect to the introduced formula (2.46)

$$S_j x = x + \frac{(d_j - d_j(x))2^K}{1_{\{j \neq 0\}} 2^{K-j+1}},$$

where $d_0(x) = q(x)$.

Thus, in one-dimensional case we have

$$
\begin{aligned}
S_0 x &= x + 2^K, \\
S_0^{-1} x &= x - 2^K, \\
S_j x &= x + d_j 2^{j-1}, \\
S_j^{-1} x &= x - d_j(x) 2^{j-1}.
\end{aligned}
$$

2.6.1 Policy-iteration algorithm description

Step 0. **Begin.**

Enter the initial date:

Integer: B, K;

Real: λ, μ_k, c_k, $(k = \overline{1, K})$, ϵ;

For the NJM–problem all the values $c_k = 1$.

Define variables:

Real: $g, v = \{v(x) : x = \overline{0, I-1}\}$;

Integer: $f = \{f(x) : x = \overline{0, I-1}\}$;

For the NJM–problem arrange the servers in order of the increasing mean service times μ_k^{-1}

$$\mu_1^{-1} \leq \mu_2^{-1} \leq \cdots \leq \mu_K^{-1}$$

For the PCM–problem arrange the servers in order to increasing of the value γ_k

$$\frac{c_1}{\mu_1} \leq \frac{c_2}{\mu_2} \leq \cdots \leq \frac{c_K}{\mu_K}.$$

Put: $n = 0$, $f_0(x) = \min\{k : d_k(x) = 0\}$, and $v_0(x) = c(x)$ for all $x = \overline{0, I-1}$. Here, and troughout this section, for the NJM–problem the function $c(x) = l(x)$ is introduced in (2.4) and denotes the number of jobs in the state x and for the PCM–problem the function $c(x)$ is a loss rate (2.24).

Step 1. Policy Evaluation.

For given policy $f = f_n = \{f_n(x) : x = \overline{0, I-1}\}$ beginning from $n = 0$ solve with given accuracy ϵ the equation (2.8) or (2.25) for NJM– and PCM–problems, respectively,

$$
\begin{aligned}
v_n(x) \;=\; & \frac{1}{\lambda + M}\Big[c(x) + \lambda v_n(S_{f_n(x)}x) + M_0(x)v_n(x) \\
& + \; 1_{\{q(x)=0\}} \sum_{j \in J_1(x)} \mu_j\, v(S_j^{-1}x) \\
& + \; 1_{\{q(x)>0\}} \sum_{j \in J_1(x)} \mu_j\, v(S_{f_n(x)}S_j^{-1}S_0^{-1}x) - g_n\Big]
\end{aligned}
$$

for all $x = \overline{0, I-1}$ under condition $v_n(0) = 0$.

To do that the successive approximation method in the following sub algorithm is used

Sub Algorithm.

Step 1.0. Begin. Beginning from $m = 0$, $\{v_n^{(m)}(x) = v_n(x),\ x = \overline{0, I-1}\}$

Step 1.1. Calculation of the successive approximation.

Calculate

$$
\begin{aligned}
g_n^{(m+1)} \;=\; & \frac{1}{\lambda + M}\Big[\lambda v_n^{(m)}(S_{f_n(0)}0) - g_n^{(m)}\Big], \\
v_n^{(m+1)}(x) \;=\; & \frac{1}{\lambda + M}\Big[c(x) + \lambda v_n^{(m)}(S_{f_n(x)}x) + M_0(x)\, v_n^{(m)}(x) \\
& + \; 1_{\{q(x)=0\}} \sum_{j \in J_1(x)} \mu_j v_n^{(m)}(S_j^{-1}x) + \\
& + \; 1_{\{q(x)>0\}} \sum_{j \in J_1(x)} \mu_j v_n^{(m)}(S_{f_n(x)}S_j^{-1}S_0^{-1}x) - g_n^{(m+1)}\Big].
\end{aligned}
$$

Step 1.2. **Calculation of the accuracy.**
    Find

$$\epsilon_1 = \max\left[\max_{\{\text{over all } x\}} |v_n^{(m+1)}(x) - v_n^{(m+1)}(x)|, \; |g_n^{(m+1)} - g_n^{(m)}|\right].$$

Step 1.3. **Testing of the accuracy.**
    Test: if $\epsilon_1 < \epsilon$, remember $v_n = v_n^{(m)}$, go to step 2; if not, change m by $m + 1$, $v_n^{(m)}(x)$ by $v_n^{(m+1)}(x)$ go to step 1.1.

Step 2. **Policy Improvement.**
    For given solution $v_n = \{v_n(x) : \; x = \overline{0, I-1}\}$ find new policy $f_{n+1} = \{f_{n+1}(x) : \; x = \overline{0, I-1}\}$, which minimize Bellman function of the model (2.12),

$$f_{n+1}(x) = \operatorname*{argmin}_{k \in A_0(x)} v_n(x + e_k) \tag{2.47}$$

Step 3. **Test.**
    Test: if $f_{n+1}(x) = f_n(x)$ for all x go to step 4; if not, change n by $n + 1$ and f_n by f_{n+1}, then go to step 1.

Step 4. **End.**
    Print results $g = g_n$, $v = v_n = \{v_n(x) : \; x = \overline{1, I-1}\}$, $f = f_n = \{f_n(x) : \; x = \overline{1, I-1}\}$. Stop.

2.6.2 Value-iteration algorithm description

In some cases it is better to use value-iteration algorithm mentioned in Section 1.4. The value-iteration algorithm computes recursively the value function $v(x)$ from

$$v(x) = \frac{1}{\lambda + M_1(x)} \min_a \left[c(x) + \lambda v(S_{a_0}x) + \sum_{j \in J_1(x)} \mu_j \, v(S_{a_j} S_j^{-1} S_0^{-1} x)\right] \tag{2.48}$$

starting with an arbitrary chosen function $v_0(x)$, $x \in E$. Here the quantity $v(x)$ can be interpreted as the minimal total expected costs per unit of time when the current state is x. This interpretation suggests that for large time period $t \to \infty$

the difference $v_n(x) - v_{n-1}(x)$ on the neighbor iterations will come very close to the minimal average cost per unit time, while the stationary policy minimizes the right side of (2.48) for all x will be very close in costs to the minimal average costs (for a proof see Tijms [75]). Thus, if we introduce the bounds

$$M_n = \max_{x \in E}\{v_n(x) - v_{n-1}(x)\},$$
$$m_n = \min_{x \in E}\{v_n(x) - v_{n-1}(x)\},$$

in [75] it was proved, that

$$m_n \leq g \leq M_n.$$

Now we can present the main elements of this algorithm.

Step 0. Begin. Initialization of system parameters.

This part is the same as in previous algorithm with exception of value g.

Step 1. Policy Evaluation.

For given policy $f = f_n = \{f_n(x) : x = \overline{0, I-1}\}$ beginning from $n = 0$ solve with given accuracy ϵ the equation (2.48),

$$
\begin{aligned}
v_n(x) \;=\; &\frac{1}{\lambda + M}\Bigg[c(x) + \lambda v_n(S_{f_n(x)}x) + M_0(x)v_n(x) \\
&+\; 1_{\{q(x)=0\}}\sum_{j \in J_1(x)} \mu_j\, v(S_j^{-1}x) \\
&+\; 1_{\{q(x)>0\}}\sum_{j \in J_1(x)} \mu_j\, v(S_{f_n(x)}S_j^{-1}S_0^{-1}x)\Bigg]
\end{aligned}
$$

for all $x = \overline{0, I-1}$ under condition $v_n(0) = 0$.

Sub Algorithm.

Step 1.0. Begin. Beginning from $m = 0$, $\{v_n^{(m)}(x) = v_n(x),\ x = \overline{0, I-1}\}$

Step 1.1. Calculation of the successive approximation.

Calculate

$$
\begin{aligned}
v_n^{(m+1)}(x) &= \frac{1}{\lambda + M}\Bigg[c(x) + \lambda v_n^{(m)}(S_{f_n(x)}x) + M_0(x)\, v_n^{(m)}(x) \\
&+ 1_{\{q(x)=0\}} \sum_{j \in J_1(x)} \mu_j v_n^{(m)}(S_j^{-1}x) + \\
&+ 1_{\{q(x)>0\}} \sum_{j \in J_1(x)} \mu_j v_n^{(m)}(S_{f_n(x)}S_j^{-1}S_0^{-1}x) - g_n^{(m+1)}\Bigg].
\end{aligned}
$$

Step 1.2. Compute the bounds.

$$
\begin{aligned}
M_n &= \max_{x \in E}\{v_n(x) - v_{n-1}(x)\}, \\
m_n &= \min_{x \in E}\{v_n(x) - v_{n-1}(x)\},
\end{aligned}
$$

Step 1.3. Calculation of the accuracy.
Find

$$
\epsilon_1 \geq \frac{M_n - m_n}{m_n}.
$$

Step 1.4. Testing of the accuracy.

Test: if $\epsilon_1 < \epsilon$, remember $v_n = v_n^{(m)}$, go to step 2; if not, change m by $m + 1$, $v_n^{(m)}(x)$ by $v_n^{(m+1)}(x)$ go to step 1.1.

Steps 2-4 are the same as in previous algorithm.

The finite convergence of the policy-iteration and value iteration algorithms was discussed by Puterman in [58] and Tijms in [75].

2.6.3 Routine

The computer program was written in C++ with using objective oriented tools. It was often used dynamic data structure for the program members description. The program was created as standard application for Windows and has quite friendly interface, so it is very simple to use it by any user which has not much experience in programming. This program was adapted for Linux operational system as well. The charts were constructed by means of the programs Advanced Grapher and

Gnuplot. The program has several regimes to obtain the results which should be chosen from the main menu. One of them allows to obtain unit result for fixed initial parameters, while another one deals with varied parameters and allows to obtain series of results which can be used to build the diagrams.

Input information consists of the number of servers K, buffer size B, as well as initial parameters, such as arrival λ and service μ_k $(k = \overline{1, K})$ intensities, waiting c_0 and using c_k $(k = \overline{1, K})$ costs, and accuracy ϵ. The values of these parameters can be entered from keyboard or from some file. As output the program gives the optimal policy in form of a table for unit result regime, or in form of diagrams for multiple results regime.

The convergence rate is strongly associate with the values of initial parameters but the policy-iteration algorithm requires typically quite small number of iterations regardless of the problem size. For the most examples to achieve accuracy to four decimal places, policy improvement requires 3 iterations (on average) and policy evaluation requires 200, 50 and 10 iterations (on average) for each policy improvement, consequently. The processing time of the program strongly depends on values of initial system parameters but for most of examples is negligible: e.g. if the number of states is about 10000, the pure processing time does not exceed in average the value 2.325 seconds for processor Pentium II 500 MHz. Therefore, the number of states in the system has to be restricted only in the case of operating storage lack.

The value iteration algorithm has less iterations for small number of system states but it depends strongly on the specific problem, in particular, on the number of system states.

2.7   Numerical analysis

Numerical analysis is based on the series of experiments. The queueing systems are assumed to be with K=5 or K=3 servers and the buffer size is quite large B=100 in order to simulate the system with infinite buffer. The optimal control policies can be represented by means of *control tables* and *control diagrams*. While in the control tables we obtain the optimal control rule for each system state when the values of system parameters are fixed, the control diagrams allow to estimate the behavior of optimal policies when the values of system parameters are varied. In the present section we use the both of optimal control policies representations.

By means of experiments we confirm the theoretical results and conjectures, and also provide the investigation of threshold function behavior with varied system parameters. The numerical examples in this section organized as follows.

In Section 2.7.1 we investigate the influence of the slower server on the behavior of thresholds. For most values of system parameters, the optimal threshold does not depend on the states of slower servers. But it is interesting to consider the reasons of its appearance. In Section 2.7.2 the NJM–problem without penalties for waiting in queue and server usage costs. In Section 2.7.3 and 2.7.4 experiments for the PCM–problem with set-up penalties for waiting in the queue and server usage costs are discussed. In Section 2.7.3 we investigate the optimal policy for the system with condition for initial parameters (2.29) and (2.30). In Section 2.7.4 we discuss the PCM–problem under condition (2.31).

2.7.1 Dependence of thresholds on the state of slow servers

In this section we consider some numerical examples for the $M/M/K$ queueing system with $K = 3$ servers. The aim of this example consists in the following: With respect to the system states $x = (q, 1, 0, 0)$ and $y = (q, 1, 0, 1)$ the assignment to the second server can depend not only on the number of jobs in the queue, but also on the state of the third server. In this example it is optimal to make an assignment in state x but not in state y. Without loss of generality we consider such system parameters that $\lambda + M_0 + M_1 = \lambda + M = 1$, where M as before is a total service intensity of all servers. We solve optimality equation for the NJM–problem with the following parameters:

- $\lambda = 0.238$, $\mu_1 = 0.621$, $\mu_2 = 0.071$ and $\mu_3 = 0.070$,

- $\lambda = 0.477$, $\mu_1 = 0.356$, $\mu_2 = 0.096$ and $\mu_3 = 0.070$.

The results of optimal solution for the first and second group of system parameters are represented in control Table 2.23 and control Table 2.24, respectively.

We notice that for most parameter values the optimal decision can be made independently of the states of the slower servers. But we intend to consider the reasons of such possible dependence. It is evident that in the NJM–problem setting with arrivals, the optimal policy assigns a job to the fastest free server in states for which this would not be optimal if there were no arrivals. This is because the system should be ready for possible arrivals, which, if they occur, will wish to see a less congested system.

Table 2.23 Optimal control for any system state

System State x	Queue length $q(x)$																	
(d_1, d_2, d_3)	0	1	2	3	4	5	6	7	8	9	10	11	12	13	14	15	16	...
(0,0,0)	1	1	1	1	1	1	1	1	1	1	1	1	1	1	1	1	1	1
(1,0,0)	0	0	0	0	0	**2**	2	2	2	2	2	2	2	2	2	2	2	2
(0,1,0)	1	1	1	1	1	1	1	1	1	1	1	1	1	1	1	1	1	1
(1,1,0)	0	0	0	0	0	**3**	3	3	3	3	3	3	3	3	3	3	3	3
(0,0,1)	1	1	1	1	1	1	1	1	1	1	1	1	1	1	1	1	1	1
(1,0,1)	0	0	0	0	**2**	2	2	2	2	2	2	2	2	2	2	2	2	2
(0,1,1)	1	1	1	1	1	1	1	1	1	1	1	1	1	1	1	1	1	1
(1,1,1)	0	0	0	0	0	0	0	0	0	0	0	0	0	0	0	0	0	0

Table 2.24

System State x	Queue length $q(x)$																	
(d_1, d_2, d_3)	0	1	2	3	4	5	6	7	8	9	10	11	12	13	14	15	16	...
(0,0,0)	1	1	1	1	1	1	1	1	1	1	1	1	1	1	1	1	1	1
(1,0,0)	0	**2**	2	2	2	2	2	2	2	2	2	2	2	2	2	2	2	2
(0,1,0)	1	1	1	1	1	1	1	1	1	1	1	1	1	1	1	1	1	1
(1,1,0)	0	**3**	3	3	3	3	3	3	3	3	3	3	3	3	3	3	3	3
(0,0,1)	1	1	1	1	1	1	1	1	1	1	1	1	1	1	1	1	1	1
(1,0,1)	**2**	2	2	2	2	2	2	2	2	2	2	2	2	2	2	2	2	2
(0,1,1)	1	1	1	1	1	1	1	1	1	1	1	1	1	1	1	1	1	1
(1,1,1)	0	0	0	0	0	0	0	0	0	0	0	0	0	0	0	0	0	0

Consider the system with three servers in the states $S_0 S_1 x$ and $S_1 S_2 x$, where $x = (0, \ldots, 0)$. Let us consider the case of potential service completion at the second server, taking into account a large number q of accompanied arrivals. Because of large q it is optimal to occupy all accessible idle servers. The mentioned above states become $S_0^{q-1} S_1 S_2 S_3 x$ and $S_0^{q-2} S_1 S_2 S_3 x$. Thus, the difference $v(S_0^{q-1} S_1 S_2 S_3 x) - v(S_0^{q-2} S_1 S_2 S_3 x)$ measures the advantage that will be obtained in the case if the assignment to the second processor $S_0 S_1 x \to S_1 S_2 x$. The events of service completion on the second server provide the incentive to make an assignment to the second server. But, if the two initial states are $S_0 S_1 S_3 x$ and $S_1 S_2 S_3 x$, the measure of advantage if service completion takes place is $v(S_0^q S_1 S_2 S_3 x) - v(S_0^{q-1} S_1 S_2 S_3 x)$. Because we expect that the value function $v(S_0^q S_1 S_2 S_3 x)$ is convex in q, it is plausible that the incentive to make an assignment to the second server is greater in state $S_0 S_1 S_3 x$ than in $S_0 S_1 x$. Numerical examples proposed in Table 2.25 confirm our expectations.

Numerical examples show that the threshold levels have a weak dependence of slower servers' states. According to our observations, the optimal threshold may vary by at most 1 when the state of a slower server changes.

Table 2.25 Value function for system states

System State x	value function $v(x)$	
(q, d_1, d_2, d_3)	example 1	example 2
(0,0,0,0)	0	0
(0,1,0,0)	2.6034	19.4480
(0,0,1,0)	14.0865	28.3810
(0,0,0,1)	14.2872	33.7009
(1,1,0,0)	7.7979	51.3142
(0,1,1,0)	16.6905	51.4444
(0,1,0,1)	16.8910	55.9981
(0,0,1,1)	28.3747	65.9866
(2,1,0,0)	15.5520	96.1454
(1,1,1,0)	21.8874	90.3521
(1,1,0,1)	22.0873	93.2714
(0,1,1,1)	30.9798	93.2581
(3,1,0,0)	25.7823	154.6580
(2,1,1,0)	29.6487	142.7630
(2,1,0,1)	29.8469	145.4230
(1,1,1,1)	36.1809	140.4050
...	...	-
(6,1,0,0)	68.3382	-
(5,1,1,0)	66.8622	-
(5,1,0,1)	66.9946	-
(4,1,1,1)	66.9830	-
(7,1,0,0)	85.9322	-
(6,1,1,0)	82.9672	-
(6,1,0,1)	83.0730	-
(5,1,1,1)	81.9234	-

2.7.2 Numerical examples. NJM–problem. Threshold function

In this section we consider some numerical examples for the NJM–problem. Values of service intensities μ_i for the system with $K=5$ servers are presented in Tables 2.26. The optimal control policies if the input intensity $\lambda=0.01$ are given in control Table 2.27.

The optimal control rules which show the first using of the slower servers are underlined.

Table 2.26 Values of initial system parameters for $M/M/5/100$ queue

i	1	2	3	4	5
μ_i	1.90	0.63	0.52	0.45	0.30

Table 2.27 Optimal control in each system state

System State x	Queue length $q(x)$																
$(d_1, d_2, d_3, d_4, d_5)$	0	1	2	3	4	5	6	7	8	9	10	11	12	13	14	15	...
$(0,*,*,*,*)$	<u>1</u>	1	1	1	1	1	1	1	1	1	1	1	1	1	1	1	1
$(1,0,*,*,*)$	0	<u>2</u>	2	2	2	2	2	2	2	2	2	2	2	2	2	2	2
$(1,1,0,*,*)$	0	0	<u>3</u>	3	3	3	3	3	3	3	3	3	3	3	3	3	3
$(1,1,1,0,*)$	0	0	0	<u>4</u>	4	4	4	4	4	4	4	4	4	4	4	4	4
$(1,1,1,1,0)$	0	0	0	0	0	0	0	<u>5</u>	5	5	5	5	5	5	5	5	5
$(1,1,1,1,1)$	0	0	0	0	0	0	0	0	0	0	0	0	0	0	0	0	0

The results given in this control table verify the theoretical results about the threshold structure of an optimal control rule. While the fastest server is always activated, each slower server has threshold which prescribes the switching on these servers. Therefore, the optimal control rule can be described by means of threshold sequence

$$0 = q_1^* \le q_2^* \le \cdots \le q_K^*,$$

and the slower server $s = 1, \ldots, l$ are used when the number of jobs in the queue is between the levels q_l^* and q_{l+1}^* with $q_{K+1}^* = \infty$. The theoretical optimality of this control rule is discussed in Section 2.4.

Now the aim is to investigate the behavior of optimal control policies when input intensity λ and service intensities μ_k are varied.
With respect to the formula (2.21) for the system in light traffic, that is $\frac{\lambda}{M_1} \to 0$, it is possible analytically obtain optimal thresholds. But in the case of an ordinary traffic, by means of the formula (2.21) we can obtain only the upper bound of the possible thresholds, that will be the main goal of a discussion in the present section.
In Table 2.28 some results of optimal threshold levels using the computer program and the NJM threshold formula for the system with varied values of initial system parameters are shown. In these examples one of the parameters is being changed while all others are fixed.

Table 2.28 Optimal thresholds behavior

System parameters			
λ	μ_1	μ_2	μ_3
0.1	0.40	0.10	0.05

Varied par.	Threshold levels comp. program			Threshold levels formula		
	q_1^*	q_2^*	q_3^*	q_1^*	q_2^*	q_3^*
$\lambda = 0.01$	0	2	7	0	2	7
$\lambda = 0.26$	0	1	4	0	2	7
$\lambda = 0.51$	0	1	2	0	2	7
$\mu_1 = 0.400$	0	2	6	0	2	7
$\mu_1 = 1.000$	0	8	18	0	8	19
$\mu_1 = 1.500$	0	13	28	0	13	29
$\mu_2 = 0.100$	0	2	6	0	2	7
$\mu_2 = 0.200$	0	0	8	0	0	9
$\mu_2 = 0.300$	0	0	10	0	0	11
$\mu_3 = 0.050$	0	2	6	0	2	7
$\mu_3 = 0.070$	0	2	4	0	2	5
$\mu_3 = 0.090$	0	2	2	0	2	3

Some results of the optimal policies calculations for the NJM–problem are summarized in control diagrams shown in Figures 1.1-1.6 in Appendix 2.9.1. The
input intensities are varied over the figures:

- $\lambda = 0.51$ in Figures 1.1, 1.4 ,

- $\lambda = 0.26$ in Figures 1.2, 1.5 ,

- $\lambda = 0.01$ in Figures 1.3, 1.6 .

In diagrams presented in Figures 1.1–1.3 the changing of threshold levels q_2^* for
the second (pictures labeled by letter "a") and q_3^* for the third (pictures labeled by
letter "b") servers as functions of first service intensity μ_1 for different values of
the second service intensity μ_2, are shown.
One can see that in the pictures "b" the server with largest service intensity much
more influences the thresholds of the slowest server than the second server does.
These diagrams show that the curves have a stepped structure that demonstrates
threshold phenomenon of the optimal policies for the model under consideration.
The threshold functions depend on the service intensities in such a manner that the
threshold levels monotonously increase when the first and the second service intensities increase. Moreover, they increase also whenthe input intensity decreases.
Thus, the value obtained by the NJM threshold formula (2.21) calculates the upper
bound for using the fastest available in state x server.
    The diagrams, presented in Figures 1.4–1.6, illustrate the threshold levels q_3^* as
the function of the sum $\mu_1 + \mu_2$ (pictures labeled by letter "a") for some fixed third
service intensity, and (pictures labeled by letter "b") for different values of μ_3. The

arrival intensities λ were varied over the figures as before. From these diagrams one can see that the threshold for the third server depends on the sum $\mu_1 + \mu_2$ as in the formula (2.21), also if $\lambda \neq 0$. The threshold function for the second server has a weak dependence on the arrival rate λ and can be approximately obtained by (2.21)

$$q_2^* = \frac{\mu_1}{\mu_2} - 1.$$

The threshold function for the third server is more sensitive to the increasing of λ, therefore by virtue of (2.21)

$$q_3^* = \frac{\mu_1 + \mu_2}{\mu_3} - 2$$

one can obtain the upper level for possible thresholds.

2.7.3 Numerical examples. PCM–problem. Threshold function

In this section we consider some numerical examples for the PCM–problem under the conditions (2.28) and (2.31), that is when the usage costs of the servers decrease slower than the corresponding service intensities. The service intensities (K=5) are presented in Table 2.29. The results of optimal policy calculation for the system with input intensity λ=0.1 are given in control Table 2.30.

Table 2.29 Values of initial system parameters for $M/M/5/100$ **queue**

i	0	1	2	3	4	5
c_i	1.00	3.00	2.80	2.60	2.40	2.00
μ_i	-	1.90	0.63	0.52	0.45	0.30
γ_i	-	1.58	4.44	5.00	5.53	6.66

Table 2.30 Optimal control for any system state

System State x	Queue length $q(x)$																
(d_1,d_2,d_3,d_4,d_5)	0	1	2	3	4	5	6	7	8	9	10	11	12	13	14	15	...
(0,*,*,*,*)	**1**	1	1	1	1	1	1	1	1	1	1	1	1	1	1	1	1
(1,0,*,*,*)	0	0	0	0	0	**2**	2	2	2	2	2	2	2	2	2	2	2
(1,1,0,*,*)	0	0	0	0	0	0	**3**	3	3	3	3	3	3	3	3	3	3
(1,1,1,0,*)	0	0	0	0	0	0	0	**4**	4	4	4	4	4	4	4	4	4
(1,1,1,1,0)	0	0	0	0	0	0	0	0	0	0	0	0	**5**	5	5	5	5
(1,1,1,1,1)	0	0	0	0	0	0	0	0	0	0	0	0	0	0	0	0	0

It is possible to see that the optimal control rule as in previous case can be represented by the following threshold sequence

$$0 = q_1^* \leq q_2^* \leq \cdots \leq q_K^*.$$

As we have mentioned above, the members of this control sequence have quite a weak dependence of the system states, i.e. the weak dependence of slower servers state, see Section 2.7.1. Therefore we omit the argument of the system state x. With respect to this control rule the server with the lowest mean usage cost $\gamma_1 = \min_{j \in J_0(x)} \{\gamma_j\}$ is always activated and provides the service with the largest service intensity $\mu_1 = \max_{j \in J_0(x)} \{\mu_j\}$. The slower servers $s = 1, \ldots, l$ are used when the number of jobs in the system is between the levels q_l^* and q_{l+1}^* where $q_{K+1}^* = \infty$. Thus, this numerical results verify the theoretical optimality of this control rule, discussed in Section 2.5.

In Table 2.31 we show some results of the optimal threshold levels calculation by means of the program and the PCM threshold formula (2.33) in case of light–traffic operation. In these examples one of the parameters is being changed while all others are fixed.

Another possible way of numerical investigation is a control diagram. Some results of the optimal policies calculation for the PCM–problem with servers' arrangement (2.28) under conditions (2.29) and (2.30) are summarized in the control diagrams shown in Figures 2.1, 2.2 and 3.1–3.9 in Appendices 2.9.2 and 2.9.3, respectively. Because of the numerous parameters which influence the decision choice, we need three–dimensional diagrams. Such diagrams are represented in Figure 2.1 and 2.2 of Appendix 2.9.2. The vertical axis denotes the queue length q for a optimal threshold level, the horizontal axis denotes the values of the first service intensity μ_1 and the third one denotes the values of the usage cost for the first server c_1. In these pictures the threshold levels q_2^* for the second server (Figure 1) and the threshold levels q_3^* for the third server (Figure 2) represent the threshold function under variation of the following values: The input intensity ($\lambda = 1.0$ on the picture labeled by letter "a" and $\lambda = 0.5$ on the picture labeled by letter "b"), the first and second service intensities (μ_1 and μ_2), usage costs (c_1 and c_2).

Table 2.31 Optimal thresholds behavior

System parameters							
λ	c_0	c_1	μ_1	c_2	μ_2	c_3	μ_3
0.1	1.00	2.00	0.40	1.50	0.10	1.00	0.05

Varied par.	Threshold levels comp. program			Threshold levels formula		
	q_1^*	q_2^*	q_3^*	q_1^*	q_2^*	q_3^*
$\lambda = 0.01$	0	3	6	0	3	6
$\lambda = 0.26$	0	2	3	0	3	6
$\lambda = 0.51$	0	1	2	0	3	6
$c_0 = 0.20$	0	15	25	0	19	31
$c_0 = 0.50$	0	6	10	0	7	12
$c_0 = 1.00$	0	3	5	0	3	6
$\mu_1 = 0.400$	0	3	5	0	3	6
$\mu_1 = 1.000$	0	11	16	0	12	18
$\mu_1 = 1.500$	0	19	26	0	20	28
$c_1 = 2.00$	0	3	5	0	3	6
$c_1 = 4.00$	0	1	3	0	1	4
$c_1 = 5.50$	0	0	2	0	0	2
$\mu_2 = 0.10$	0	3	5	0	3	6
$\mu_2 = 0.20$	0	0	7	0	0	8
$\mu_2 = 0.30$	0	0	9	0	0	10
$c_2 = 1.50$	0	3	5	0	3	6
$c_2 = 1.70$	0	3	4	0	4	6
$c_2 = 1.90$	0	4	4	0	5	5
$\mu_3 = 0.02$	0	3	17	0	3	21
$\mu_3 = 0.05$	0	3	5	0	3	6
$\mu_3 = 0.06$	0	3	3	0	3	4
$c_3 = 0.80$	0	3	3	0	3	4
$c_3 = 1.00$	0	3	5	0	3	6
$c_3 = 1.40$	0	3	8	0	3	10

Curves of different types are used for different service intensities of the second server, and several curves of the same group have different shades [1] corresponding to different values of the second server usage costs.

Keep in mind that in these figures the servers are arranged according to the rule (2.28) in order of their mean usage costs increasing, i.e.

$$\frac{c_1}{\mu_1} \leq \frac{c_2}{\mu_2} \leq \frac{c_3}{\mu_3},$$

and the rule (2.29). Notice that if all costs c_0, c_1, c_2, c_3 are equal to one, the problem turns into the problem of minimizing the mean number of jobs in the system.

The values of the service intensities and the usage costs were chosen according to the introduced inequalities. The waiting cost c_0 as well as the parameters of the third server were fixed at $c_0 = c_3 = 1.0$, $\mu_3 = 0.1$ which gives $\gamma_3 = 10.0$. Other parameters were varied in the following way:

---

[1] In the screen these curves have given with different colors, which looks in the figures like curves of different shades.

- The curves labeled with the number 1 correspond to the case when $\mu_2 = 0.1$, $c_2 = 1.0$ with $\gamma_2 = 10.0$;

- The curves labeled with the number 2 correspond to the case when $\mu_2 = 0.3$, and according to the above condition we consider different possible values of the usage cost $c_2 = \{1.0; 2.0; 3.0\}$, thus $\gamma_2 = \{3.3; 6.6; 10.0\}$, respectively;

- The curves labeled with the number 3 represent the case when $\mu_2 = 0.5$, and as before, we consider different possible values of the usage cost $c_2 = \{1.0; 2.0; 3.0; 4.0; 5.0\}$ with $\gamma_2 = \{2.0; 4.0; 6.0; 8.0; 10.0\}$.

The highest curve of the same shade on these diagrams corresponds to the highest usage cost of the second server. Each associated bottom curve of the same shade corresponds to the (decreasing) values of the usage cost c_2.

These figures provide the following conclusions:

The optimal policies for the PCM–problem as well as for the NJM–problem are of threshold type. The behavior of the threshold levels depends not only on the values of arrival and service intensities but also depends on the usage costs of the servers. The optimal control which specifies which of the server should be switched on depends strongly on the values of γ_k.

One can see from the diagrams that the optimal threshold levels monotonously increase in the following cases:

1. The service intensity of the first server increases and/or the appropriate usage cost decreases.

2. The service intensity of the second server decreases and/or the appropriate usage cost increases.

3. Input intensity decreases.

These results justify the theoretical results obtained in previous sections for the system with imposed arrangement (2.28) under conditions (2.29) and (2.30).

Now we shall consider the threshold function behavior and estimate the influence of the parameter γ_k on the optimal control. To analyze the results of a program we also considered two-dimensional diagrams for the threshold levels behavior. In Figures 3.1–3.3 in Appendix 2.9.3 we give the results which represent the threshold functions q_2^* for the second (pictures labeled by letter "a") and

q_3^* for the third (pictures labeled by letter "b") servers The input intensities are varied over the figures:

- $\lambda = 0.51$ in Figure 3.1,

- $\lambda = 0.26$ in Figure 3.2,

- $\lambda = 0.01$ in Figure 3.3.

In all of these examples the value of waiting cost was fixed $c_0=1$. In the tables below the values of system parameters for the function q_2^* and q_3^* are given.

Table 2.32 Values of system parameters for the function q_2^* (a)

Figure	a: $\gamma_2 = \frac{c_2}{\mu_2} = 30.00$, $\gamma_3 = \frac{c_3}{\mu_3} = 40.00$					
	c_1	μ_1	c_2	μ_2	c_3	μ_3
3.1	1.00	0.45	1.50	0.05	0.40	0.01
λ=0.51	3.00	0.46	3.00	0.10	0.80	0.02
3.2	5.00	0.47	4.50	0.15	1.20	0.03
λ=0.26	8.00	0.48	6.00	0.20	1.60	0.04
3.3	12.00	0.49	7.50	0.25	2.00	0.05
λ =0.01		. . .				

Table 2.33 Values of system parameters for the functions q_3^* (b)

Figure	b: $\gamma_3 = \frac{c_3}{\mu_3} = 40.00$							
	c_1	μ_1	c_2	μ_2	c_3	μ_3	$c_1 + c_2$	$\mu_1 + \mu_2$
3.1	1.00	0.45	1.50	0.05	0.40	0.01	2.50	0.50
λ=0.51	1.50	0.46	1.00	0.10	0.80	0.02	4.50	. . .
	1.00	0.47	3.50	0.15	1.20	0.03	6.50	0.55
3.2	2.50	0.48	2.00	0.20	1.60	0.04	9.50	. . .
λ=0.26	2.00	0.49	4.50	0.25	2.00	0.05	13.50	0.60
	4.00	. . .	2.50					. . .
3.3	4.00		5.50					0.65
λ =0.01	6.00		3.50					. . .
	7.50		6.00					0.70
	8.50		5.00					. . .

The curves q_2^* represent the threshold function under variation of arguments μ_1 and c_1. The values c_2 and μ_2 as well as c_3 and μ_3 are chosen in such a way that $\gamma_2 = \frac{c_2}{\mu_2}=30.00$ and $\gamma_3 = \frac{c_3}{\mu_3}=40.00$. The threshold function for the second server for the fixed parameters c_0, γ_2 and γ_3 depends mainly on the values of c_1 and μ_1. The word "mainly" means that only in some cases of normal and heavy traffic we have small fluctuations of the curves because of different values of c_2 and μ_2. With small decreasing of the traffic capacity, these fluctuations also decrease and vanish. One more evident result is that the threshold levels for the second server have weak dependence of the arrival intensity λ. Therefore, assuming an independence on the input intensity, to obtain the optimal threshold levels q_2^* for the second server it is possible to use the formula (2.33)

$$q_2^* \approx \frac{\mu_1}{c_0}\left[\gamma_2 - \gamma_1\right].$$

The curves q_3^* is presented as a function of arguments $\mu_1 + \mu_2$ and $c_1 + c_2$. In the case of large input intensity λ in Figures 3.1 (b) and 3.2 (b) the threshold functions have small dependence of the different values of c_1, c_2 and μ_1, μ_2. While the input intensity λ is getting smaller, e.g. in the Figure 3.3 (b), the thresholds levels depend only on the sums $\mu_1 + \mu_2$ and $c_1 + c_2$. The arrival intensity strongly influences the threshold functions for the third server, i.e. if the input intensity increases threshold levels decreases. This conjecture seems quite reasonable, since if arrival intensity is getting higher, there is a need to be ready for possible future arrivals, therefore, the controller uses the sever with smaller ratio γ_k more often, that is when the queue length is smaller. In this case the formula (2.33)

$$q_3^* \leq \frac{\mu_1 + \mu_2}{c_0}\left[\gamma_3 - \frac{c_1 + c_2}{\mu_1 + \mu_2}\right]$$

represents only the upper bound for possible threshold levels for the switching on the third server.

In Figures 3.4–3.6 and 3.7–3.9 in Appendix 2.9.3 the diagrams for the threshold levels behavior depending on the parameters γ_1, γ_2 and $\frac{c_1+c_2}{\mu_1+\mu_2}$,$\gamma_3$ for the second q_2^* and the third q_3^* servers are shown, respectively. They represent the changing of the threshold levels for the second server as a function under variation of the γ_1, γ_2. For the third server the curves represent a threshold function under variation of the ratio $\frac{c_1+c_2}{\mu_1+\mu_2}$, γ_3 with input intensity $\lambda = 0.51$.
The curves in these pictures correspond to the same value of γ_2 and γ_3, but with different values of c_2, μ_2 and c_3, μ_3 marked directly on the figures.
The values of system parameters are given below.

Table 2.34 Values of system parameters for the function q_2^*

Figure	a, $\gamma_2 = \frac{c_2}{\mu_2} = 6.67$	b, $\gamma_2 = \frac{c_2}{\mu_2} = 9.70$	$\gamma_3 = \frac{c_3}{\mu_3} = 10.00$
3.4	$\gamma_2 = \frac{2.00}{0.30}$	$\gamma_2 = \frac{2.91}{0.30}$	$\gamma_3 = \frac{1.00}{0.10}$
3.5	$\gamma_2 = \frac{3.33}{0.50}$	$\gamma_2 = \frac{4.85}{0.50}$	$\gamma_3 = \frac{1.00}{0.10}$
3.6	$\gamma_2 = \frac{5.33}{0.80}$	$\gamma_2 = \frac{7.76}{0.80}$	$\gamma_3 = \frac{1.00}{0.10}$

Table 2.35 Values of system parameters for the function q_3^*

Figure	a, $\gamma_2 = \frac{c_2}{\mu_2} = 6.67$	b, $\gamma_2 = \frac{c_2}{\mu_2} = 9.70$	$\gamma_3 = \frac{c_3}{\mu_3} = 10.00$
3.7	$\gamma_2 = \frac{3.33}{0.50}$	$\gamma_2 = \frac{4.85}{0.50}$	$\gamma_3 = \frac{1.00}{0.10}$
3.8	$\gamma_2 = \frac{3.33}{0.50}$	$\gamma_2 = \frac{4.85}{0.50}$	$\gamma_3 = \frac{3.00}{0.30}$
3.9	$\gamma_2 = \frac{3.33}{0.50}$	$\gamma_2 = \frac{4.85}{0.50}$	$\gamma_3 = \frac{4.00}{0.40}$

It is possible to see that the appropriate curves have the analogous structure. Thus we obtain the numerical evidence of a conjecture that the optimal threshold levels for the second server essentially depends on the values of the first service intensity μ_1 and the appropriate usage cost c_1. Nevertheless, the appropriate curves for different values of γ_2 have the analogous structure, and it shows that the threshold level of the second server mainly depends on the parameter γ_2. The optimal threshold levels for the third server essentially depends on the values of the sum $\mu_1 + \mu_2$ and $c_1 + c_2$. Similar to the second server, the appropriate curves for different values of γ_3 have also the analogous structure and show that threshold level for the third server mainly depends on the parameter γ_3.

The threshold level for the second server monotonously increases when γ_1 decreases and γ_2 increases. For the third server the thresholds monotonously increase when γ_1, γ_2 decreases and the ration $\frac{c_1+c_2}{\mu_1+\mu_2}$ increases. Moreover, thresholds for the second server exist only if $\gamma_1 < \gamma_2$ and in turn, the thresholds for the third server exist only if $\gamma_2 < \gamma_3$, according to the introduced order of the servers. Therefore, if $\gamma_1 = \gamma_2$, both of the servers are used under the same condition. If $\gamma_1 > \gamma_2$, the first and the second servers are interchanged and the thresholds appear for the first server. Finally, if the value of γ_1 becomes greater then γ_3 the first server becomes the third one.

In all these examples with a fixed value of the waiting cost $c_0 = 1$, the first server with smallest γ_1 is used immediately after an arrival, without putting the customer into the buffer. In other words, there the threshold level for the first server $q_1^* = 0$.

2.7.4 Numerical examples. PCM–problem. Two-level function

In this section we give some numerical results of an optimal policy calculation for the PCM–problem under the conditions (2.28) and (2.31), that is when the usage costs of the servers increase faster than the corresponding service intensities.

Table 2.36 Values of initial system parameters for $M/M/5/100$ queue

i	0	1	2	3	4	5
c_i	0.20	1.00	1.70	2.30	3.50	7.00
μ_i	-	0.30	0.45	0.52	0.63	0.90
γ_i	-	3.33	3.78	4.42	5.56	7.78

Table 2.37 Optimal control for any system state

System State x	Queue length $q(x)$																
(d_1,d_2,d_3,d_4,d_5)	0	1	2	3	4	...	10	11	12	...	19	20	21	...	23	24	...
(0,0,0,0,0)	1	1	1	2	2	2	2	3	3	3	3	4	4	4	4	5	5
(1,0,0,0,0)	0	2	2	2	2	2	2	2	2	2	2	2	3	3	3	3	3
(0,1,0,0,0)	1	1	1	1	1	1	3	3	3	3	3	3	3	3	3	3	3
(1,1,0,0,0)	0	0	0	3	3	3	3	3	3	3	3	3	3	3	3	3	3
(0,0,1,0,0)	1	1	1	1	2	2	2	2	2	2	2	2	2	2	2	2	2
(1,0,1,0,0)	0	2	2	2	2	2	2	2	2	2	2	2	2	2	2	2	2
(0,1,1,0,0)	1	1	1	1	1	1	1	1	1	1	1	1	1	1	1	1	1
(1,1,1,0,0)	0	0	0	0	0	0	4	4	4	4	4	4	4	4	4	4	4
(0,0,0,1,0)	1	1	1	1	2	2	2	2	2	2	2	2	2	2	2	3	3
(1,0,0,1,0)	0	2	2	2	2	2	2	2	2	2	2	2	2	2	2	2	2
(0,1,0,1,0)	1	1	1	1	1	1	1	1	1	3	3	3	3	3	3	3	3
(1,1,0,1,0)	0	0	0	3	3	3	3	3	3	3	3	3	3	3	3	3	3
(0,0,1,1,0)	1	1	1	1	2	2	2	2	2	2	2	2	2	2	2	2	2
(1,0,1,1,0)	0	2	2	2	2	2	2	2	2	2	2	2	2	2	2	2	2
(0,1,1,1,0)	1	1	1	1	1	1	1	1	1	1	1	1	1	1	1	1	1
(1,1,1,1,0)	0	0	0	0	0	0	0	0	0	0	0	0	0	0	0	0	0
(0,0,0,0,1)	1	1	1	1	2	2	2	2	2	2	2	2	2	2	2	3	3
(1,0,0,0,1)	0	2	2	2	2	2	2	2	2	2	2	2	2	2	2	2	2
(0,1,0,0,1)	1	1	1	1	1	1	1	1	1	3	3	3	3	3	3	3	3
(1,1,0,0,1)	0	0	0	3	3	3	3	3	3	3	3	3	3	3	3	3	3
(0,0,1,0,1)	1	1	1	1	1	1	2	2	2	2	2	2	2	2	2	2	2
(1,0,1,0,1)	0	2	2	2	2	2	2	2	2	2	2	2	2	2	2	2	2
(0,1,1,0,1)	1	1	1	1	1	1	1	1	1	1	1	1	1	1	1	1	1
(1,1,1,0,1)	0	0	0	0	0	0	4	4	4	4	4	4	4	4	4	4	4
(0,0,0,1,1)	1	1	1	1	1	1	2	2	2	2	2	2	2	2	2	2	2
(1,0,0,1,1)	0	2	2	2	2	2	2	2	2	2	2	2	2	2	2	2	2
(0,1,0,1,1)	1	1	1	1	1	1	1	1	1	3	3	3	3	3	3	3	3
(1,1,0,1,1)	0	0	0	3	3	3	3	3	3	3	3	3	3	3	3	3	3
(0,0,1,1,1)	1	1	1	1	1	1	2	2	2	2	2	2	2	2	2	2	2
(1,0,1,1,1)	0	2	2	2	2	2	2	2	2	2	2	2	2	2	2	2	2
(0,1,1,1,1)	1	1	1	1	1	1	1	1	1	1	1	1	1	1	1	1	1
(1,1,1,1,1)	0	0	0	0	0	0	0	0	0	0	0	0	0	0	0	0	0

The structure of an optimal control rule for this type of model for the system with K=5 servers, for input intensity λ=0.1 and with parameters in Table 2.36 is presented in control Table 2.37.

The optimal control policies for each system state are proposed in Table 2.37 where threshold levels are marked by bold font and underlined. In this example, if the queue length $q(x) > 90$ for any servers state, the optimal control rule consists in using the server with the largest mean usage cost (the fastest and the most expensive). Thus, for each state the optimal control rule is characterized by a threshold sequence for any available server in that state

$$0 \leq q_j^*(x) \leq q_{j+1}^*(x) \cdots \leq q_{i-1}^* \leq q_i^*(x) < q_{i+1}^*(x) = \infty,$$

where $j, j + 1, i \in J_0(x)$, $j \leq i$ with $i = \max\{j : j \in J_0(x)\}$. With respect to this switching rule, j-th server is used only if the current queue length satisfies the condition $0 \leq q_j^*(x) \leq q(x) < q_{j+1}^*(x)$, $j + 1$-st server is used if $q_{j+1}^*(x) \leq q(x) < q_{j+2}^*(x)$ and so on. The last available in state x server with $i = \max\limits_{k} \gamma_k$ has to be switched on only if $q(x) \geq q_i^*(x)$ and $q_{K+1}^* = \infty$.

To analyze the behavior of the threshold sequences in each state when the values of system parameters are varied we consider the system with K=3 servers and a large buffer B=100.

In Table 2.38 the results of optimal threshold levels are proposed for each system state where they exist. On the top of the table the values of initial system parameters are given. Then one of them is varied while all others are fixed. Now we give some explanations to proposed results. The optimal values of thresholds $q_j^*(x)$ depend strongly on the specific value of system parameters. With increasing arrival intensity λ threshold levels decrease, that is the faster but more expensive server is getting more preferable. The same behavior takes place in the case when the waiting cost c_0 increases. If the service intensity μ_1 of the cheapest server grows, the thresholds for using the faster but more expensive servers increase. If the service intensity μ_2 increases then the threshold level for the second server decreases, but for the third server the threshold increases. If the third service intensity μ_3 increases, then only the thresholds for the third server change, namely, they decrease. Finally, if we increase the values of the usage costs c_1, c_2 and c_3, the contrary to the corresponding service intensities effect takes place.

The numerical results show that if no arrivals taking into account the controller at the beginning of the queue length growth has to use available server with the fewest ratio γ_k, that is, the server with smallest index k. Also it is true in the case of light traffic $\lambda \approx 0$.

Table 2.38 Optimal thresholds behavior for each system state

System parameters							
λ	c_0	c_1	μ_1	c_2	μ_2	c_3	μ_3
0.010	0.200	1.000	0.020	5.000	0.050	50.00	0.450

(d_1, d_2, d_3)	(0,0,0)	(0,0,1)	(1,0,0)	(1,0,1)	(1,1,0)	(0,1,0)
Varied par.	q_1^* q_2^* q_3^*	q_1^* q_2^*	q_2^* q_3^*	q_2^*	q_3^*	q_1^* q_3^*
$\lambda = 0.005$	0,5,11	0,10,-	-,2,15	-,2,-	-,-,12	0,-,15
$\lambda = 0.050$	0,3,8	0,4,-	-,0,10	-,0,-	-,-,5	0,-,8
$\lambda = 0.150$	0,1,6	0,1,-	-,0,8	-,0,-	-,-,2	0,-,6
$c_0 = 0.200$	0,5,12	0,9,-	-,2,14	-,2,-	-,-,11	0,-,14
$c_0 = 0.500$	0,2,5	0,4,-	-,0,6	-,0,-	-,-,4	0,-,6
$c_0 = 1.000$	0,1,2	0,3,-	-,0,3	-,0,-	-,-,2	0,-,3
$\mu_1 = 0.020$	0,5,12	0,9,-	-,2,14	-,2,-	-,-,11	0,-,14
$\mu_1 = 0.023$	0,8,12	0,13,-	-,2,16	-,2,-	-,-,13	0,-,15
$\mu_1 = 0.025$	0,11,12	0,17,-	-,3,17	-,3,-	-,-,14	0,-,17
$c_1 = 0.500$	0,9,12	0,15,-	-,3,16	-,3,-	-,-,13	0,-,16
$c_1 = 1.000$	0,5,12	0,9,-	-,2,14	-,2,-	-,-,11	0,-,14
$c_1 = 1.500$	0,2,11	0,3,-	-,0,13	-,0,-	-,-,10	0,-,12
$\mu_2 = 0.050$	0,5,12	0,9,-	-,2,14	-,2,-	-,-,11	0,-,14
$\mu_2 = 0.080$	0,2,27	0,4,-	-,0,34	-,0,-	-,-,22	0,-,25
$\mu_2 = 0.100$	0,0,46	0,0,-	-,0,66	-,0,-	-,-,33	0,-,36
$c_2 = 4.000$	0,3,18	0,5,-	-,1,21	-,1,-	-,-,16	0,-,19
$c_2 = 5.000$	0,5,12	0,9,-	-,2,14	-,2,-	-,-,11	0,-,14
$c_2 = 5.500$	0,6,7	0,11,-	-,2,11	-,2,-	-,-,9	0,-,11
$\mu_3 = 0.350$	0,5,27	0,9,-	-,2,33	-,2,-	-,-,22	0,-,26
$\mu_3 = 0.400$	0,5,18	0,9,-	-,2,21	-,2,-	-,-,16	0,-,19
$\mu_3 = 0.450$	0,5,12	0,9,-	-,2,14	-,2,-	-,-,11	0,-,14
$c_3 = 45.00$	0,5,6	0,9,-	-,2,10	-,2,-	-,-,7	0,-,10
$c_3 = 50.00$	0,5,12	0,9,-	-,2,14	-,2,-	-,-,11	0,-,14
$c_3 = 60.00$	0,5,22	0,9,-	-,2,24	-,2,-	-,-,19	0,-,22

Otherwise, the first server which is used by controller may not be necessary with the fewest γ_k.

In the case of light traffic the threshold levels for the servers in the state $(0, 0, 0)$ can be obtained directly, that is in this state the threshold sequence is $0 = q_1^*(x) \leq q_2^*(x) \leq q_3^*(x) \leq q_4^*(x) = \infty$ where

$$q_1^*(x) = 0,$$

$$q_2^*(x) = \frac{1}{c_0}\left[\frac{1}{\mu_1} - \frac{1}{\mu_2}\right]^{-1}\left[\gamma_2 - \gamma_1\right],$$

$$q_3^*(x) = \frac{1}{c_0} \left[\frac{1}{\mu_2} - \frac{1}{\mu_3} \right]^{-1} \left[\gamma_3 - \gamma_2 \right],$$
$$q_4^*(x) = \infty,$$

and j-th server is used only if $q_j^*(x) \leq q(x) < q_{j+1}^*(x)$. Also this formula can be successfully applied to the system with two servers. For multi-server case threshold levels q_j^* for each server strongly depend on which other servers are busy. Therefore, it is necessary to use for the functions $q_j^*(x)$ the argument x and the above formulas can not be used to calculate thresholds in the states where some other servers are busy.

Threshold levels for the first exploitable server can be obtained as before by

$$q_2^* = \frac{1}{c_0} \left[\frac{1}{\mu_1} \right]^{-1} \left[\gamma_2 - \gamma_1 \right],$$
$$q_3^* = \frac{1}{c_0} \left[\frac{1}{\mu_1 + \mu_2} \right]^{-1} \left[\gamma_3 - \frac{c_1 + c_2}{\mu_1 + \mu_2} \right]$$

and independ on the states of servers with larger mean usage costs.

The examples of dynamic behavior of threshold levels when the values of the initial system parameters are varied are proposed in control diagrams shown in Figures 4.1–4.5 of Appendix 2.9.4. As mentioned above for this type of the PCM–problem the values of the initial system parameters satisfy the conditions (2.28) and (2.31).

The dynamic behavior of two-level threshold functions and thresholds between queue and server are proposed for each state of the system under consideration as follows

- $x = (0,0,0)$, two-level thresholds $[q_1^*(x), q_2^*(x)), [q_2^*(x), q_3^*(x)), [q_3^*(x), q_4^*(x)),$
  in Figure 4.1 $\lambda = 0.01$ and
  in Figure 4.2 $\lambda = 0.1$;

- $x = (0,0,1)$, two-level thresholds $[q_1^*(x), q_2^*(x)), [q_2^*(x), q_4^*(x))$
  in Figure 4.1 $\lambda = 0.01$ and
  in Figure 4.2 $\lambda = 0.1$;

- $x = (1,0,0)$, two-level thresholds $[q_2^*(x), q_3^*(x)), [q_3^*(x), q_4^*(x))$, thresholds between queue and second server $q_2^* = q_2^*(x)$,
  in Figure 4.3 $\lambda = 0.01$ and
  in Figure 4.4 $\lambda = 0.1$;

- $x = (1, 0, 1)$, thresholds between queue and second server q_2^*,
  in Figure 4.3 $\lambda = 0.01$ and
  in Figure 4.4 $\lambda = 0.1$;

- $x = (1, 1, 0)$, threshold between queue and third server q_3^*,
  in Figure 4.3 $\lambda = 0.01$ and
  in Figure 4.4 $\lambda = 0.1$;

- $x = (0, 0, 0)$, two-level thresholds $[q_1^*(x), q_3^*(x)), [q_3^*(x), q_4^*(x))$,
  in Figure 4.5 (a) $\lambda = 0.01$ and
  in Figure 4.5 (b) $\lambda = 0.1$;

- $x = (0, 1, 0)$, two-level thresholds $[q_1^*(x), q_3^*(x)), [q_3^*(x), q_4^*(x))$,
  in Figure 4.5 (a) $\lambda = 0.01$ and
  in Figure 4.5 (b),(c) $\lambda = 0.1$;

In all these examples $q_1^* = q_1^*(x) = 0$ and $q_4^*(x) = \infty$. In the diagrams presented the changing of the two-level thresholds are shown as the threshold functions under variation of the first service intensity μ_1, first usage cost c_1, second μ_2 and third μ_3 service intensities. The values of the initial system parameters are varied over the figures as follows:

- $\gamma_2 = \frac{c_2}{\mu_2} = \frac{5.00}{0.05} = 100.00$,
  $\gamma_3 = \frac{c_3}{\mu_3} = \frac{50.00}{0.45} = 111.11$,
  Figures 4.1–4.4, pictures labeled by letter "a", Figure 4.5, pictures labeled by letter "a" and "b";

- $\gamma_2 = \frac{c_2}{\mu_2} = \frac{5.00}{0.10} = 50.00$,
  $\gamma_3 = \frac{c_3}{\mu_3} = \frac{50.00}{0.40} = 125.00$,
  Figures 4.1–4.4, pictures labeled by letter "b", Figure 4.5, picture labeled by letter "c";

- $\gamma_2 = \frac{c_2}{\mu_2} = \frac{5.00}{0.15} = 33.33$,
  $\gamma_3 = \frac{c_3}{\mu_3} = \frac{50.00}{0.35} = 142.86$,
  Figures 4.1–4.4, pictures labeled by letter "c".

The first usage cost takes its values $c_1 = \{1, 2, 3, 4\}$. The curves of the specified shades correspond to the case $c_1 = 1$. All other similar curves represent the cases

$c_1 = \{2, 3, 4\}$, respectively.

Proposed control diagrams allow us to make some conclusions about the behavior of the two-level thresholds when the values of system parameters are varied. With respect to observation when the service intensity of the cheaper servers increases or/and when the usage cost of the slower servers decreases, the incentive to make an assignment to the servers with the lower mean usage cost is getting higher Otherwise, the incentive to make an assignment decreases. All the servers which are used by controller in a certain state have the order of mean usage cost increasing with respect to the growth of the queue length. But it is not necessary at all that controller uses all available servers in some state. Under some values of system parameters with respect to the optimal control rule the controller can miss some available servers and at once switch on the server with the larger mean usage cost. This case is proposed in control diagrams shown in Figure 4.5 when in the state $x = (0, 0, 0)$ the controller at first uses the first server and then it turns on the third one missing the second server.

Numerical examples show that in each state there exist a threshold sequence which includes two threshold levels for available servers. If the queue length is greater some level $q(x) > q^*$, then in any system state x the optimal control rule consists in using the server with the largest mean usage cost. Therefore, if the queue length is quite small then the main characteristic which is used by controller to choose an optimal server is server's usage cost. While the queue length increases more important becomes the information about the service intensity.

2.8 Conclusions

In this chapter we have considered the problem of controlling a multi-server queueing system like $M/M/K/B$. We presented a novel use of iteration procedures for queueing systems which constitutes the combination of dynamic programming and probabilistic arguments. We have shown that an optimal policy of job allocation for such a system with respect to minimization the mean number of jobs in the system is of threshold type, and the decision maker has to activate the server with highest intensity, if necessary. In some cases the exact or approximate value of the optimal threshold can be obtained analytically.

The problem of total processing cost minimization includes also usage costs for servers and the problem is divided into two subcases with respect to different system parameters, such as the usage cost c_k and the service intensity μ_k. In the first subcase, when the usage costs of the servers decrease slower than the service intensities, we have shown and numerically verified that the optimal policy is also of threshold type and the decision maker should use the server with minimal value of mean usage cost γ_k. In the second subcase, when the usage costs of the servers increase faster than the service intensities, the optimal policy has more difficult structure, i.e. the optimal allocation rule represents a threshold sequence and any available in the certain state server can be switched on but only if the current queue length is between some low and some upper levels. Thus, for each server there exists two–level threshold policy which depend on the states of all busy servers.

2.9   Appendices

2.9.1   Threshold functions for NJM–problem.

Figure 1.1   **(a)**   **(b)**

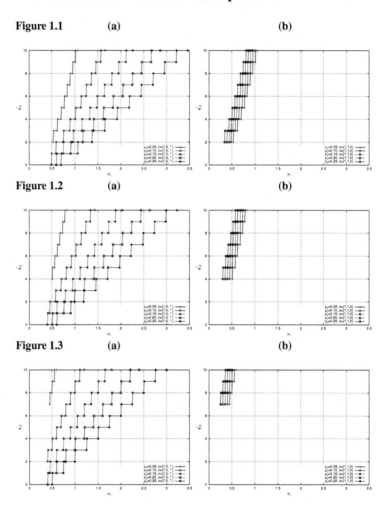

Figure 1.2   **(a)**   **(b)**

Figure 1.3   **(a)**   **(b)**

Figure 1.4   **(a)**   **(b)**

Figure 1.5   **(a)**   **(b)**

Figure 1.6   **(a)**   **(b)**

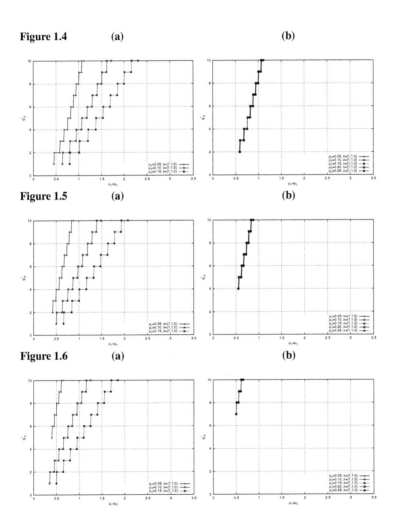

2.9.2 3–dimensional diagrams of threshold function for PCM–problem.

(a)

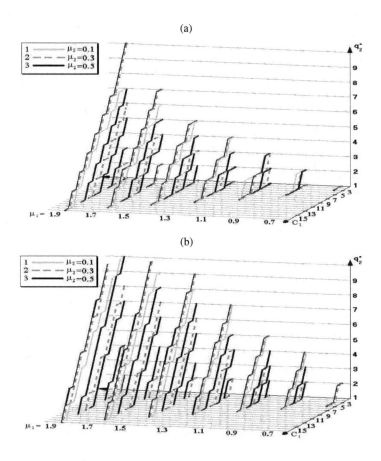

(b)

Fig. 2.1. The threshold level functions for input intensity (a) $\lambda=1.0$ and (b) $\lambda=0.5$.

(a)

(b)

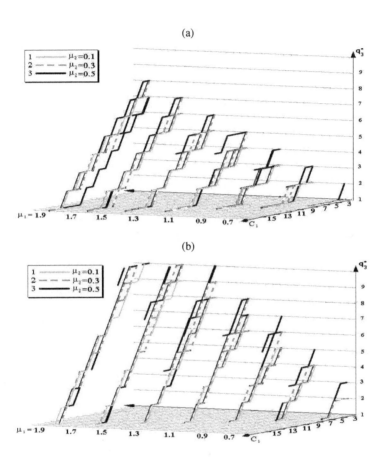

Fig. 2.2. The threshold level functions for input intensity (a) $\lambda=1.0$ and (b) $\lambda=0.5$.

2.9.3 2–dimensional diagrams of threshold function for PCM–problem.

Figure 3.1   **(a)**   **(b)**

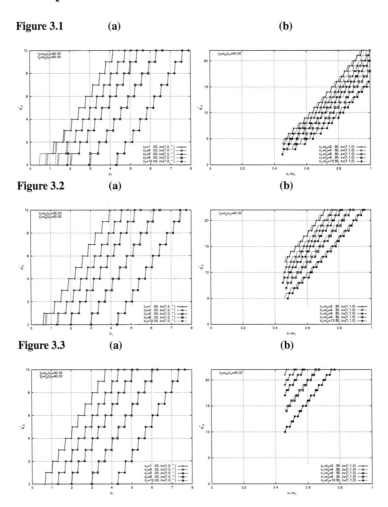

Figure 3.2   **(a)**   **(b)**

Figure 3.3   **(a)**   **(b)**

Figure 3.4   **(a)**   **(b)**

Figure 3.5   **(a)**   **(b)**

Figure 3.6   **(a)**   **(b)**

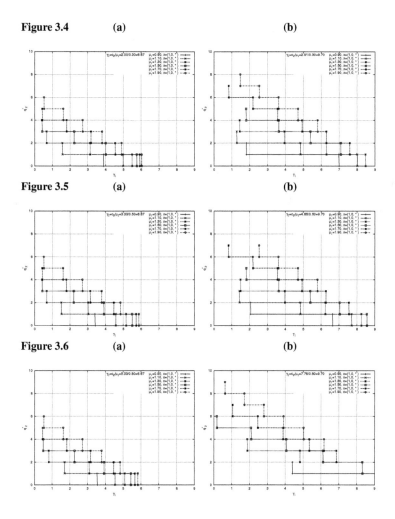

Figure 3.7   **(a)**   **(b)**

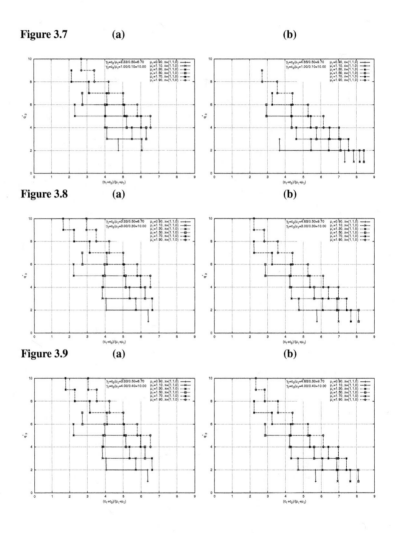

Figure 3.8   **(a)**   **(b)**

Figure 3.9   **(a)**   **(b)**

2.9.4 Two-level threshold function for PCM–problem.

Figure 4.1   **(a)**   **Figure 4.2**   **(a)**

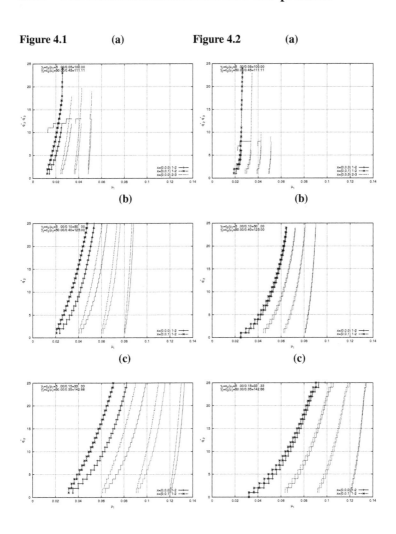

(b)   **(b)**

(c)   **(c)**

Figure 4.3   **(a)**   **Figure 4.4**   **(a)**

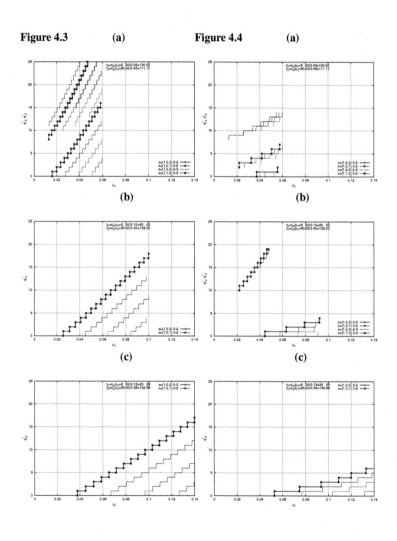

Figure 4.5 **(a)**

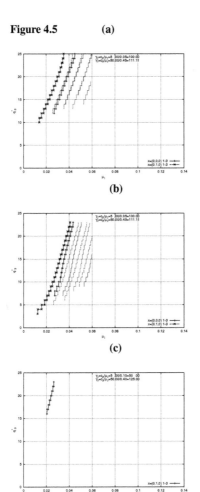

(b)

(c)

Chapter 3

Arrivals with modulating phases

This chapter extends the model of the preceding chapter in that now more general arrival streams with modulating arrival phases allowed. We analyze such arrival streams as Erlang (E) and Phase-type (PH), as well as Markov modulated Poisson process (MMPP) and Markov additive arrival process (MAP). Again we consider NJM and PCM optimization problems, and demonstrate that the optimal control policy is of threshold type, with threshold levels depending on the arrival modulating state.

3.1 Introduction.

In the system with m-phase (stage) Erlangian arrival a job arrival is assumed complete (and thus the customer can be forwarded for service) if all m phases of arrival have been completed. The times spending by a job on the phases are independent and equally distributed according to the exponential low with some parameter.

The PH-type arrival process is more complex since the distribution of times between events is expressed as the distribution of the first exit time from a set of states of continuous time Markov chain, as described by Neuts in [52].

Markovian additive arrival process (MAP), introduced by Neuts [53], is a generalization of the PH-type distribution. A MAP is associated with a finite absorbing Markov chain but instead of having only one initial probability vector, it requires as many as the number of transient states in the underlying Markov chain, i.e. one initial probability vector per transient state. This means that once the Markov chain has entered the absorbing state and a single MAP random variable is generated, the process restarts from the transient part again for the next random variable "remembering" the last transient state that reached absorption. Therefore, the MAP is formally represented by two matrices (Λ, N) rather than a matrix and a vector as in the PH-distribution case and is in general a non-renewal process. The most popular case of a MAP is known as Markov Modulated Poisson Process (MMPP) where the matrix Λ has all entries zero except the diagonal ones. Even a Poisson process is a MAP with only one single transient state in the underlying Markov chain.

The importance of arrivals with modulating phases lies in their ability to be more effective and powerful traffic models, that in its turn can be a better approximation of physical systems than the simple Poisson process. The systems with Erlangian arrivals in a communication network could be the case when the job, or a message, arrives in parts, for example m packets, in a network node and is served as a whole when all parts have arrived. Such a system with two heterogeneous servers has been investigated by Viniotis and Ephremides [81], who give a threshold policy definition for this model. The queueing systems with MAP are useful extention since for many interesting applications, especially in B-ISDN networks with very bursty arrival streams and with significant correlation between successive interarrival times, it has been shown that this burstiness has a significant impact on the behaviour of the system (see e.g. [15]). A method to derive the stationary waiting time distribution for a single-server system with MMPP was demonstrated in [48] and in a multi-server case in [10].

This chapter is organized as follows. In the next Section 3.3 the system with Erlangian arrivals is introduced. The systems with PH-type interarrival time distribution and MAP are discussed in Sections 3.4 and 3.5, respectively. For each queue we obtain the optimality equations and investigate a typical properties of corresponding optimal policies.

The great attention in this chapter is payed to numerical analysis of optimal policy structure when the values of initial system parameters vary. We note that for numerical analysis of different queueing systems in order to compare the results we use such initial system parameters that the average characteristics, namely mean arrival rates, are equal.

3.2   Problem description

Consider queueing system with K heterogeneous servers of intensities μ_k ($k = \overline{1, K}$), B places in the buffer ($K \leq B < \infty$), which can be symbolically represented in Figure 3.1

Figure 3.1 Queueing system

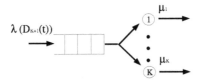

In this picture $D_{K+1}(t)$ is a modulating process for arrival stream that will be discussed below and specified for each particular case.

The formulation and notations of the optimization problem with respect to this type of queueing system are analogous to the previous (Markovian) case. But now the modulating phase at a decision epoch is a part of the system state. Therefore, the controlled queueing system is modelled by the stochastic Markov decision process $\{Z(t)\} = \{X(t), U(t)\}$. Here, the observed process $\{X(t)\}_{t \geq 0}$ with state space $E = \mathbf{N} \times \{0, 1\}^K \times \{1, ..., m\}$ includes one additional component $D_{K+1}(t)$, which denotes irreducible finite state modulating process with state space $\{1, \ldots, m\}$. Thus, for each state $x = (d_0, d_1, \ldots, d_K, d_{K+1})$, $d_{K+1}(x)$ denotes the state of the arrival process in the system state x, i.e. $d_{K+1}: 1 \to 2 \to \cdots \to m$. The value $m - d_{K+1}(x)$ denotes the residual interarrival time in the certain state x.

Denote by $e_i = (\underbrace{0, \ldots, 0}_{i}, 1, \underbrace{0, \ldots, 0}_{K+1-i})$ the $K + 2$ - dimensional vector for which the i-th component is one and all others are zeros. Consider the same shift operators S_0, S_j and S_0^{-1}, S_j^{-1} on the state space E introduced in (2.2), when arrivals and service completions take place in the queue. Additionally, one needs one more shift operator for modulating phase changing. Let $d_{K+1}(y) = \alpha$ is a new state of the modulating process after phase changing in a current state x. Now, the operator S_{K+1}^{α} can be introduced for changing the $K + 1$-st coordinate of the vector $x = (d_0, d_1, \ldots, d_K, d_{K+1})$,

$$S_{K+1}^{\alpha} x = x + [\alpha - d_{K+1}(x)] e_{K+1}. \tag{3.1}$$

We note, that with respect to different modulating phases $\alpha \neq \beta$ the following equalities hold

$$J_0(S_{K+1}^{\alpha}x) = J_0(S_{K+1}^{\beta}x), \qquad J_1(S_{K+1}^{\alpha}x) = J_1(S_{K+1}^{\beta}x),$$
$$M_0(S_{K+1}^{\alpha}x) = M_0(S_{K+1}^{\beta}x), \qquad M_1(S_{K+1}^{\alpha}x) = M_1(S_{K+1}^{\beta}x),$$
$$l(S_{K+1}^{\alpha}x) = l(S_{K+1}^{\beta}x), \qquad c(S_{K+1}^{\alpha}x) = c(S_{K+1}^{\beta}x).$$

Below the long-run average cost optimization problem is specified for queueing systems with different interarrival time distributions.

3.3   Controlled $E/M/K$ queue

In this section we consider the queueing system with m-stage Erlangian arrival process which is symbolically shown in Figure 3.2

Figure 3.2 Arrival process

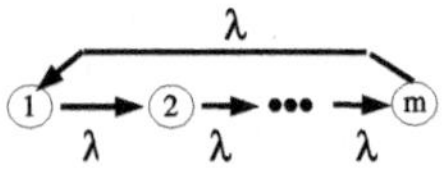

Each job arrives to the system in m-stages, $m \geq 1$. When $m = 1$, this model reduces to the $M/M/K/B$ model studied in Chapter 2. The overall arrival rate is $\overline{\lambda} = \frac{\lambda}{m}$, where λ is a rate per stage.

The equilibrium condition for an infinite buffer size

$$\overline{\lambda} = \frac{\lambda}{m} < \sum_{k=1}^{K} \mu_k. \tag{3.2}$$

We note that if the current Erlangian phase $d_{K+1}(x) < m$, in the state x only service completions take place, and if $d_{K+1}(x) = m$, then a new arrival and the service completions can be considered as the decision epochs.

To introduce optimality equation we have to represent the transition intensities of the process $\{Z(t)\}$. Using the notations of shift operators for vector state

$x = \{q, d_1 \ldots, d_K, d_{K+1}\}$ and properties of Erlang distribution the transition intensities $\lambda_{xy}(a)$ to go from state x to state y when action a is selected, can be represented in the form

$$\lambda_{xy}(a) = \begin{cases} \lambda, & y = S_{K+1}^{\alpha+1}x, d_{K+1}(x) = \alpha < m, \, d_{K+1}(y) = \alpha+1, \\ \lambda, & y = S_{a_0}S_{K+1}^1x, d_{K+1}(x) = m, \, d_{K+1}(y) = 1, \\ \mu_j, & y = S_{a_j}S_0^{-1}S_j^{-1}x, \quad j \in J_1(x), \\ -(\lambda + \sum_{j \in J_1(x)} \mu_j), & y = x, \\ 0, & \text{otherwise,} \end{cases}$$

where $a = a_0 \in A(x)$ denotes the control which has to be chosen in the case of an arrival to the state x, $a = a_j \in A(S_j^{-1}S_0^{-1}x)$ denotes the control in the case of a service completion on the j-th server.
In this matrix:

- the first case corresponds to phase changing without arrivals;

- the second case corresponds to the phase changing with new job arrival if the final modulating phase is completed;

- the third case corresponds to the service completion.

The fourth line represents diagonal elements of transition intensity matrix.

The possible transitions from the state x just after arrival and service completion epochs can be illustrated by the graph shown in Figure 3.3 (a) and (b), respectively

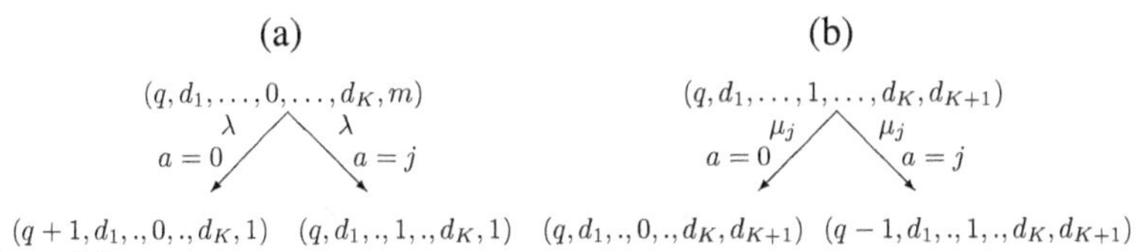

(a)   (b)

$(q, d_1, \ldots, 0, \ldots, d_K, m)$ $(q, d_1, \ldots, 1, \ldots, d_K, d_{K+1})$

$\lambda \quad\quad \lambda$ $\mu_j \quad\quad \mu_j$

$a = 0 \quad\quad a = j$ $a = 0 \quad\quad a = j$

$(q+1, d_1, ., 0, ., d_K, 1) \quad (q, d_1, ., 1, ., d_K, 1) \quad (q, d_1, ., 0, ., d_K, d_{K+1}) \quad (q-1, d_1, ., 1, ., d_K, d_{K+1})$

Figure 3.3

3.3.1 Optimality equation

To represent the optimality equation, consider the function $V(x,\,t) = \inf_{\delta} \mathbf{E}_x^{\delta} Y(t)$, that denotes the minimal total operating cost of the system during time t. For some small interval h the following equation can be obtained

$$
\begin{aligned}
V(x, t+h) = {}& c(x)h + (1 - [\lambda + M_1]h)V(x,t)(x) \\
& + \mathbf{1}_{\{d_{K+1}(x)=m\}}\lambda h \min_{a_0 \in A(x)} V(S_{a_0} S_{K+1}^1 x, t) \\
& + \mathbf{1}_{\{d_{K+1}(x)=i<m\}}\lambda h \, V(S_{K+1}^{i+1} x) \\
& + \mathbf{1}_{\{q(x)=0\}} \sum_{j \in J_1(x)} \mu_j h \, V(S_j^{-1} x, t) \\
& + \mathbf{1}_{\{q(x)>0\}} \sum_{j \in J_1(x)} \mu_j h \min_{a_j \in A(S_j^{-1} S_0^{-1} x)} V(S_{a_j} S_j^{-1} S_0^{-1} x, t).
\end{aligned}
$$

In this equation the first member in the right–hand side represents the loss of the system up to time h, the second one represents the total loss of the system during the following time t in the case that no modulating phase changes and service completions occur in the system, the next one denotes the total loss of the system during time t in the case that a new customer arrives before the service completion. The next item is a modulating phase changing without arrival. The following member represents the loss of the system in the case of service completion with non-empty queue before new customer arrival, the last member deals with the total loss of the system in the case that one of the served customers leaves the system with empty queue before some customer arrives.

After some transformations taking into account the asymptotic behavior (2.6) of the function $V(x,\,t)$ when $t \to \infty$ and passing to the limit $h \to 0$, the previous equation assumes the form

$$
\begin{aligned}
v(x) = \frac{1}{\lambda + M_1} \bigg[& c(x) + \lambda \bigg(\mathbf{1}_{\{d_{K+1}(x)=m\}} T_0 v(S_{K+1}^1 x) \qquad\qquad (3.3) \\
& + \mathbf{1}_{\{d_{K+1}(x)=i<m\}} v(S_{K+1}^{i+1} x) \bigg) \\
& + \sum_{j \in J_1(x)} \mu_j T_j v(x) - g \bigg] = Bv(x),
\end{aligned}
$$

where operators T_0 and T_j given by formula (2.9) and $Bv(x)$ denotes (see Section 2.4) the transform operator for the value function $v(x)$.

The optimal policy $f = \{f(x) : x \in E\}$ is determined by the definitions (2.11) and (2.12).

3.3.2 Monotonicity properties. Dependence on arrival phases

In this section we extend the monotonicity results obtained in Chapter 2 for the system with Erlangian arrivals. The form of optimality equation (3.3) shows that the formulation of monotonicity properties is analogous to the previous model since the introduced in the previous chapter inequalities for the value function do not depend on the arrival statistics.

For this model the modulating phase (stage) or the residual interarrival time at a decision epoch is a part of the system state. Therefore we exploit a partial ordering (2.14) and (2.15) of the state space E, and the order with respect to the different Erlangian phases α and β

$$S_{K+1}^{\beta} x \geq S_{K+1}^{\alpha} x, \qquad \alpha \leq \beta. \tag{3.4}$$

This order is also partial. Now assuming that an optimal policy exists and is unique we can conclude that the optimal policy is of threshold type.

Theorem 3.4 *The optimal policy for the NJM– and the PCM–problems for the system with Erlangian arrivals is of threshold type with finite thresholds $q_k^*(d_{K+1})$ for each phase.*

Proof: Let us consider the states $S_{K+1}^{\alpha} x$ and $S_{K+1}^{\beta} x$ with different Erlangian phases α and β. As we have mentioned above, the different states of arrival process do not change a threshold nature of optimal control rule. Thus, the value function $v(x)$ is submodular that can be proved in similar way as in Section 2.4.6. Therefore, for each phase holds the inequality

$$(1 - S_0)(S_0 - S_k)v(S_{K+1}^{\alpha} x) \leq 0,$$
$$(1 - S_0)(S_0 - S_k)v(S_{K+1}^{\beta} x) \leq 0$$

and the optimal policy is of threshold type with finite threshold levels for k-th server $q_k^*(\alpha)$ and $q_k^*(\beta)$ which depend on modulating phases (residual interarrival time).
$\square$

Thus, for the NJM–problem the optimal policy is of threshold type with threshold values for j-th server $q_j^*(d_{K+1})$ which are independ on the states of slower servers (in light traffic case, i.e. $\frac{\lambda}{m} < \mu_K$) or have weak dependence (in heavy traffic, i.e. $\frac{\lambda}{m} \approx M_0 + M_1$) and are decreasing in Erlangian phase d_{K+1}. The optimal control in this case consists in using the fastest available server, if necessary.

For the PCM–problem with servers arrangement (2.28) under conditions (2.29) and (2.30), i.e. the usage costs decrease slower than the service intensities, the optimal policy is also of threshold type with levels $q_j^*(d_{K+1})$ for j-th server depending on Erlangian phase d_{K+1} as for the NJM–problem. The controller uses the server with fewest mean usage cost, if necessary.

For the PCM–problem under condition (2.31), i.e. the usage costs increase faster than the service intensities, there exist two-level threshold policy $(q_j^*(x),$ $q_{j+1}^*(x))$ which depend on the state x. The controller in this case can use any of available servers in increasing oder of the mean usage costs when the queue length increases. Moreover, starting from some queue level q^* the optimal control in any state consists in using the server with largest mean usage cost.

As for the system $M/M/K$, in the case of light traffic when $\lambda < \mu_K$, the threshold levels can be determined by (2.21) and (2.33). Otherwise, we use numerical analysis, see Section 3.3.4 and while the value of arrival intensity per stage λ increases, the threshold levels $q_j^*(\lambda, d_{K+1})$ is also decreasing when λ increases.

Now consider a two-state modulating process. With respect to introduced partial order in our special case we show that the threshold levels $q_k^*(\alpha)$ and $q_k^*(\beta)$ may be different, moreover $q_k^*(\alpha) \geq q_k^*(\beta)$, when $\alpha \leq \beta$.

Theorem 3.5 *Assume the bounded, nondecreasing function $v(x)$ has the following property*

$$v(S_{K+1}^\beta x) \geq v(S_{K+1}^\alpha x), \; \alpha \leq \beta,$$

or for residual interarrival time $m - \alpha \geq m - \beta$. Then the operator B introduced in (3.3) also retains this property for the value function of the model,

$$Bv(S_{K+1}^\beta x) \geq Bv(S_{K+1}^\alpha x), \; \alpha \leq \beta.$$

Proof: At first, for operator T_0 we have

$$T_0 v(S_{K+1}^\alpha x) = \min_{k \in A(S_{K+1}^\alpha x)} v(S_k S_{K+1}^\alpha x) \geq v(S_{K+1}^\alpha x),$$

$$T_0 v(S_{K+1}^\beta x) = \min_{k \in A(S_{K+1}^\beta x)} v(S_k S_{K+1}^\beta x) \geq \min_{k \in A(S_{K+1}^\alpha x)} v(S_k S_{K+1}^\alpha x) = T_0 v(S_{K+1}^\alpha x),$$

by virtue of assumption about nondecreasing property of the value function
$v(S_k S_{K+1}^\alpha x) \geq v(x)$ and $v(S_{K+1}^\beta x) \geq v(S_{K+1}^\alpha x)$ when $\alpha \leq \beta$ and the fact that
set of controls does not vary in directions S_{K+1}^α and S_{K+1}^β, that is $A(S_{K+1}^\alpha x) = A(S_{K+1}^\beta x)$. Operator T_j also retains the latter property according to the definition (2.9).
Without loss of generality, we assume that $2\lambda + \sum_{j \in J_1(x)} \mu_j = 1$. Now for operator
B and $\alpha \leq \beta$ we get

$$
\begin{aligned}
Bv(S_{K+1}^\beta x) - Bv(S_{K+1}^\alpha x) &= [c(S_{K+1}^\beta x) - c(S_{K+1}^\alpha x)] \\
&+ \lambda[T_0 v(S_{K+1}^\alpha x) + v(S_{K+1}^\beta x)] - \lambda[v(S_{K+1}^\beta x)] + v(S_{K+1}^\alpha x)] \\
&+ \sum_{j \in J_1(x)} \mu_j[T_j v(S_{K+1}^\beta x) - T_j v(S_{K+1}^\alpha x)] \geq 0,
\end{aligned}
$$

by virtue of the property that $c(x)$ is constant with respect to the shifts S_{K+1}^α and
S_{K+1}^β; and the properties of operators T_0, T_j.

Now the statement of the theorem follows from the fact that the value function
of the model $v = \{v(x) : x \in E\}$ is a fixed point of operator B.
□

Remark 3.6 We have not been able to prove successfully Theorem 3.5 for any
number of the phases m, nevertheless the statement of the theorem is confirmed
by the numerical results.

Using the last theorem we expect that with decreasing of the residual interarrival
time the incentive to make an assignment to the slower servers is getting higher.
That means that for some server k the threshold levels for different modulating
phases satisfy $q_k^*(\alpha) \geq q_k^*(\beta)$, when $\alpha \leq \beta$. For this, it is sufficiently, that

$$
f(S_{K+1}^\beta x) = 0 \quad \Rightarrow \quad f(S_{K+1}^\alpha x) = 0.
$$

It is possible to rewrite the last statement in accordance with the definition of
optimal policy in the form

$$
v(S_0 S_{K+1}^\beta x) \leq v(S_k S_{K+1}^\beta x) \Rightarrow v(S_0 S_{K+1}^\alpha x) \leq v(S_k S_{K+1}^\alpha x).
$$

For the last inequalities we get

$$
v(S_0 S_{K+1}^\alpha x) - v(S_k S_{K+1}^\alpha x) - v(S_0 S_{K+1}^\beta x) + v(S_k S_{K+1}^\beta x) \leq 0,
$$

or in operator form

$$
(S_0 - S_k)(S_{K+1}^\alpha - S_{K+1}^\beta)v(x) \leq 0 \quad \text{for all } k \in J_0(x), \ \alpha \leq \beta. \tag{3.5}
$$

3.3.3   Algorithm

To analyze numerically the behavior of optimal strategies the servers will be arranged for the NJM–problem in order (2.13) of their service intensities decreasing and for the PCM–problem in order (2.28) of their mean usage costs increasing under conditions (2.29)–(2.31).

The algorithm as before consists of two basic steps

Strategy estimation. For a given policy $f = \{f_n(x) : x = \overline{1, I}\}$ solve up to an accuracy ε by a successive approximation method the equation

- if $d_{K+1}(x) = i < m$ then

$$v_n(x) = \frac{1}{\lambda + M_1}\left[c(x) + \lambda v_n(S_{K+1}^{i+1}x)\right.$$
$$\left. + \sum_{j \in J_1(x)} \mu_j v_n(S_{f_n(S_j^{-1}S_0^{-1}x)}S_j^{-1}S_0^{-1}x) - g_n\right]$$

- if $d_{K+1}(x) = m$

$$v_n(x) = \frac{1}{\lambda + M_1}\left[c(x) + \lambda v_n(S_{f_n(S_{K+1}^1x)}S_{K+1}^1x)\right.$$
$$\left. + \sum_{j \in J_1(x)} \mu_j v_n(S_{f_n(S_j^{-1}S_0^{-1}x)}S_j^{-1}S_0^{-1}x) - g_n\right]$$

for all $x \in E$ under the condition $v(0) = 0$.

Strategy improvement. For a given solution $v_n = \{v_n(x) : x \in E\}$ find a new policy $f_{n+1} = \{f_{n+1}(x) : x \in E\}$, which minimizes the Bellman function (2.11) of the model:

$$f_{n+1}(x) = \operatorname*{argmin}_{k \in A(x)} v_n(x + e_k), \quad k = \overline{0, K}.$$

We note, that in the case of new arrival, that is $d_{K+1}(x) = m$, the optimal control is associated with the state S_{K+1}^1x after phase changing.

The algorithm stops when two successive iterations yield the same policy.

The realization of this algorithm with respect to the multidimensional system states is quite complex and requires a lot of processing time to obtain the results.

Therefore, for description of system state changing at the control epochs we consider the one-to-one correspondence between the multidimensional representation of the system state x and the index of such a state. Namely,

$$\#(x) = 2^K(d_0(x)m_{K+1} + d_{K+1}(x) - 1) + \sum_{j=1}^{K} 2^{j-1}d_j(x)\mathbf{1}_{\{j>1\}} \equiv x \quad (3.6)$$

and the number of system states is $2^K m(B - K + 1)$.

Now, if y_j is the state after possible transition from the j-th coordinate it can be obtained with respect to introduced formula

$$y_j = x + \frac{(d_j - d_j(x))2^K \mathbf{1}_{\{j=0\}}m_{K+1}}{\mathbf{1}_{\{1 \leq j \leq K\}}2^{K-j+1}}. \quad (3.7)$$

Thus, in one-dimensional case we have

$$
\begin{aligned}
S_0 x &= x + m2^K, &\quad (3.8)\\
S_0^{-1} x &= x - m2^K, \\
S_j x &= x + 2^{j-1}, \\
S_j^{-1} x &= x - 2^{j-1}, \\
S_{K+1}^i &= x + (i - d_{K+1}(x))2^K.
\end{aligned}
$$

3.3.4 Numerical analysis

In this section we consider some numerical examples of optimal policy structure for the system with Erlangian arrivals. At first, we consider examples for the NJM–problem. For the system $E_5/M/5/100$, if number of phases $m = 5$, arrival intensity per stage $\lambda = 0.05$, the mean arrival rate $\overline{\lambda} = \frac{\lambda}{m} = 0.01$ and values of service intensities μ_i given in Table 3.7 are presented in control Table 3.8.

Table 3.7 Values of initial system parameters for $E_5/M/5/100$ queue

i	1	2	3	4	5
μ_i	1.90	0.63	0.52	0.45	0.30

Table 3.8 Optimal control for any system state

System State x $(d_1, d_2, d_3, d_4, d_5, d_6)$	Queue length $q(x)$													
	0	1	2	3	4	5	6	7	8	9	10	11	12	...
$(0,*,*,*,*,*)$	<u>1</u>	1	1	1	1	1	1	1	1	1	1	1	1	1
$(1,0,*,*,*,1)$	0	0	<u>2</u>	2	2	2	2	2	2	2	2	2	2	2
$(1,0,*,*,*,5)$	0	<u>2</u>	2	2	2	2	2	2	2	2	2	2	2	2
$(1,1,0,*,*,*)$	0	0	<u>3</u>	3	3	3	3	3	3	3	3	3	3	3
$(1,1,1,0,*,*)$	0	0	0	<u>4</u>	4	4	4	4	4	4	4	4	4	4
$(1,1,1,1,0,1)$	0	0	0	0	0	0	0	<u>5</u>	5	5	5	5	5	5
$(1,1,1,1,0,5)$	0	0	0	0	0	0	<u>5</u>	5	5	5	5	5	5	5
$(1,1,1,1,1,*)$	0	0	0	0	0	0	0	0	0	0	0	0	0	

The optimal control rule, in accordance with threshold policy, are underlined in this control table. The results of this table show that the optimal policy for the system with Erlangian arrivals has threshold property. The fastest server is always activated. But now, the threshold sequence is depend not only on the queue length, but also can depend on the current stage of arrival process. Threshold levels take their values:

$$q_1^*(d_6) = 0, \quad d_6 = \overline{1, m};$$
$$q_2^*(d_6) = 2, \quad d_6 = \overline{1, 4};$$
$$q_2^*(d_6) = 1, \quad d_6 = 5;$$
$$q_3^*(d_6) = 2, \quad d_6 = \overline{1, m};$$
$$q_4^*(d_6) = 3, \quad d_6 = \overline{1, m};$$
$$q_5^*(d_6) = 7, \quad d_6 = \overline{1, 4};$$
$$q_5^*(d_6) = 6, \quad d_6 = 5.$$

Thus, the threshold sequence has the following form

$$0 = q_1^* \leq q_2^*(\beta) \leq q_2^*(\alpha) \leq \cdots \leq q_K^*(\beta) \leq q_K^*(\alpha) < q_{K+1}^* = \infty,$$

where α and β are the current arrival modulating phases and $\alpha \leq \beta$. The last inequality means that if the residual interarrival time decreases, the value of threshold level for the slower servers also decreases. And vice versa, as the residual interarrival time increases, the threshold level also increases. The numerical examples allow us to suspect that the optimal threshold may vary at most 1 for the states with different arrival modulating phase, that is, $q_k^*(\beta) \leq q_k^*(\alpha) \leq q_k^*(\beta) + 1$ if $\alpha \leq \beta$. In all examples it was mentioned, that the optimal threshold can changes only if the residual time for a new arrival is less than the time which the job has already spent on the modulating phase.

To investigate the dynamics of optimal threshold levels behavior for the NJM–problem we consider the system $E_5/M/3/100$ with m=5 modulating phases (stages) and $K = 3$ heterogeneous servers. The results of calculation are shown in Figures 1.1–1.6 in Appendix 3.7.1. To compare the results of the optimal policies calculation for different queues we take the same varied values of service intensities as for the system with Poisson arrivals, and the arrival rate per stage satisfies the condition $\lambda = \frac{\bar{\lambda}}{m}$, where $\bar{\lambda}$ is Poisson arrival rate for $M/M/K$ system. Therefore, the arrival intensity per stage λ is varied over the Figures 1.1–1.3 as follows

- λ=2.55, $\bar{\lambda} = \frac{\lambda}{m}$=0.51, in Figure 1.1,

- λ=1.30, $\bar{\lambda} = \frac{\lambda}{m}$=0.26, in Figure 1.2,

- λ=0.05, $\bar{\lambda} = \frac{\lambda}{m}$=0.01, in Figure 1.3.

In these diagrams the changing of threshold levels $q_2^*(d_4)$ for the second server (pictures labeled by letter "a") and $q_3^*(d_4)$ for the third server (pictures labeled by letter "b") as the threshold function with arguments of first service intensity μ_1, for different values of the second service intensity μ_2, depending on the Erlangian phase d_4 are shown.

From the pictures one can see that the threshold functions have the same structure as for the model with Poisson arrivals, but now to each value of second server service intensity corresponds the family of curves which consists of the threshold functions for each value of Erlangian arrival phase. This shows possible difference of threshold levels for different modulating phases. In all examples the incentive to make an assignment to the second server is greater in state $x = (1, 0, *, \beta)$ than in state $x = (1, 0, *, \alpha)$, and to the third server is greater in state $x = (1, 1, 0, \beta)$ than in state $x = (1, 1, 0, \alpha)$, if $\alpha \leq \beta$, or for the residual interarrival time $m - \alpha \geq m - \beta$. The legend for the diagrams represents the upper and low bounds for each family of curves. The upper bound denotes the thresholds when a new customer starts its generation, that is $d_{K+1} = 1$, and the low bound denotes — the thresholds, when $d_{K+1} = m = 5$. All other curves of the family correspond to the cases when $d_{K+1} = \overline{2,4}$. In the case of small arrival intensity per stage, the upper and low bounds tend to coincide.

The influence of the number of modulating phases on the form of threshold diagrams is shown on the Figures 1.4–1.6, where $\lambda = 1.30$, $\bar{\lambda} = 0.26$ (pictures labeled by letter "a") and $\lambda = 0.05$, $\bar{\lambda} = 0.01$ (pictures labeled by letter "b"). The number of modulating phases is changed over the figures, so

- m=5   in Figure 1.4,
- m=10   in Figure 1.5,
- m=20   in Figure 1.6.

In these diagrams the curve family structure remains the same but the number of the curves between two bounds increases as increases the number of modulating Erlangian phases.

For the PCM–problem we propose only control tables since the pictures for optimal threshold policy are the same as for $M/M/K$ queue but depending now on Erlangian phases in similar way as before.

For arrangement of the servers (2.28) and in the case of $\mu_1 \geq \mu_2 \geq \cdots \geq \mu_5$ for the parameters in Table 3.9 the results are illustrated in control Table 3.10.

Table 3.9 Values of initial system parameters for $E_5/M/5/100$ queue

i	0	1	2	3	4	5
c_i	1.00	3.00	2.80	2.60	2.40	2.00
μ_i	-	1.90	0.63	0.52	0.45	0.30
γ_i	-	1.58	4.44	5.00	5.53	6.66

Table 3.10 Optimal control for any system state

System State x	Queue length $q(x)$													
$(d_1, d_2, d_3, d_4, d_5, d_6)$	0	1	2	3	4	5	6	7	8	9	10	11	12	...
(0,*,*,*,*,*)	**1**	1	1	1	1	1	1	1	1	1	1	1	1	1
(1,0,*,*,*,1)	0	0	0	0	0	**2**	2	2	2	2	2	2	2	2
(1,0,*,*,*,5)	0	0	0	0	**2**	2	2	2	2	2	2	2	2	2
(1,1,0,*,*,*)	0	0	0	0	0	0	**3**	3	3	3	3	3	3	3
(1,1,1,0,*,*)	0	0	0	0	0	0	0	**4**	4	4	4	4	4	4
(1,1,1,1,0,*)	0	0	0	0	0	0	0	0	0	0	0	**5**	5	
(1,1,1,1,1,*)	0	0	0	0	0	0	0	0	0	0	0	0	0	

In this case of the PCM–problem the optimal control is of threshold type and has the same structure as for the NJM–problem. In this example threshold sequence consists of the following elements

$$q_1^*(d_6) = 0, \quad d_6 = \overline{1, m};$$
$$q_2^*(d_6) = 5, \quad d_6 = \overline{1, 4};$$
$$q_2^*(d_6) = 4, \quad d_6 = 5;$$
$$q_3^*(d_6) = 6, \quad d_6 = \overline{1, m};$$
$$q_4^*(d_6) = 7, \quad d_6 = \overline{1, m};$$

$$q_5^*(d_6) = 12, \quad d_6 = \overline{1,m}.$$

Table 3.11 Values of initial system parameters for $E_5/M/5/100$ **queue**

i	0	1	2	3	4	5
c_i	0.20	1.00	1.70	2.30	3.50	7.00
μ_i	-	0.30	0.45	0.52	0.63	0.90
γ_i	-	3.33	3.78	4.42	5.56	7.78

Table 3.12 Optimal control for any system state

System State x	Modulating phase d_6				
(d_1,d_2,d_3,d_4,d_5)	1	2	3	4	5
(0,0,0,0,0)	0,2,11,17,24	0,2,11,18,25	0,2,12,18,26	0,3,12,20,30	0,3,15,26,37
(1,0,0,0,0)	-,0,21,33,46	-,0,21,33,46	-,0,22,34,48	-,0,22,36,51	-,0,24,41,58
(0,1,0,0,0)	0,-,10,34,46	0,-,10,34,47	0,-,10,35,48	0,-,10,37,52	0,-,10,41,59
(1,1,0,0,0)	-,-,3,49,68	-,-,3,50,68	-,-,3,50,69	-,-,3,51,72	-,-,2,55,78
(0,0,1,0,0)	0,5,-,30,47	0,5,-,30,47	0,5,-,30,49	0,5,-,32,52	0,4,-,35,58
(1,0,1,0,0)	-,0,-,42,68	-,0,-,42,68	-,0,-,43,69	-,0,-,44,72	-,0,-,47,78
(0,1,1,0,0)	0,-,-,25,69	0,-,-,25,69	0,-,-,25,70	0,-,-,25,73	0,-,-,26,79
(1,1,1,0,0)	-,-,-,10,89	-,-,-,10,89	-,-,-,10,90	-,-,-,10,91	-,-,-,9,96
(0,0,0,1,0)	0,5,22,-,43	0,5,22,-,44	0,5,22,-,45	0,5,23,-,48	0,5,25,-,54
(1,0,0,1,0)	-,0,31,-,62	-,0,31,-,63	-,0,31,-,63	-,0,31,-,66	-,0,33,-,71
(0,1,0,1,0)	0,-,14,-,63	0,-,14,-,63	0,-,14,-,64	0,-,13,-,66	0,-,13,-,72
(1,1,0,1,0)	-,-,3,-,81	-,-,3,-,81	-,-,3,-,82	-,-,3,-,83	-,-,2,-,88
(0,0,1,1,0)	0,5,-,-,59	0,5,-,-,59	0,5,-,-,59	0,5,-,-,61	0,5,-,-,66
(1,0,1,1,0)	-,0,-,-,74	-,0,-,-,74	-,0,-,-,74	-,0,-,-,76	-,0,-,-,80
(0,1,1,1,0)	0,-,-,-,55	0,-,-,-,55	0,-,-,-,55	0,-,-,-,55	0,-,-,-,56
(1,1,1,1,0)	-,-,-,-,31	-,-,-,-,31	-,-,-,-,31	-,-,-,-,31	-,-,-,-,30
(0,0,0,0,1)	0,5,22,35,-	0,5,23,35,-	0,5,23,35,-	0,5,23,37,-	0,5,25,42,-
(1,0,0,0,1)	-,0,31,50,-	-,0,31,50,-	-,0,31,51,-	-,0,31,52,-	-,0,33,56,-
(0,1,0,0,1)	0,-,14,50,-	0,-,14,50,-	0,-,14,51,-	0,-,14,53,-	0,-,13,56,-
(1,1,0,0,1)	-,-,3,63,-	-,-,3,63,-	-,-,3,63,-	-,-,3,63,-	-,-,2,67,-
(0,0,1,0,1)	0,6,-,44,-	0,6,-,44,-	0,6,-,44,-	0,5,-,45,-	0,5,-,48,-
(1,0,1,0,1)	-,0,-,54,-	-,0,-,54,-	-,0,-,54,-	-,0,-,54,-	-,0,-,55,-
(0,1,1,0,1)	0,-,-,31,-	0,-,-,31,-	0,-,-,31,-	0,-,-,31,-	0,-,-,30,-
(1,1,1,0,1)	-,-,-,10,-	-,-,-,10,-	-,-,-,10,-	-,-,-,10,-	-,-,-,9,-
(0,0,0,1,1)	0,6,32,-,-	0,6,32,-,-	0,6,32,-,-	0,6,32,-,-	0,5,34,-,-
(1,0,0,1,1)	-,0,40,-,-	-,0,40,-,-	-,0,40,-,-	-,0,40,-,-	-,0,40,-,-
(0,1,0,1,1)	0,-,15,-,-	0,-,15,-,-	0,-,15,-,-	0,-,15,-,-	0,-,14,-,-
(1,1,0,1,1)	-,-,3,-,-	-,-,3,-,-	-,-,3,-,-	-,-,3,-,-	-,-,2,-,-
(0,0,1,1,1)	0,6,-,-,-	0,6,-,-,-	0,6,-,-,-	0,6,-,-,-	0,5,-,-,-
(1,0,1,1,1)	-,0,-,-,-	-,0,-,-,-	-,0,-,-,-	-,0,-,-,-	-,0,-,-,-
(0,1,1,1,1)	0,-,-,-,-	0,-,-,-,-	0,-,-,-,-	0,-,-,-,-	0,-,-,-,-

Now consider the case for server arrangement (2.28) and parameters $\mu_1 \leq \mu_2 \leq \cdots \leq \mu_5$ and $c_1 \leq c_2 \leq \cdots \leq c_5$. The control table has quite complex structure since for such group of initial system parameters the optimal control rule represents threshold sequences which are different for different system states. In the table Table 3.12 we consider system states with modulating phases $d_{K+1} = \{1, 2, 3, 4, 5\}$. The optimal control policies are presented as threshold sequences $q_1^*(x)$, $q_2^*(x), \ldots, q_K^*(x)$.

From the Table 3.12 one can see that when the queue length $q \geq q^* = 96$ the controller in all system states always uses the server with largest mean usage cost, which is the fastest and the most expensive one. Otherwise, the slower but cheaper servers can be used by controller. Taking into account future arrivals the controller prefers cheaper but slower servers while the residual interarrival time decreases.

3.4   Controlled $PH/M/K$ queue

In this section we consider the queueing system $PH/M/K/B$ in which Phase-type interarrival time distribution has a representation (η, Λ). The vector $\eta = (\eta^1, \ldots, \eta^m)$ of dimension m is an initial modulating phase distribution and matrix $\Lambda = [\lambda_{ij}]$, $m \times m$ — transition intensities of PH-distribution. PH-type arrival process symbolically can be represented in Figure 3.13

Figure 3.13 Arrival process

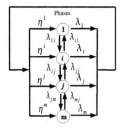

The equilibrium condition in this case

$$\bar{\lambda} = (-\eta^T \Lambda^{-1} \vec{1})^{-1} < \sum_{k=1}^{K} \mu_k. \tag{3.9}$$

The decision times in any state consists of arrivals and service completions epochs.
The transition intensities of the process $\{Z(t)\}$ are the following

$$
\lambda_{xy}(a) = \begin{cases}
\lambda_{\alpha\beta}, & y = S_{K+1}^{\beta}x, & d_{K+1}(x) = \alpha,\ d_{K+1}(y) = \beta, \\
\eta^{\beta}\lambda_{\alpha}, & y = S_{a_0}S_{K+1}^{\beta}x, & d_{K+1}(x) = \alpha,\ d_{K+1}(y) = \beta, \\
\mu_j, & y = S_{a_j}S_0^{-1}S_j^{-1}x, & j \in J_1(x), \\
\lambda_{\alpha\alpha} - \sum_{j \in J_1(x)}\mu_j, & y = x, & d_{K+1}(x) = \alpha, \\
0, & \text{otherwise,}
\end{cases}
$$

where $\lambda_j = -\Lambda\vec{1}$. As before, $a = a_0 \in A(x)$ denotes the control which has to be chosen in the case of an arrival to the state x, $a = a_j \in A(S_j^{-1}S_0^{-1}x)$ denotes the control in the case of a service completion on the j-th server.
In this matrix:

- the first case corresponds to phase changing without arrivals;

- the second case corresponds to the phase changing with new job arrival;

- the third case corresponds to the service completion.

The diagonal elements of this matrix (the fourth line) equal to the sum of its elements along the row with negative sign.
    The possible transitions after the arrival or service completion can be illustrated by means of the graph shown in Figure 3.14 (a) and (b), respectively

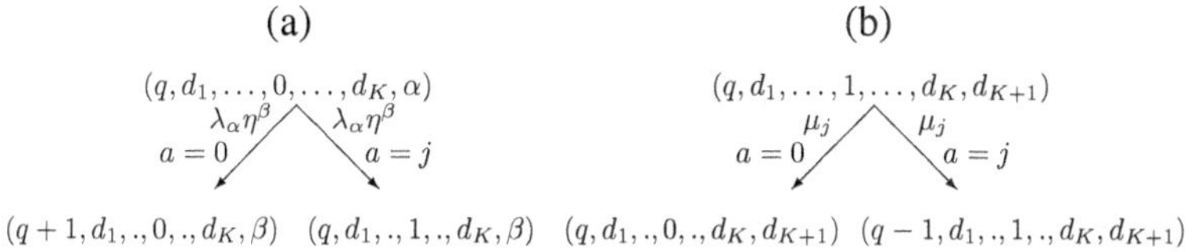

(a)

$(q, d_1, \ldots, 0, \ldots, d_K, \alpha)$

$\lambda_\alpha \eta^\beta$ $\lambda_\alpha \eta^\beta$

$a = 0$ $a = j$

$(q+1, d_1, ., 0, ., d_K, \beta)$ $(q, d_1, ., 1, ., d_K, \beta)$

(b)

$(q, d_1, \ldots, 1, \ldots, d_K, d_{K+1})$

μ_j μ_j

$a = 0$ $a = j$

$(q, d_1, ., 0, ., d_K, d_{K+1})$ $(q-1, d_1, ., 1, ., d_K, d_{K+1})$

Figure 3.14

3.4.1   Optimality equation

As usual, for the function $V(x, t)$ and small interval h we have

$$V(x, t+h) = c(x)h + (1 + [\lambda_{d_{K+1}(x)\, d_{K+1}(x)} - M_1]h)V(x,t)(x)$$

$$+ \lambda_{d_{K+1}(x)} \sum_{i=1}^{m} \eta^i h \min_{a_0 \in A(x)} V(S_{a_0} S_{K+1}^i x, t)$$

$$+ \sum_{\substack{i \neq \\ d_{K+1}(x)}} \lambda_{d_{K+1}(x)\, i} h\, V(S_{K+1}^i x)$$

$$+ \mathbf{1}_{\{q(x)=0\}} \sum_{j \in J_1(x)} \mu_j h\, V(S_j^{-1} x, t)$$

$$+ \mathbf{1}_{\{q(x)>0\}} \sum_{j \in J_1(x)} \mu_j h \min_{a_j \in A(S_j^{-1} S_0^{-1} x)} V(S_{a_j} S_j^{-1} S_0^{-1} x, t),$$

In this equation, the first member on the right–hand side represents the loss of the system up to time h, the second one represents the total loss of the system during the following time t in the case that no modulating phase changes and service completions occur in the system, the next one represents the total loss of the system during the following time t in the case that a new customer arrives before the service completion. The next item denotes the modulating phase changing without arrival. The last two members represent the total loss of the system in the case that one of the served customers leaves the system with empty queue before some customer arrives and the loss of the system in the case of service completion with non-empty queue before new customer arrival.

Due to the asymptotic behavior of the function $V(x, t)$ (2.6) for $h \to \infty$ the optimality equation can be written in the form

$$v(x) = \frac{1}{\lambda_x} \left[c(x) + C_1(x) + C_2(x) - g \right. \tag{3.10}$$

$$\left. + \lambda_{d_{K+1}(x)} \sum_{i=1}^{m} \eta^i T_0 v(S_{K+1}^i x) + \sum_{j \in J_1(x)} \mu_j T_j v(x) \right] = Bv(x).$$

In this representation

$$\lambda_x = -\left(\lambda_{d_{K+1}(x) d_{K+1}(x)} - \sum_{j \in J_1(x)} \mu_j \right)$$

is intensity of state x changing;

$$C_1(x) = \sum_{i \neq d_{K+1}(x)} \lambda_{d_{K+1}(x)i} v(S^i_{K+1} x)$$

is loss rate due to phase changing without decision making;

$$C_2(x) = \sum_{\substack{j \in J_1(x) \\ d_0(x)=0}} \mu_j v(S_j^{-1} x)$$

is loss rate due to service completion with empty queue;

Operators T_0 and T_j given by formula (2.9) denote minimal loss in the case of a new job arrival and minimal loss in the case of service completion and appropriate decision making.

The optimal policy $f = \{f(x) : x \in E\}$ as before is determined by the definitions (2.11) and (2.12).

3.4.2   Monotonicity properties. Dependence on arrival phases

Let the arrival phases are arranged in such a way that for any two phases α and β, $\lambda_\alpha \geq \lambda_\beta$ when $\alpha \leq \beta$. Let

$$S^\alpha_{K+1} x \geq S^\beta_{K+1} x, \quad \lambda_\alpha \geq \lambda_\beta \tag{3.11}$$

be the introduced order for different phases. Thus, the inequalities (2.14), (2.15) and (3.11) form the partial order on the state space E. Similar to the system with Erlangian arrivals we investigate some monotonicity properties of optimal control rule in the case of PH-type interarrival time distribution.

Using the same arguments as in previous section one can state that the value function of the model $v(x)$ is supermodular, that is

Theorem 3.15 *The optimal policy for the NJM– and the PCM–problems for the system with PH-type interarrival time distribution is of threshold type with finite thresholds* $q^*_k(d_{K+1})$ *for each phase.*

In the case of light traffic denote by λ the maximal rate of transitions occurring in state i, that is $\lambda = \max\{\lambda_i + \sum_{j \neq i} \lambda_{ij}\}$. As it was discussed in [60] this parameter λ is not really the rate of the PH renewal process since there are less than λ renewals per unit time. It is better to interpret λ as a scale that is proportional to the rate, i.e. if there are n transitions, on the average, between visits to instantaneous state $m + 1$, then the true rate is λ/n. Thus, when $\lambda \approx 0$ the PH renewal process is in light traffic. For the system under consideration in this case we require $\lambda < \mu_K$ and the formulas (2.21) and (2.33) can be applied for this model.

Consider now two-state arrival process. Below we show that if $\lambda_\alpha \geq \lambda_\beta$ then the threshold levels for the k-th server satisfy $q_k^*(\alpha) \leq q_k^*(\beta)$.

Theorem 3.16 *Assume the bounded, nondecreasing function $v(x)$ has the following property*

$$v(S_{K+1}^\alpha x) \geq v(S_{K+1}^\beta x), \quad \lambda_\alpha \geq \lambda_\beta.$$

Then the operator B introduced in (3.10), also retains the property of nondecreasing function for the value function of the model

$$Bv(S_{K+1}^\alpha x) \geq Bv(S_{K+1}^\beta x), \quad \lambda_\alpha \geq \lambda_\beta.$$

Proof: As before, for the operators T_0 and T_j we have

$$T_0 v(S_{K+1}^\alpha x) \geq v(S_{K+1}^\alpha x),$$
$$T_0 v(S_{K+1}^\alpha x) \geq T_0 v(S_{K+1}^\beta x),$$
$$T_j v(S_{K+1}^\alpha x) \geq T_j v(S_{K+1}^\beta x).$$

Without loss of generality, we assume that $\lambda_\alpha + \lambda_\beta + \sum_{j \in J_1(x)} \mu_j = 1$.
Now, for operator B we obtain

$$\begin{aligned}
Bv(S_{K+1}^\alpha x) - Bv(S_{K+1}^\beta x) &= [c(S_{K+1}^\alpha x) - c(S_{K+1}^\beta x)] \\
&+ \sum_{j=J_1(x)} \mu_j [T_j v(S_{K+1}^\alpha x) - T_j v(S_{K+1}^\beta x)] \\
&+ \lambda_\alpha [\eta^\alpha T_0 v(S_{K+1}^\alpha x) + \eta^\beta T_0 v(S_{K+1}^\beta x) - (\eta^\alpha + \eta^\beta) v(S_{K+1}^\beta x)] \\
&- \lambda_\beta [\eta^\alpha T_0 v(S_{K+1}^\alpha x) + \eta^\beta T_0 v(S_{K+1}^\beta x) - (\eta^\alpha + \eta^\beta) v(S_{K+1}^\alpha x)].
\end{aligned}$$

The first two items of the latter expression is nonnegative by virtue of the properties for the function $c(x)$ and operator T_j. For the last two items we get

$$
\lambda_\alpha[\eta^\alpha[T_0 v(S^\alpha_{K+1}x) - v(S^\beta_{K+1}x)] + \eta^\beta[T_0 v(S^\beta_{K+1}x) - v(S^\beta_{K+1}x)]]
$$
$$
- \lambda_\beta[\eta^\alpha[T_0 v(S^\alpha_{K+1}x) - v(S^\alpha_{K+1}x)] + \eta^\beta[T_0 v(S^\beta_{K+1}x) - v(S^\alpha_{K+1}x)]]
$$
$$
\geq \lambda_\alpha[\eta^\alpha[T_0 v(S^\alpha_{K+1}x) - v(S^\alpha_{K+1}x)] + \eta^\beta[T_0 v(S^\beta_{K+1}x) - v(S^\beta_{K+1}x)]]
$$
$$
- \lambda_\beta[\eta^\alpha[T_0 v(S^\alpha_{K+1}x) - v(S^\alpha_{K+1}x)] + \eta^\beta[T_0 v(S^\beta_{K+1}x) - v(S^\beta_{K+1}x)]] \geq 0,
$$

when $\lambda_\alpha \geq \lambda_\beta$.

Now using the fact that the value function of the model $v = \{v(x) : x \in E\}$ is a fixed point of the operator B we obtain the necessary result.
□

Here we expect, that as the arrival rate λ_α increases, the slow server will be used more often in optimal control law, since the chance is then higher that the reduction of the queue length will indeed be translated in a shorter waiting time or fewer processing cost for a future arrival. Therefore, it is sufficiently, that

$$
(S_0 - S_k)(S^\beta_{K+1} - S^\alpha_{K+1})v(x) \leq 0, \quad k \in J_1(x), \ \lambda_\alpha \geq \lambda_\beta.
$$

3.4.3 Algorithm

To analyze numerically the behavior of optimal strategies the servers will be arranged in order (2.13) for the NJM–problem and in order (2.28) for the PCM–problem under conditions (2.29)–(2.31).

The steps of algorithm are the same as before and differ only by the form of optimality equation.

Strategy estimation. For a given policy $f = \{f_n(x) : x = \overline{1, I}\}$ solve up to an accuracy ε by a successive approximation method the equation

$$
v_n(x) = \frac{1}{\lambda_x}\left[c(x) + C_1(x) + C_2(x) - g_n \right.
$$
$$
\left. + \lambda_{d_{K+1}(x)}\sum_{i=1}^{m}\eta^i v_n(S_{f_n(x)}S^i_{K+1}x) + \sum_{j\in J_1(x)}\mu_j v_n(S_{f_n(S_j^{-1}S_0^{-1}x)}S_j^{-1}S_0^{-1}x)\right]
$$

for all $x \in E$ under the condition $v(0) = 0$.

Strategy improvement. For a given solution $v_n = \{v_n(x) : x \in E\}$ find a new policy $f_{n+1} = \{f_{n+1}(x) : x \in E\}$, which minimizes the Bellman function (2.11) of the model:

$$f_{n+1}(x) = \operatorname*{argmin}_{k \in A(x)} v_n(x + e_k), \quad k = \overline{0, K}.$$

The algorithm stops when two successive iterations yield the same policy.

The description of system states changing at the control epochs by means of one dimensional representation was introduced in previous section by (3.6)-(3.8)

3.4.4   Numerical analysis

In this section we consider some numerical examples of optimal policy structure for the system with PH-type arrivals. This type of model is quite difficult for numerical investigation because of large number of different elements which can influence on optimal policy behavior. Therefore, we consider some selective typical examples.

As before, we consider examples for the NJM–problem. Optimal controls for the system $PH/M/5/100$, if number of phases $m = 5$ are presented in control Table 3.18. The mean arrival rate $\overline{\lambda} = 0.01$, initial modulating phases distribution η, arrival transition intensities matrix Λ, arrival intensities from the phases λ_i as well as values of service intensities μ_i are given below.

$$\Lambda = \lambda_{ij} = \begin{pmatrix} -0.130 & 0.010 & 0.020 & 0.030 & 0.040 \\ 0.040 & -0.120 & 0.030 & 0.020 & 0.010 \\ 0.020 & 0.030 & -0.110 & 0.040 & 0.010 \\ 0.030 & 0.040 & 0.010 & -0.105 & 0.020 \\ 0.010 & 0.030 & 0.040 & 0.020 & -0.101 \end{pmatrix}$$

$$\lambda_i = -\Lambda \overline{1} = \begin{pmatrix} 0.030 \\ 0.020 \\ 0.010 \\ 0.005 \\ 0.001 \end{pmatrix}, \; \eta = [\eta^k] = \begin{pmatrix} 0.010 \\ 0.020 \\ 0.050 \\ 0.170 \\ 0.750 \end{pmatrix}$$

and arrival intensity from the phases.

The results show that the optimal policy for the system with PH-type interarrival time distribution has threshold property.

Table 3.17 **Values of initial system parameters for** $PH/M/5/100$ **queue**

i	1	2	3	4	5
μ_i	1.90	0.63	0.52	0.45	0.30

Table 3.18 Optimal control for any system state

System State x	Queue length $q(x)$													
$(d_1,d_2,d_3,d_4,d_5,d_6)$	0	1	2	3	4	5	6	7	8	9	10	11	12	...
$(0,*,*,*,*,*)$	**1**	1	1	1	1	1	1	1	1	1	1	1	1	1
$(1,0,*,*,*,1)$	0	2	2	2	2	2	2	2	2	2	2	2	2	2
$(1,0,*,*,3)$	0	0	2	2	2	2	2	2	2	2	2	2	2	2
$(1,1,0,*,*)$	0	0	3	3	3	3	3	3	3	3	3	3	3	3
$(1,1,1,0,*,*)$	0	0	0	4	4	4	4	4	4	4	4	4	4	4
$(1,1,1,1,0,*)$	0	0	0	0	0	0	0	5	5	5	5	5	5	5
$(1,1,1,1,1,*)$	0	0	0	0	0	0	0	0	0	0	0	0	0	0

The fastest server is always activated. The threshold sequence depends not only on the queue length but also can depend on the phase of new arrival. Threshold levels take their value:

$$q_1^*(d_6) = 0, \quad d_6 = \overline{1,m};$$
$$q_2^*(d_6) = 1, \quad d_6 = \overline{1,2};$$
$$q_2^*(d_6) = 2, \quad d_6 = \overline{3,5};$$
$$q_3^*(d_6) = 2, \quad d_6 = \overline{1,m};$$
$$q_4^*(d_6) = 3, \quad d_6 = \overline{1,m};$$
$$q_5^*(d_6) = 7, \quad d_6 = \overline{1,m}.$$

In this example the incentive to make an assignment to the slower servers is greater in the states with less index of arrival phases where, the arrival intensity from such phases is larger.

Thus, in this case, the threshold sequence has the following form

$$0 = q_1^* \leq q_2^*(\alpha) \leq q_2^*(\beta) \leq \cdots \leq q_K^*(\alpha) \leq q_K^*(\beta),$$

where α and β is current arrival modulating phases and $\lambda_\alpha \geq \lambda_\beta$.

The numerical examples allow us to suspect that the optimal threshold may vary at most 1 for the states with different arrival modulating phase, that is $q_k^*(\alpha) \leq q_k^*(\beta) \leq q_k^*(\alpha) + 1$ if $\lambda_\alpha \geq \lambda_\beta$.

To investigate the dynamics of optimal threshold levels behavior for the NJM–
problem we consider the system $PH/M/3/100$ with $m = 2$ arrival phases and
$K = 3$ heterogeneous servers. The results of calculation are gathered in Figures
2.1–2.6 in Appendix 3.7.2. The transition arrival intensities matrix Λ, arrival intensities from the phases λ_i and initial modulating phases distribution η are varied
over the figures as follows

- $\Lambda = \begin{pmatrix} -1.30 & 0.60 \\ 0.01 & -0.46 \end{pmatrix}, \lambda_i = \begin{pmatrix} 0.70 \\ 0.45 \end{pmatrix}, \eta = \begin{pmatrix} 0.60 \\ 0.40 \end{pmatrix}$ in Figure 2.1,

- $\Lambda = \begin{pmatrix} -0.45 & 0.10 \\ 0.04 & -0.24 \end{pmatrix}, \lambda_i = \begin{pmatrix} 0.35 \\ 0.20 \end{pmatrix}, \eta = \begin{pmatrix} 0.60 \\ 0.40 \end{pmatrix}$ in Figure 2.2,

- $\Lambda = \begin{pmatrix} -0.68 & 0.65 \\ 0.02 & -0.03 \end{pmatrix}, \lambda_i = \begin{pmatrix} 0.03 \\ 0.01 \end{pmatrix}, \eta = \begin{pmatrix} 0.60 \\ 0.40 \end{pmatrix}$ in Figure 2.3,

- $\Lambda = \begin{pmatrix} -1.60 & 0.60 \\ 0.11 & -0.55 \end{pmatrix}, \lambda_i = \begin{pmatrix} 1.00 \\ 0.44 \end{pmatrix}, \eta = \begin{pmatrix} 0.20 \\ 0.80 \end{pmatrix}$ in Figure 2.4,

- $\Lambda = \begin{pmatrix} -0.81 & 0.50 \\ 0.10 & -0.35 \end{pmatrix}, \lambda_i = \begin{pmatrix} 0.31 \\ 0.25 \end{pmatrix}, \eta = \begin{pmatrix} 0.20 \\ 0.80 \end{pmatrix}$ in Figure 2.5,

- $\Lambda = \begin{pmatrix} -0.02 & 0.01 \\ 0.01 & -0.02 \end{pmatrix}, \lambda_i = \begin{pmatrix} 0.01 \\ 0.01 \end{pmatrix}, \eta = \begin{pmatrix} 0.20 \\ 0.80 \end{pmatrix}$ in Figure 2.6.

According to given values of parameters the average arrival rates $\overline{\lambda} = (-\eta^T \Lambda^{-1} \vec{1})^{-1}$
are follows

- $\overline{\lambda}=0.51$ in Figures 2.1 and 2.4,

- $\overline{\lambda}=0.26$ in Figures 2.2 and 2.5,

- $\overline{\lambda}=0.01$ in Figures 2.3 and 2.6.

As usual, in theses diagrams the changing of threshold levels $q_2^*(d_4)$ for the second server (pictures labeled by letter "a") and $q_3^*(d_4)$ for the third server (pictures
labeled by letter "b") as the threshold function with arguments of first service intensity μ_1 for different values of the second service intensity μ_2 depending on
arrival phases d_4 are shown.

As we can see from proposed control diagrams the incentive to make an assignment to the second server is greater in state $x = (1, 0, *, \alpha)$ than in state $x = (1, 0, *, \beta)$, and to the third server is greater in state $x = (1, 1, 0, \alpha)$ than in state $x = (1, 1, 0, \beta)$ if $\lambda_\alpha \geq \lambda_\beta$ and in this case $\alpha \leq \beta$. Therefore, the upper curve of each family denotes thresholds for the states with $d_{K+1} = 2$ and the low for the states with $d_{K+1} = 1$. Thus we can conclude, that the main characteristic which influences on the decision making with respect to different arrival phases is arrival intensity from the certain phase.

For the PCM–problem when arrangement of the servers (2.28) and in the case of $\mu_1 \geq \mu_2 \geq \cdots \geq \mu_5$, for the parameters in Table 3.19 we have

Table 3.19 Values of initial system parameters for $PH/M/5/100$ queue

i	0	1	2	3	4	5
c_i	1.00	3.00	2.80	2.60	2.40	2.00
μ_i	-	1.90	0.63	0.52	0.45	0.30
γ_i	-	1.58	4.44	5.00	5.53	6.66

Table 3.20 Optimal control for any system state

System State x	Queue length $q(x)$													
$(d_1, d_2, d_3, d_4, d_5, d_6)$	0	1	2	3	4	5	6	7	8	9	10	11	12	...
$(0, *, *, *, *, *)$	**1**	1	1	1	1	1	1	1	1	1	1	1	1	1
$(1, 0, *, *, *, 1)$	0	0	0	0	**2**	2	2	2	2	2	2	2	2	2
$(1, 0, *, *, *, 5)$	0	0	0	0	0	**2**	2	2	2	2	2	2	2	2
$(1, 1, 0, *, *, *)$	0	0	0	0	0	0	**3**	3	3	3	3	3	3	3
$(1, 1, 1, 0, *, *)$	0	0	0	0	0	0	0	**4**	4	4	4	4	4	4
$(1, 1, 1, 1, 0, *)$	0	0	0	0	0	0	0	0	0	0	0	0	**5**	5
$(1, 1, 1, 1, 1, *)$	0	0	0	0	0	0	0	0	0	0	0	0	0	0

In this case of the PCM–problem the optimal control is of threshold type and has the same structure as for the NJM–problem with following threshold sequence

$$q_1^*(d_6) = 0, \quad d_6 = \overline{1, m};$$
$$q_2^*(d_6) = 4, \quad d_6 = \overline{1, 4};$$
$$q_2^*(d_6) = 5, \quad d_6 = 5;$$
$$q_3^*(d_6) = 6, \quad d_6 = \overline{1, m};$$
$$q_4^*(d_6) = 7, \quad d_6 = \overline{1, m};$$
$$q_5^*(d_6) = 12, \quad d_6 = \overline{1, m}.$$

Now we discuss the case for arrangement of the servers (2.28) and parameters $\mu_1 \leq \mu_2 \leq \cdots \leq \mu_5$ and $c_1 \leq c_2 \leq \cdots \leq c_5$. In the Table 3.22 we consider system states with modulating phases $d_{K+1} = \{1, 2, 3, 4, 5\}$. The optimal control policies are presented as threshold sequences $q_1^*(x)$, $q_2^*(x)$, ..., $q_K^*(x)$.

Table 3.21 Values of initial system parameters for $PH/M/5/100$ queue

i	0	1	2	3	4	5
c_i	0.20	1.00	1.70	2.30	3.50	7.00
μ_i	-	0.30	0.45	0.52	0.63	0.90
γ_i	-	3.33	3.78	4.42	5.56	7.78

Table 3.22 Optimal control for any system state

System State x	Modulating phase d_6				
$(d_1, d_2, d_3, d_4, d_5)$	1	2	3	4	5
(0,0,0,0,0)	0,3,12,21,29	0,3,12,20,29	0,3,12,19,28	0,3,12,19,27	0,3,12,19,27
(1,0,0,0,0)	-,0,23,36,51	-,0,22,36,51	-,0,22,35,49	-,0,22,35,49	-,0,22,35,48
(0,1,0,0,0)	0,-,10,37,52	0,-,10,37,52	0,-,10,36,50	0,-,10,36,50	0,-,10,35,49
(1,1,0,0,0)	-,-,2,52,73	-,-,2,52,72	-,-,3,51,71	-,-,3,51,71	-,-,3,50,70
(0,0,1,0,0)	0,5,-,32,52	0,5,-,32,52	0,5,-,31,50	0,5,-,31,50	0,5,-,31,49
(1,0,1,0,0)	-,0,-,44,73	-,0,-,44,72	-,0,-,44,71	-,0,-,43,71	-,0,-,43,70
(0,1,1,0,0)	0,-,-,25,73	0,-,-,25,73	0,-,-,25,72	0,-,-,25,72	0,-,-,25,71
(1,1,1,0,0)	-,-,-,10,92	-,-,-,10,92	-,-,-,10,91	-,-,-,10,91	-,-,-,10,90
(0,0,0,1,0)	0,5,23,-,48	0,5,23,-,48	0,5,23,-,47	0,5,23,-,46	0,5,23,-,46
(1,0,0,1,0)	-,0,32,-,66	-,0,32,-,66	-,0,31,-,65	-,0,31,-,65	-,0,31,-,64
(0,1,0,1,0)	0,-,13,-,67	0,-,13,-,66	0,-,13,-,66	0,-,13,-,65	0,-,14,-,65
(1,1,0,1,0)	-,-,2,-,84	-,-,2,-,84	-,-,3,-,83	-,-,3,-,83	-,-,3,-,82
(0,0,1,1,0)	0,5,-,-,61	0,5,-,-,61	0,5,-,-,61	0,5,-,-,60	0,5,-,-,60
(1,0,1,1,0)	-,0,-,-,76	-,0,-,-,76	-,0,-,-,75	-,0,-,-,75	-,0,-,-,75
(0,1,1,1,0)	0,-,-,-,55	0,-,-,-,55	0,-,-,-,55	0,-,-,-,55	0,-,-,-,55
(1,1,1,1,0)	-,-,-,-,31	-,-,-,-,31	-,-,-,-,31	-,-,-,-,31	-,-,-,-,31
(0,0,0,0,1)	0,5,24,38,-	0,5,24,37,-	0,5,23,37,-	0,5,23,36,-	0,5,23,36,-
(1,0,0,0,1)	-,0,32,52,-	-,0,32,52,-	-,0,31,52,-	-,0,31,51,-	-,0,31,51,-
(0,1,0,0,1)	0,-,14,53,-	0,-,14,53,-	0,-,14,52,-	0,-,14,52,-	0,-,14,52,-
(1,1,0,0,1)	-,-,2,64,-	-,-,2,64,-	-,-,3,64,-	-,-,3,63,-	-,-,3,63,-
(0,0,1,0,1)	0,5,-,45,-	0,5,-,45,-	0,5,-,45,-	0,5,-,45,-	0,6,-,44,-
(1,0,1,0,1)	-,0,-,54,-	-,0,-,54,-	-,0,-,54,-	-,0,-,54,-	-,0,-,54,-
(0,1,1,0,1)	0,-,-,31,-	0,-,-,31,-	0,-,-,31,-	0,-,-,31,-	0,-,-,31,-
(1,1,1,0,1)	-,-,-,10,-	-,-,-,10,-	-,-,-,10,-	-,-,-,10,-	-,-,-,10,-
(0,0,0,1,1)	0,6,33,-,-	0,6,33,-,-	0,6,32,-,-	0,6,32,-,-	0,6,32,-,-
(1,0,0,1,1)	-,0,40,-,-	-,0,40,-,-	-,0,40,-,-	-,0,40,-,-	-,0,40,-,-
(0,1,0,1,1)	0,-,14,-,-	0,-,15,-,-	0,-,15,-,-	0,-,15,-,-	0,-,15,-,-
(1,1,0,1,1)	-,-,2,-,-	-,-,2,-,-	-,-,3,-,-	-,-,3,-,-	-,-,3,-,-
(0,0,1,1,1)	0,6,-,-,-	0,6,-,-,-	0,6,-,-,-	0,6,-,-,-	0,6,-,-,-
(1,0,1,1,1)	-,0,-,-,-	-,0,-,-,-	-,0,-,-,-	-,0,-,-,-	-,0,-,-,-
(0,1,1,1,1)	0,-,-,-,-	0,-,-,-,-	0,-,-,-,-	0,-,-,-,-	0,-,-,-,-

For introduced values of initial system parameters with increasing of modulating phase index d_{K+1} more expensive but faster servers are more preferable by controller. In this example if the queue length $q \geq 92$ the controller uses only the fastest available servers.

From this control table one can see that the incentive to make an assignment to the servers with larger mean usage costs is larger in states x with greater value of arrival intensity $\lambda_{d_{K+1}(x)}$.

3.5 Controlled $MAP/M/K$ queue

Consider a $MAP/M/K/B$ queueing system. As we have mentioned above, the Markovian arrival process parameterized by rate matrices $\Lambda = [\lambda_{ij}]$ which specifies intensities of phase transition without arrivals and $N = [\nu_{ij}]$ specifies intensities of phase transition accompanied by arrivals, whose sum $\Lambda + N$ is an irreducible infinitesimal generator of order m. The particular case of MAP is a Markov modulated Poisson process which is determined only by matrix N.

The equilibrium condition in this case

$$\overline{\lambda} = \sum_{i=1}^{m} \sum_{j=1}^{m} \pi_{D_{K+1}}(i)\nu_{ij} < \sum_{k=1}^{K} \mu_k, \tag{3.12}$$

where $\pi_{D_{K+1}}$ is the equilibrium distribution of the process $D_{K+1}(t)$ which satisfies

$$\pi_{D_{K+1}}^T (\Lambda + N) = 0, \quad \pi_{D_{K+1}}^T \vec{1} = 1.$$

The elements $\lambda_{xy}(a)$ of transition intensities matrix for the Markov decision process $\{Z(t)\}$ have the form

$$\lambda_{xy}(a) = \begin{cases} \lambda_{\alpha\beta}, & y = S_{K+1}^{\beta} x, & d_{K+1}(x) = \alpha, \, d_{K+1}(y) = \beta, \\ \nu_{\alpha\beta}, & y = S_{a_0} S_{K+1}^{\beta} x, & d_{K+1}(x) = \alpha, \, d_{K+1}(y) = \beta, \\ \mu_j, & y = S_{a_j} S_0^{-1} S_j^{-1} x, & j \in J_1(x), \\ \lambda_{\alpha\alpha} - \sum_{j \in J_1(x)} \mu_j, & y = x, & d_{K+1}(x) = \alpha, \\ 0, & \text{otherwise}, \end{cases}$$

where $a = a_0 \in A(x)$ denotes the control which has to be chosen in the case of an arrival to the state x, $a = a_j \in A(S_j^{-1} S_0^{-1} x)$ denotes the control in the case of a service completion on the j-th server.

In this matrix:

- the first case corresponds to the MAP phase changing without new job arrival;

- the second case corresponds to an arrival of a new job in the system and sending it to the queue or to some server in accordance with the decision rule;

- the third case corresponds to the service completion

The diagonal elements of this matrix equal to the sum of its elements along the row with negative sign.

The arrival and service completion transitions are illustrated by the graph shown in Figure 3.23 (a) and (b), respectively

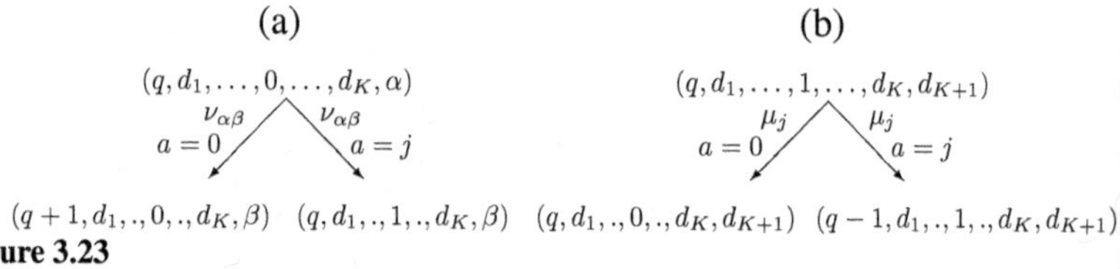

(a)

$(q, d_1, \ldots, 0, \ldots, d_K, \alpha)$

$\nu_{\alpha\beta} \qquad \nu_{\alpha\beta}$

$a = 0 \qquad\qquad a = j$

(b)

$(q, d_1, \ldots, 1, \ldots, d_K, d_{K+1})$

$\mu_j \qquad \mu_j$

$a = 0 \qquad\qquad a = j$

$(q+1, d_1, ., 0, ., d_K, \beta) \quad (q, d_1, ., 1, ., d_K, \beta) \quad (q, d_1, ., 0, ., d_K, d_{K+1}) \quad (q-1, d_1, ., 1, ., d_K, d_{K+1})$

Figure 3.23

3.5.1   Optimality equation

As usual, for the function $V(x, h)$ and small interval h we have

$$V(x, t+h) = l(x)h + \left(1 + \left[\lambda_{d_{K+1}(x)d_{K+1}(x)} + \sum_{j \in J_1(x)} \mu_j\right]h\right)V(x, t)(x)$$

$$+ \sum_{i=1}^{m} \nu_{d_{K+1}(x)i}h \min_{a_0 \in A(x)} V(S_{a_0}S_{K+1}^i x, t)$$

$$+ \sum_{\substack{i \neq \\ d_{K+1}(x)}} \lambda_{d_{K+1}(x)i}hV(S_{K+1}^i x, t)$$

$$+ \mathbf{1}_{\{q(x)=0\}} \sum_{j \in J_1(x)} \mu_j h V(S_j^{-1} x, t)$$

$$+ \mathbf{1}_{\{q(x)>0\}} \sum_{j \in J_1(x)} \mu_j h \min_{a_j \in A(S_j^{-1} S_0^{-1} x)} V(S_{a_j} S_j^{-1} S_0^{-1} x, t).$$

In this equation, the first member of the right–hand side represents the loss of the system up to time h, the second one represents the total loss of the system during the following time t in the case that no phase changes occur in the system, the next one represents the total loss of the system during the following time t in the case that a new customer arrives before the service completion. The following member represents the loss of the system in the case of service completion with non-empty queue before new customer arrival, the next two members deal with the total loss of the system in the case that one of the served customers leaves the system with empty queue before some customer arrives and phase changes without arrivals.

For the system under consideration, taking into account the asymptotic behavior of the function $V(x, t)$ the previous equation assumes the form

$$v(x) = \frac{1}{\lambda_x} \left[l(x) + C_1(x) + C_2(x) - g \right. \tag{3.13}$$

$$\left. + \sum_{i=1}^{m} v_{d_{K+1}(x)i} T_0 v(S_{K+1}^i x) + \sum_{j \in J_1(x)} \mu_j T_j v(x) \right] = Bv(x).$$

In this representation

$$\lambda_x = -\left(\lambda_{d_{K+1}(x)d_{K+1}(x)} - \sum_{j \in J_1(x)} \mu_j \right)$$

is intensity of state x changing;

$$C_1(x) = \sum_{d_{K+1} \neq d_{K+1}(x)} \lambda_{d_{K+1}(x)d_{K+1}} v(S_{K+1}^{d_{K+1}} x)$$

is loss rate due to MAP phase changing without decision making;

$$C_2(x) = \sum_{\substack{j \in J_1(x) \\ q(x)=0}} \mu_j v(S_j^{-1} x)$$

is loss rate due to service completion with empty queue. Operators T_0 and T_j are given by formula (2.9).

The optimal policy $f = \{f(x) : x \in E\}$ as before is determined by the definitions (2.11) and (2.12).

3.5.2   Monotonicity properties. Dependence on arrival phases

For two phases α and β we introduce the order

$$S_{K+1}^\alpha x \geq S_{K+1}^\beta x, \quad \nu_\alpha \geq \nu_\beta, \, \alpha \leq \beta,$$

where for two-state arrival process $\nu_\alpha = \nu_{\alpha\alpha} + \nu_{\alpha\beta}$ and $\nu_\beta = \nu_{\beta\beta} + \nu_{\beta\alpha}$.

Analogously, for this system the value function $v(x)$ is supermodular and the optimal control policy is of threshold type.

Theorem 3.24 *The optimal policy for the NJM– and the PCM–problems for the system with MAP is of threshold type with finite thresholds $q_k^*(d_{K+1})$ for each modulating phase.*

The light traffic results, see [60], obtained in Chapter 2 holds for this system if

$$\lambda = \max_i \{ \sum_{j=1}^m \nu_{ij} + \sum_{\substack{j=1 \\ j \neq i}}^m \lambda_{ij} \} < \mu_K.$$

Now we show, that for two-state arrival process, if $\nu_\alpha \geq \nu_\beta$, the threshold levels satisfy $q_k^*(\alpha) \leq q_k^*(\beta)$.

Theorem 3.25 *Assume the bounded, nondecreasing function $v(x)$ has the following property*

$$v(S_{K+1}^\alpha x) \geq v(S_{K+1}^\beta x), \quad \nu_\alpha \geq \nu_\beta.$$

Then, the operator B introduced in (3.13), also retains this property of nondecreasing function for the value function of the model,

$$Bv(S_{K+1}^\alpha x) \geq Bv(S_{K+1}^\beta x), \quad \nu_\alpha \geq \nu_\beta.$$

Proof: For the operators T_0 and T_j with respect to shifts S_{K+1}^α and S_{K+1}^β we have

$$T_0 v(S_{K+1}^\alpha x) \geq v(S_{K+1}^\alpha x),$$
$$T_0 v(S_{K+1}^\alpha x) \geq T_0 v(S_{K+1}^\beta x),$$
$$T_j v(S_{K+1}^\alpha x) \geq T_j v(S_{K+1}^\beta x).$$

Now by virtue of definition (3.13) of operator B we have

$$Bv(S_{K+1}^\alpha x) - Bv(S_{K+1}^\beta x)$$
$$= c(S_{K+1}^\alpha x) - c(S_{K+1}^\beta x) + \sum_{j \in J_1(x)} \mu_j[T_j v(S_{K+1}^\alpha x) - T_j v(S_{K+1}^\beta x)]$$
$$+ \nu_{\alpha\alpha} T_0 v(S_{K+1}^\alpha x) + \nu_{\alpha\beta} T_0 v(S_{K+1}^\beta x) + \nu_{\beta\beta} T_0 v(S_{K+1}^\alpha x) + \nu_{\beta\alpha} T_0 v(S_{K+1}^\alpha x)$$
$$+ \lambda_{\alpha\beta} v(S_{K+1}^\beta x) + \lambda_{\beta\alpha} v(S_{K+1}^\alpha x)$$
$$- \nu_{\beta\beta} T_0 v(S_{K+1}^\beta x) - \nu_{\beta\alpha} T_0 v(S_{K+1}^\alpha x) - \nu_{\alpha\alpha} T_0 v(S_{K+1}^\beta x) - \nu_{\alpha\beta} T_0 v(S_{K+1}^\beta x)$$
$$- \lambda_{\beta\alpha} v(S_{K+1}^\alpha x) - \lambda_{\alpha\beta} v(S_{K+1}^\beta x).$$

In this expression the first two items is nonnegative since $c(S_{K+1}^\alpha x) - c(S_{K+1}^\beta x) = 0$ and $\sum_{j \in J_1(x)} \mu_j[T_j v(S_{K+1}^\alpha x) - T_j v(S_{K+1}^\beta x)] \geq 0$ by virtue of the properties for function $v(x)$ and operators T_j.

We note that for two state (α, β) MAP the expression does not depend on phase changing rates without arrivals. In this case we get

$$\nu_{\alpha\alpha}[T_0 v(S_{K+1}^\alpha x) - v(S_{K+1}^\beta x)] - \nu_{\beta\beta}[T_0 v(S_{K+1}^\beta x) - v(S_{K+1}^\alpha x)]$$
$$+ \nu_{\alpha\beta}[T_0 v(S_{K+1}^\beta x) - v(S_{K+1}^\beta x)] - \nu_{\beta\alpha}[T_0 v(S_{K+1}^\alpha x) - v(S_{K+1}^\alpha x)]$$
$$\geq \nu_{\alpha\alpha}[T_0 v(S_{K+1}^\alpha x) - v(S_{K+1}^\alpha x)] - \nu_{\beta\beta}[T_0 v(S_{K+1}^\beta x) - v(S_{K+1}^\alpha x)]$$
$$+ \nu_{\alpha\beta}[T_0 v(S_{K+1}^\beta x) - v(S_{K+1}^\alpha x)] - \nu_{\beta\alpha}[T_0 v(S_{K+1}^\alpha x) - v(S_{K+1}^\alpha x)]$$
$$= (\nu_{\alpha\alpha} - \nu_{\beta\alpha})[T_0 v(S_{K+1}^\alpha x) - v(S_{K+1}^\alpha x)] - (\nu_{\beta\beta} - \nu_{\alpha\beta})[T_0 v(S_{K+1}^\beta x) - v(S_{K+1}^\alpha x)] \geq 0,$$

by virtue of inequalities $v(S_{K+1}^\alpha x) \geq v(S_{K+1}^\beta x)$, $T_0 v(S_{K+1}^\alpha x) \geq T_0 v(S_{K+1}^\beta x)$ and the condition

$$\nu_{\alpha\alpha} - \nu_{\beta\alpha} \geq \nu_{\beta\beta} - \nu_{\alpha\beta}$$

that follows from inequality $\nu_\alpha \geq \nu_\beta$.

The statement of the theorem for the value function of the model $v = \{v(x) : x \in E\}$ follows from the fact that it is a fixed point of operator B.
$\square$

For the system under consideration again we expect that as the arrival rate ν_α increases, the incentive to make an assignment to the slower server is getting higher. Thus, we can require, that

$$(S_0 - S_k)(S_{K+1}^\beta - S_{K+1}^\alpha)v(x) \leq 0, \quad k \in J_0(x), \ \nu_\alpha \geq \nu_\beta.$$

3.5.3 Algorithm

To analyze numerically the behavior of optimal strategies the servers will be arranged in order (2.13) of their service intensities decreasing for the NJM–problem and in order (2.28) of their mean usage cost increasing for the PCM–problem under conditions (2.29)–(2.31).

Strategy estimation. For a given policy $f = \{f_n(x) : x = \overline{1,I}\}$ solve up to an accuracy ε by a successive approximation method the equation

$$
v_n(x) = \frac{1}{\lambda_x} \Bigg[c(x) + C_1(x) + C_2(x) - g_n
$$
$$
+ \sum_{i=1}^{m} \nu_{d_{K+1}(x)i} v_n(S_{f_n(x)} S_{K+1}^i x) + \sum_{j \in J_1(x)} \mu_j v_n(S_{f_n(S_j^{-1} S_0^{-1} x)} S_j^{-1} S_0^{-1} x) \Bigg]
$$

for all $x \in E$ under the condition $v(0) = 0$.

Strategy improvement. For a given solution $v_n = \{v_n(x) : x \in E\}$ find a new policy $f_{n+1} = \{f_{n+1}(x) : x \in E\}$, which minimizes the Bellman function (2.11) of the model:

$$
f_{n+1}(x) = \operatorname*{argmin}_{k \in A(x)} v_n(x + e_k), \quad k = \overline{0, K}.
$$

The algorithm stops when two successive iterations yield the same policy.

The description of system states changing at the control epochs by means of one dimensional representation was introduced in previous section by (3.6)-(3.8)

3.5.4 Numerical analysis

This type of model is very close to the previous one, therefore numerical results should be very close. At first we consider examples for the NJM–problem. Optimal controls of the system $MAP/M/5/100$ if number of phases $m = 5$ are given in control Table 3.26. The elements of the matrix $\Lambda = [\lambda_{ij}]$ are the same as in analogous example for the PH-type arrivals. The elements of the matrix N can be found by $N = \vec{\lambda}\eta^T$, where $\vec{\lambda}$ denotes the vector of arrival intensities from the phases for the PH-type arrivals, see previous system. Therefore, the total arrival intensity from the phases satisfy the property $\nu_\alpha \geq \nu_\beta$ when $\alpha \leq \beta$.

Table 3.26 Values of initial system parameters for $MAP/M/5/100$ **queue**

i	1	2	3	4	5
μ_i	1.90	0.63	0.52	0.45	0.30

Table 3.27 Optimal control for any system state

System State x $(d_1, d_2, d_3, d_4, d_5, d_6)$	Queue length $q(x)$													
	0	1	2	3	4	5	6	7	8	9	10	11	12	...
$(0,*,*,*,*,*)$	**1**	1	1	1	1	1	1	1	1	1	1	1	1	1
$(1,0,*,*,*,1)$	0	**2**	2	2	2	2	2	2	2	2	2	2	2	2
$(1,0,*,*,*,3)$	0	0	**2**	2	2	2	2	2	2	2	2	2	2	2
$(1,1,0,*,*,*)$	0	0	**3**	3	3	3	3	3	3	3	3	3	3	3
$(1,1,1,*,*,*)$	0	0	0	**4**	4	4	4	4	4	4	4	4	4	4
$(1,1,1,1,0,*)$	0	0	0	0	0	0	0	**5**	5	5	5	5	5	5
$(1,1,1,1,1,*)$	0	0	0	0	0	0	0	0	0	0	0	0	0	0

This control table shows the same results as for the previous system. The fastest server is always activated. The threshold sequence is depend on the queue length and the phase of new arrival. Threshold levels take their value:

$$q_1^*(d_6) = 0, \quad d_6 = \overline{1, m};$$
$$q_2^*(d_6) = 1, \quad d_6 = \overline{1, 2};$$
$$q_2^*(d_6) = 2, \quad d_6 = \overline{3, 5};$$
$$q_3^*(d_6) = 2, \quad d_6 = \overline{1, m};$$
$$q_4^*(d_6) = 3, \quad d_6 = \overline{1, m};$$
$$q_5^*(d_6) = 7, \quad d_6 = \overline{1, m}.$$

Thus, in this case the threshold sequence has the following form

$$0 = q_1^* \le q_2^*(\alpha) \le q_2^*(\beta) \le \cdots \le q_K^*(\alpha) \le q_K^*(\beta) < q_{K+1}^* = \infty,$$

where α and β is current arrival modulating phases and $\nu_\alpha \le \nu_\beta$, $\alpha \le \beta$.

The numerical examples allow us to suspect that the optimal threshold may vary at most 1 for the states with different arrival modulating phase, that is $q_k^*(\alpha) \le q_k^*(\beta) \le q_k^*(\alpha) + 1$ if $\nu_\alpha \ge \nu_\beta$.

As before the dynamic behavior of optimal threshold levels for the NJM–problem can be represented by means of the control-diagrams. We propose the diagrams for the systems with MMPP and MAP arrival streams.

$MMPP/M/K$ **queue**

Figures 3.1–3.6 in Appendix 3.7.3 illustrate threshold curves for the system $MMPP/M/3/100$ which is the particular case of the system with MAP. The average arrival rates $\overline{\lambda} = \{0.51, 0.26, 0.01\}$ are varied over the figures in the following way

- $N = \begin{pmatrix} 0.500 & 0.100 \\ 0.200 & 0.130 \end{pmatrix}$ in Figure 3.1,

- $N = \begin{pmatrix} 0.300 & 0.100 \\ 0.090 & 0.050 \end{pmatrix}$ in Figure 3.2,

- $N = \begin{pmatrix} 0.050 & 0.005 \\ 0.001 & 0.001 \end{pmatrix}$ in Figure 3.3.

The results of optimal threshold calculation with different values of arrival intensities from the phases for the second and third servers are shown in Figures 3.4–3.6 (a,b). The average arrival intensity in these examples $\overline{\lambda} = 0.51$ but the elements of the matrix N are changed

- $N = \begin{pmatrix} 0.000 & 0.340 \\ 1.000 & 0.000 \end{pmatrix}$ in Figure 3.4,

- $N = \begin{pmatrix} 0.000 & 0.810 \\ 0.300 & 0.100 \end{pmatrix}$ in Figure 3.5,

- $N = \begin{pmatrix} 0.300 & 0.330 \\ 0.300 & 0.100 \end{pmatrix}$ in Figure 3.6.

In all these examples one can see that the incentive to use the slower server as optimal control is greater in states with larger arrival intensity and respective curves are always below the others.

$MAP/M/K$ **queue**

Similar examples are introduced for MAP streams. For this system the results of optimal policies calculation are summarized in the diagrams shown in Figures 4.1–4.6 (a,b) in Appendix 3.7.4. Parameters for arrivals with average $\overline{\lambda} = \{0.51, 0.26, 0.01\}$ take the following values

- $N = \begin{pmatrix} 0.500 & 0.400 \\ 0.100 & 0.240 \end{pmatrix}$, $\Lambda = \begin{pmatrix} -1.900 & 1.000 \\ 0.500 & -0.840 \end{pmatrix}$ in Figure 4.1,

- $N = \begin{pmatrix} 0.350 & 0.180 \\ 0.100 & 0.010 \end{pmatrix}$, $\Lambda = \begin{pmatrix} -1.430 & 0.900 \\ 0.500 & -0.610 \end{pmatrix}$ in Figure 4.2,

- $N = \begin{pmatrix} 0.030 & 0.010 \\ 0.010 & 0.001 \end{pmatrix}$, $\Lambda = \begin{pmatrix} -1.040 & 1.000 \\ 0.010 & -0.021 \end{pmatrix}$ in Figure 4.3.

For the same average $\overline{\lambda} = 0.51$ but for different values of the elements in the matrices N and Λ, the results are shown in Figures 4.4–4.6 (a,b), so

- $N = \begin{pmatrix} 0.000 & 0.200 \\ 1.000 & 0.000 \end{pmatrix}$, $\Lambda = \begin{pmatrix} -0.630 & 0.430 \\ 0.000 & -1.000 \end{pmatrix}$ in Figure 4.4,

- $N = \begin{pmatrix} 0.000 & 1.500 \\ 0.440 & 0.000 \end{pmatrix}$, $\Lambda = \begin{pmatrix} -6.500 & 5.000 \\ 0.000 & -0.440 \end{pmatrix}$ in Figure 4.5,

- $N = \begin{pmatrix} 0.500 & 0.340 \\ 0.100 & 0.000 \end{pmatrix}$, $\Lambda = \begin{pmatrix} -1.840 & 1.000 \\ 1.550 & -1.650 \end{pmatrix}$ in Figure 4.6.

Table 3.28 Values of initial system parameters for $MAP/M/5/100$ **queue**

i	0	1	2	3	4	5
c_i	1.00	3.00	2.80	2.60	2.40	2.00
μ_i	-	1.90	0.63	0.52	0.45	0.30
γ_i	-	1.58	4.44	5.00	5.53	6.66

Table 3.29 Optimal control for any system state

System State x	Queue length $q(x)$													
$(d_1, d_2, d_3, d_4, d_5, d_6)$	0	1	2	3	4	5	6	7	8	9	10	11	12	...
(0,*,*,*,*,*)	**1**	1	1	1	1	1	1	1	1	1	1	1	1	1
(1,0,*,*,*,1)	0	0	0	0	**2**	2	2	2	2	2	2	2	2	2
(1,0,*,*,*,3)	0	0	0	0	0	0	**2**	2	2	2	2	2	2	2
(1,1,0,*,*,*)	0	0	0	0	0	0	0	**3**	3	3	3	3	3	3
(1,1,1,0,*,*)	0	0	0	0	0	0	0	**4**	4	4	4	4	4	4
(1,1,1,1,0,*)	0	0	0	0	0	0	0	0	0	0	0	0	**5**	5
(1,1,1,1,1,*)	0	0	0	0	0	0	0	0	0	0	0	0	0	0

As usual, in theses diagrams the changing of threshold levels $q_2^*(d_4)$ for the second server (pictures labeled by letter "a") and $q_3^*(d_4)$ for the third server (pictures labeled by letter "b") as the threshold function with arguments of first service intensity μ_1 for different values of the second service intensity μ_2 and depending on arrival phases d_4 are shown.

In these examples the incentive to make an assignment to the second servers is greater in the state $x = (1, 0, *, \alpha)$ than in state $x = (1, 0, *, \beta)$ and to the third server is greater in state $x = (1, 1, 0, \alpha)$ than in state $x = (1, 1, 0, \beta)$ if $\nu_\alpha \geq \nu_\beta$ and in our case $\alpha \leq \beta$. Therefore, each family of curves for different arrival phases has the low and upper bound. The low and upper bounds always correspond to the states with largest and fewest arrival rates ν_i, respectively.

For the PCM–problem when arrangement of the servers (2.28) and in the case of $\mu_1 \geq \mu_2 \geq \cdots \geq \mu_5$, for the parameters in Table 3.28 we illustrate the corresponding controls in table 3.29.

In this case of the PCM–problem the optimal control is of threshold type with the following threshold sequence

$$
\begin{aligned}
q_1^*(d_6) &= 0, & d_6 &= \overline{1, m}; \\
q_2^*(d_6) &= 4, & d_6 &= \overline{1, 4}; \\
q_2^*(d_6) &= 5, & d_6 &= 5; \\
q_3^*(d_6) &= 6, & d_6 &= \overline{1, m}; \\
q_4^*(d_6) &= 7, & d_6 &= \overline{1, m}; \\
q_5^*(d_6) &= 12, & d_6 &= \overline{1, m}.
\end{aligned}
$$

In this case of the PCM–problem the optimal policy has the same structure as for the NJM–problem.

Below we discuss the case for arrangement of the servers (2.28) and parameters $\mu_1 \leq \mu_2 \leq \cdots \leq \mu_5$ and $c_1 \leq c_2 \leq \cdots \leq c_5$. In Table 3.31 we consider system states with modulating phases $d_{K+1} = \{1, 2, 3, 4, 5\}$. The optimal control policies are presented as threshold sequences $q_1^*(x), q_2^*(x), \ldots, q_K^*(x)$.

For introduced values of initial system parameters with increasing of modulating phase index d_{K+1} more expensive but faster servers are more preferable by controller. In this example if the queue length $q \geq 92$ the controller uses only the fastest available servers.

Table 3.30 Values of initial system parameters for $MAP/M/5/100$ **queue**

i	0	1	2	3	4	5
c_i	1.00	3.00	2.80	2.60	2.40	2.00
μ_i	-	0.30	0.45	0.52	0.63	0.90
γ_i	-	1.58	4.44	5.00	5.53	6.66

Table 3.31 Optimal control for any system state

System State x	Modulating phase d_6				
(d_1,d_2,d_3,d_4,d_5)	1	2	3	4	5
(0,0,0,0,0)	0,3,12,21,29	0,3,12,20,29	0,3,12,19,28	0,3,12,19,27	0,3,12,19,27
(1,0,0,0,0)	-,0,23,36,51	-,0,22,36,51	-,0,22,35,49	-,0,22,35,49	-,0,22,35,48
(0,1,0,0,0)	0,-,10,37,52	0,-,10,37,52	0,-,10,36,50	0,-,10,36,50	0,-,10,35,49
(1,1,0,0,0)	-,-,2,52,73	-,-,2,52,72	-,-,3,51,71	-,-,3,51,71	-,-,3,50,70
(0,0,1,0,0)	0,5,-,32,52	0,5,-,32,52	0,5,-,31,50	0,5,-,31,50	0,5,-,31,49
(1,0,1,0,0)	-,0,-,44,73	-,0,-,44,72	-,0,-,44,71	-,0,-,43,71	-,0,-,43,70
(0,1,1,0,0)	0,-,-,25,73	0,-,-,25,73	0,-,-,25,72	0,-,-,25,72	0,-,- ,25,71
(1,1,1,0,0)	-,-,-,10,92	-,-,-,10,92	-,-,-,10,91	-,-,-,10,91	-,-,-,10,90
(0,0,0,1,0)	0,5,23,-,48	0,5,23,-,48	0,5,23,-,47	0,5,23,-,46	0,5,23,-,46
(1,0,0,1,0)	-,0,32,-,66	-,0,32,-,66	-,0,31,-,65	-,0,31,-,65	-,0,31,-,64
(0,1,0,1,0)	0,-,13,-,67	0,-,13,-,66	0,-,13,-,66	0,-,13,-,65	0,-,14,-,65
(1,1,0,1,0)	-,-,2,-,84	-,-,2,-,84	-,-,3,-,83	-,-,3,-,83	-,-,3,-,82
(0,0,1,1,0)	0,5,-,-,61	0,5,-,-,61	0,5,-,-,61	0,5,-,-,60	0,5,-,-,60
(1,0,1,1,0)	-,0,-,-,76	-,0,-,-,76	-,0,-,-,75	-,0,-,-,75	-,0,-,-,75
(0,1,1,1,0)	0,-,-,-,55	0,-,-,-,55	0,-,-,-,55	0,-,-,-,55	0,-,-,-,55
(1,1,1,1,0)	-,-,-,-,31	-,-,-,-,31	-,-,-,-,31	-,-,-,-,31	-,-,-,-,31
(0,0,0,0,1)	0,5,24,38,-	0,5,24,37,-	0,5,23,37,-	0,5,23,36,-	0,5,23,36,-
(1,0,0,0,1)	-,0,32,52,-	-,0,32,52,-	-,0,31,52,-	-,0,31,51,-	-,0,31,51,-
(0,1,0,0,1)	0,-,14,53,-	0,-,14,53,-	0,-,14,52,-	0,-,14,52,-	0,-,14,52,-
(1,1,0,0,1)	-,-,2,64,-	-,-,2,64,-	-,-,3,64,-	-,-,3,63,-	-,-,3,63,-
(0,0,1,0,1)	0,5,-,45,-	0,5,-,45,-	0,5,-,45,-	0,5,-,45,-	0,6,-,44,-
(1,0,1,0,1)	-,0,-,54,-	-,0,-,54,-	-,0,-,54,-	-,0,-,54,-	-,0,-,54,-
(0,1,1,0,1)	0,-,-,31,-	0,-,-,31,-	0,-,-,31,-	0,-,-,31,-	0,-,-,31,-
(1,1,1,0,1)	-,-,-,10,-	-,-,-,10,-	-,-,-,10,-	-,-,-,10,-	-,-,-,10,-
(0,0,0,1,1)	0,6,33,-,-	0,6,33,-,-	0,6,32,-,-	0,6,32,-,-	0,6,32,-,-
(1,0,0,1,1)	-,0,40,-,-	-,0,40,-,-	-,0,40,-,-	-,0,40,-,-	-,0,40,-,-
(0,1,0,1,1)	0,-,14,-,-	0,-,15,-,-	0,-,15,-,-	0,-,15,-,-	0,-,15,-,-
(1,1,0,1,1)	-,-,2,-,-	-,-,2,-,-	-,-,3,-,-	-,-,3,-,-	-,-,3,-,-
(0,0,1,1,1)	0,6,-,-,-	0,6,-,-,-	0,6,-,-,-	0,6,-,-,-	0,6,-,-,-
(1,0,1,1,1)	-,0,-,-,-	-,0,-,-,-	-,0,-,-,-	-,0,-,-,-	-,0,-,-,-
(0,1,1,1,1)	0,-,-,-,-	0,-,-,-,-	0,-,-,-,-	0,-,-,-,-	0,-,-,-,-

3.6 Conclusions

In this chapter we considered the controlled queueing systems with different inter-arrival time distributions. We investigated quantitative and qualitative properties of optimal control policies and presented iteration procedures for successful obtaining of the optimal controls. We have shown that different arrival statistics do not change the nature of optimal policy. Thus, we can speak about threshold phenomenon of optimal control policy also for these type of queues. For the NJM–problem the controller uses the fastest available server and for each server corresponds m threshold levels for each arrival phase.

For the PCM–problem two possible optimal rules exist depending on the values of initial system parameters. In one case the server with minimal mean usage cost should be turned on and as for the NJM–problem m threshold levels for each server exist. In other case the controller in each state can use different servers in increasing order of their mean usage costs. Thus, each available server can have several thresholds for different states of servers and in this case there exist such queue length that for all states the optimal control consists in using server with largest mean usage cost which is the fastest and the most expensive in such states.

The presence of the arrival phases information as a part of the system state influences on the threshold levels and for different values of these phases for the same states of the servers there can exist different threshold levels.

For different interarrival time distributions there exist different characteristics which influence on optimal thresholds. The threshold levels increases in the case of Erlangian arrivals when the residual interarrival time increases, in the case of PH-type distribution and MAP when the total arrival intensity from the phase decreases. Also it was noticed that the optimal threshold may vary by at most 1 for different arrival phases.

3.7 Appendices

3.7.1 $E_m/M/K$

Figure 1.1 (a) (b)

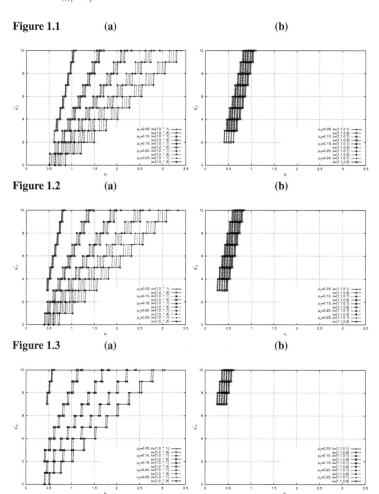

Figure 1.2 (a) (b)

Figure 1.3 (a) (b)

Figure 1.4   **(a)**   **(b)**

Figure 1.5   **(a)**   **(b)**

Figure 1.6   **(a)**   **(b)**

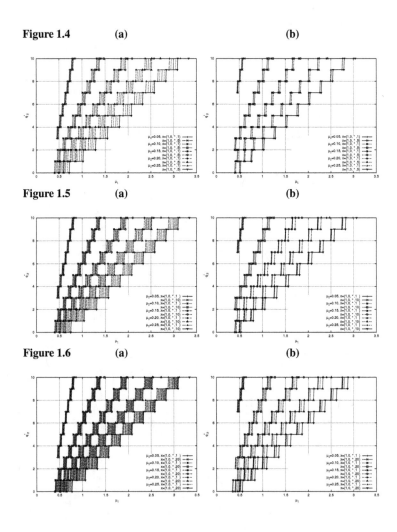

3.7.2 *PH/M/K*

Figure 2.1   (a)   (b)

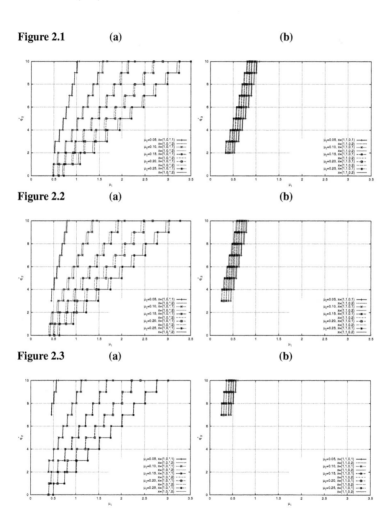

Figure 2.2   (a)   (b)

Figure 2.3   (a)   (b)

Figure 2.4   **(a)**   **(b)**

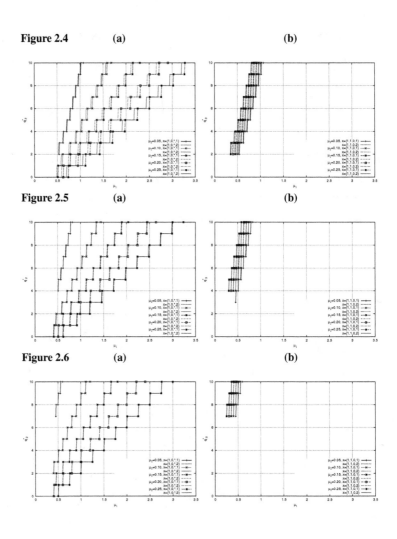

Figure 2.5   **(a)**   **(b)**

Figure 2.6   **(a)**   **(b)**

3.7.3 $MMPP/M/K$

Figure 3.1   (a)   (b)

Figure 3.2   (a)   (b)

Figure 3.3   (a)   (b)

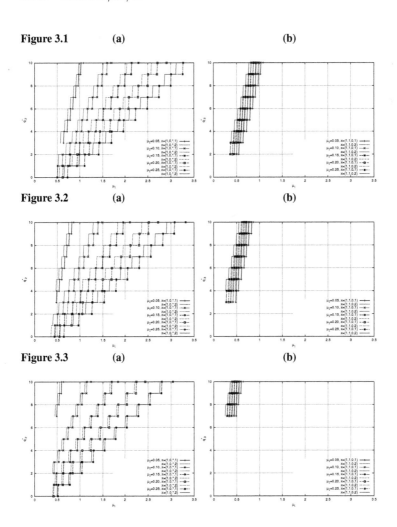

Figure 3.4   (a)   (b)

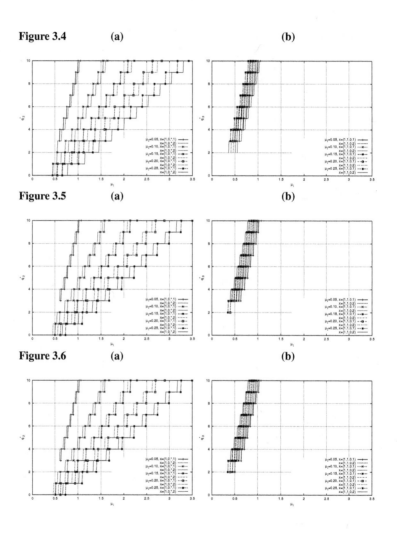

Figure 3.5   (a)   (b)

Figure 3.6   (a)   (b)

3.7.4 $MAP/M/K$

Figure 4.1   **(a)**   **(b)**

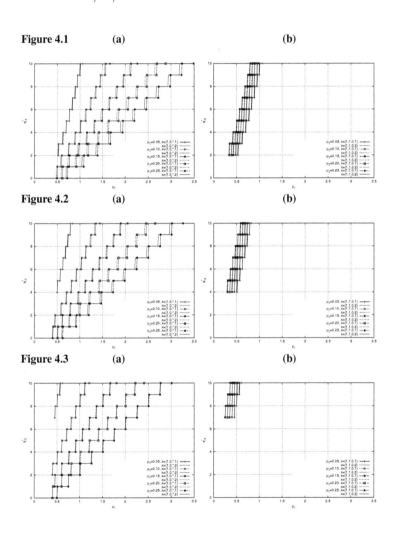

Figure 4.2   **(a)**   **(b)**

Figure 4.3   **(a)**   **(b)**

Figure 4.4   (a)   (b)

Figure 4.5   (a)   (b)

Figure 4.6   (a)   (b)

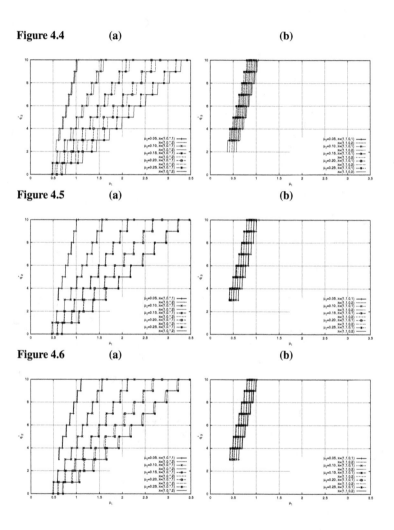

Chapter 4

Service with phases

In this chapter we consider the system with Poisson arrivals and service rates depending on a modulating Markov process. We consider m-stage Erlangian (E_m) and Phase-type (PH) service time distributions. We extend the validity of some existing results on the optimal control of multi-server queueing systems with phase-type service time distributions. It will be shown that the optimal policy of such queueing systems is also of a threshold type, with threshold levels depending on the service phases. Finally, some quantitative properties as well as numerical description of the optimal policies are presented.

4.1 Introduction.

Queueing systems with service phases allow a considerable extension of the classical controlled queueing systems. The Erlangian service-time models represents the case of general consecutive service phases (stages), with the restriction that a customer cannot enter the first phase of service until the preceding one completes the last phase. In a distributed database system, this could be the case if the job, i.e. a transaction, requests and locks either 1 or m resources. This can help when the system operates in a two phase commitment protocol to achieve atomicity of transactions. It is useful to study such a model also because an arbitrary service distribution can be approximated by a mixture of Erlangian ones, choosing appropriately the number of stages.

Phase-type service time distributions are more complex and can be used to analyze a system with superpositions of of a large number of data connections in

ATM heterogeneous links with burst durations.

The main goal of this chapter is to investigate the influence of service phases on the process of decision making and analyze the dynamic behavior of optimal policies when initial system paremeters are varied. As before we consider the NJM–problem and also discuss the PCM–problem for the mentioned systems. For each controlled queueing system we give a description and obtain optimality equation. Based on this equation an algorithm will be proposed to calculate optimal policies.

In Section 4.3 we give analysis of the queueing model with Erlangian service phases. Section 4.4 extends the previous model in that now a more general PH-type service time distribution is allowed. We note that heterogeneous servers in these systems mean unequal averages of service times.

4.2   Problem description

We consider a family of queueing systems with Poisson arrivals which symbolically can be represented in Figure 4.1.

Figure 4.1 Queueing system

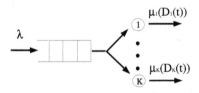

The control times are all arrival and service completion times. The task of control as before is to to put the customers to the queue or send them to one of free servers with the aim of minimizing the mean number of jobs in the system (NJM–problem) or the total processing cost (PCM–problem).

To solve the problem we introduce the Markov decision controllable process $\{Z(t)\} = \{X(t), U(t)\}$. The observed process $\{X(t)\}_{t \geq 0}$ with state space $E = \mathbf{N} \times \prod_{k=1}^{K} \{0, \ldots, m_k\}$ is a vector process with components $D_0(t), D_1(t), \ldots, D_K(t)$, where, as before, $D_0(t) = Q(t)$ is a queue length at time t, and $D_k(t)$ for $k > 0$

describes the state of the service process of the server k at this time:

$$D_k(t) = \begin{cases} 0, & \text{if the } k\text{-th server is idle at time } t \text{ and} \\ d_k = \overline{1, m_k}, & \text{if the } k\text{-th server is in phase } d_k. \end{cases}$$

For each state $x = (d_0, d_1, \ldots, d_K)$, where $d_0 := q(x)$, let $J_0(x)$ and $J_1(x)$ be the sets of labels assigned to idle and busy servers, respectively, in this state, i.e.

$$J_0(x) = \{j : d_j(x) = 0\}, \qquad J_1(x) = \{j : d_j(x) \neq 0\}.$$

Denote also by $L(t) = D_0(t) + \sum_{k=1}^{K} 1_{\{D_k(t)>0\}}$ the random process of number of jobs in the system.

The controlling process $\{U(t)\}_{t \geq 0}$ with decision sets $A(x)$ has the same description as for the previous models, see e.g. Section 2.3. The transition intensities for the process $\{Z(t)\}$ will be specified for each queue separately.

In our further investigation we will need shift operators for the state space. Therefore, denote by $e_i = (\underbrace{0, \ldots, 0}_{i}, 1, \underbrace{0, \ldots, 0}_{K-i})$ the $K+1$ - dimensional vector for which the i-th component is one and all others are zeros. Consider the shift operators S_0, $S_j^{d_j}$ when arrivals of new customers take place in the queue

$$S_0 x = x + e_0 1_{\{q(x)<B\}}, \tag{4.1}$$
$$S_j^{d_j} x = x + d_j e_j 1_{\{j \in J_0(x)\}},$$

otherwise $S_0 x = S_j^{d_j} x = x$. The same operator S_j is used to represent a phase change without service completion:

$$S_j^{d_j} x = x + [d_j - d_j(x)] e_j, \quad j \in J_1(x).$$

When a service completion takes place one considers the inverse shift operators S_0^{-1} and $S_j^{-d_j}$, respectively, that is

$$S_0^{-1} x = x - e_0, \qquad \text{if} \quad q(x) > 0,$$
$$S_j^{-d_j} x = x - d_j e_j, \qquad \text{if} \quad j \in J_1(x).$$

As before, two types of the optimization problem can be considered, the NJM–problem and the the PCM–problem with additional penalties. Therefore, in accordance with the given cost structure, the quantity functional to be minimized has the form

$$Y(t) = \int_0^t \left(c_0 Q(u) + \sum_{j:D_j(u)\neq 0} c_j \right) du.$$

For this functional the adjusted loss per unit of time is independent of the decision. For the NJM–problem the loss rate in the state x has the form

$$c(x) = q(x) + \sum_{k=1}^{K} \mathbf{1}_{\{d_k(x)>0\}} = l(x),$$

and for the PCM–problem

$$c(x) = q(x)c_0 + \sum_{j \in J_1(x)} c_j.$$

The problem consists in minimizing the mean loss per unit of time, that is

$$g(x; \delta) = \lim_{t \to \infty} \frac{1}{t} \mathbf{E}_{x_0}^{\delta} Y(t).$$

4.3 Controlled $M/E/K$ queue

Denote by m_k the number of phases (stages) and by μ_k the different rates per stage for each server $k = \overline{1, K}$. The service process is illustrated in Figure 4.2

Figure 4.2 Service process

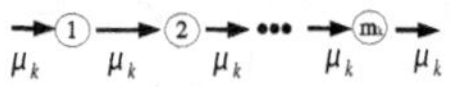

The equilibrium condition in infinite buffer case

$$\lambda < \sum_{k=1}^{K} \frac{\mu_k}{m_k}, \tag{4.2}$$

where $\frac{\mu_k}{m_k}$ is a mean service rate of the k-th server.

For this system we have to take into account that a departure from some stage $d_j(x) < m_j$, $j \in J_1(x)$ engenders the transition to the next stage $d_j(x) + 1$, while a departure from stage $d_j(x) = m_j$ signifies the service completion of the job.

Using the shift notations introduced above, we represent the transition intensities $\lambda_{xy}(a)$ of the process $\{Z(t)\}$ by

$$\lambda_{xy}(a) = \begin{cases} \lambda, & y = S^1_{a_0}x, \ a_0 \neq 0, \quad y = S_0 x, \ a_0 = 0, \\ \mu_j \mathbf{1}_{\{d_j(x)=m_j\}}[\mathbf{1}_{\{q(x)=0\}} + \\ \mathbf{1}_{\{q(x)>0, a_j=0\}}], & y = S^{-m_j}_j x, \quad j \in J_1(x) \\ \mu_j \mathbf{1}_{\{d_j(x)=m_j, q(x)>0, a>0\}}, & y = S^1_{a_j} S^{-m_j}_j S^{-1}_0 x, \ j \in J_1(x), \\ \mu_j, & y = S^{d_j(x)+1}_j x, \quad j \in J_1(x) \cap J_1(y), \\ -(\lambda + \sum_{j \in J_1(x)} \mu_j), & y = x, \\ 0, & \text{otherwise}, \end{cases}$$

where $a = a_0 \in A(x)$ denotes the control which has to be chosen in the case of an arrival to the state x, $a = a_j \in A(S^{-m_j}_j S^{-1}_0 x)$ denotes the control in the case of a service completion on the j-th server.
In this matrix:

- the first case corresponds to arrivals;

- the second case corresponds to a service completion with an empty queue or with control $a_j = 0$ when the last service phase is completed;

- the third case corresponds to a service completion and the decision to send one of the jobs from the queue to one of the available servers;

- the fifth case corresponds to a change of the service phase, for which a transition is possible only to the next service phase.

The diagonal elements of this matrix equal the negative sum of all the entries in the same row.

The transitions after an arrival and service phase completion are illustrated by the graph in Figure 4.3 (a) and (b), respectively

Figure 4.3

4.3.1   Optimality equation

As usual, to obtain the optimality equation we obtain for the function $V(x, t)$ and a small interval of length h

$$
\begin{aligned}
V(x, t+h) =& c(x)h + \left(1 - \left[\lambda + \sum_{j \in J_1(x)} \mu_j\right]h\right)V(x, t) \\
& + \lambda h \min_{a_0 \in A(x)} V(S_{a_0}x, t) \\
& + \sum_{\substack{j \in J_1(x) \\ q(x)>0}} \mathbf{1}_{\{d_j(x)=m_j\}}\mu_j h \min_{a_j \in A(S_j^{-m_j}S_0^{-1}x)} V(S_{a_j}S_j^{-m_j}S_0^{-1}x, t) \\
& + \sum_{\substack{j \in J_1(x) \\ q(x)=0}} \mathbf{1}_{\{d_j(x)=m_j\}}\mu_j h V(S_j^{-m_j}x, t) \\
& + \sum_{j \in J_1(x)} \mathbf{1}_{\{d_j(x)<m_j\}}\mu_j h\, V(S_j^{d_j(x)+1}x, t).
\end{aligned}
$$

The asymptotic behavior of the function $V(x, t)$ and the long-run problem (2.6) implies the following form of the optimality equation:

$$
\begin{aligned}
v(x) \;=\;& \frac{1}{\lambda_x}\Big[c(x) + C_1(x) + C_2(x) - g \\
& + \lambda T_0 v(x) + \sum_{\substack{j \in J_1(x) \\ q(x)>0 \\ d_j(x)=m_j}} \mu_j T_j v(x)\Big] = Bv(x).
\end{aligned} \tag{4.3}
$$

In this representation

$$
\lambda_x = \lambda + \sum_{j \in J_1(x)} \mu_j
$$

is the intensity of a transition from state x,

$$
C_1(x) = \sum_{\substack{j \in J_1(x) \\ d_j(x)<m_j}} \mu_j v(S_j^{d_j(x)+1}x)
$$

is the loss rate due to a change of the service phase without decision making,

$$
C_2(x) = \sum_{\substack{j \in J_1(x) \\ q(x)=0 \\ d_j(x)=m_j}} \mu_j v(S_j^{-m_j}x)
$$

is the loss rate due to a service completion with an empty queue,

$$T_0 v(x) = \min \left\{ v(S_0 x), v(S_k^1 x) : \ k = \overline{1, K} \right\} \tag{4.4}$$

is the minimal loss in case of a new job arrival,

$$T_j v(x) = T_0 v(S_0^{-1} S_j^{-m_j} x) \mathbf{1}_{\{q(x)>0\}} \tag{4.5}$$

is the minimal loss in case of a service completion and the appropriate decision making.

It is possible to see from this system of equations that the optimal policy

$$f = \{ f(x) : x \in E \}$$

minimizes the function $b = \{ b(x, a) : x \in E, a \in A \}$ with

$$b(x, a) = \mathbf{1}_{\{a=0\}} v(S_a x) + \mathbf{1}_{\{a=k\}} v(S_a^1 x) \tag{4.6}$$

and has the form

$$f(x) = \operatorname{argmin}[b(x, a) : \ a \in A(x)]. \tag{4.7}$$

This means that it is also determined by the value function

$$v = \{ v(x) : \ x \in E \}$$

of the model, which is a solution of the optimality equation (4.3).

4.3.2 Monotonicity properties. Dependence on service phases

Let the servers be arranged for the NJM–problem in decreasing order of their mean service intensities

$$\frac{\mu_1}{m_1} \geq \frac{\mu_2}{m_2} \geq \cdots \geq \frac{\mu_K}{m_K} \tag{4.8}$$

and for the PCM–problem in increasing order of their mean usage cost

$$\frac{c_1 m_1}{\mu_1} \leq \frac{c_2 m_2}{\mu_2} \leq \cdots \leq \frac{c_K m_K}{\mu_K} \tag{4.9}$$

with different possible values of initial parameters, e.g.

- $$0 \leq m_1\mu_1^{-1} \leq m_2\mu_2^{-1} \leq \cdots \leq m_K\mu_K^{-1}, \quad c_1 \leq c_2 \leq \cdots \leq c_K; \quad (4.10)$$
- $$0 \leq m_1\mu_1^{-1} \leq m_2\mu_2^{-1} \leq \cdots \leq m_K\mu_K^{-1}, \quad c_1 > c_2 > \cdots > c_K; \quad (4.11)$$
- $$0 < m_K\mu_K^{-1} < \cdots < m_2\mu_2^{-1} < m_1\mu_1^{-1}, \quad c_1 \leq c_2 \leq \cdots \leq c_K; \quad (4.12)$$

The system under consideration with Phase-type service time distributions is much more difficult than the Markovian queue. Based on the numerical results we expect that this system must have the similar monotonicity properties. These properties can be formalized as the following conjectures

Conjecture 4.4 *An optimal policy in the NJM–problem has the property that whenever it assigns a job to an available server it makes the assignment to an available server with minimal mean service time (4.8). In the PCM–problem, if the values of initial system parameters satisfy the conditions (4.9)-(4.11), the controller always assigns a job to the server with minimal mean usage cost. Under the conditions (4.9) and (4.12), the controller can use any of available servers but while the queue length increases, more expensive but faster server can be used.*

Conjecture 4.5 *The optimal control policy is of threshold type with one finite threshold for each service phase of each server in the NJM- and the PCM–problem under the conditions (4.9)-(4.11). The optimal control policy is of threshold type with different finite thresholds for each service phase of each server in the PCM–problem under the conditions (4.9) and (4.12).*

We note that only some of the statements in the Conjectures 4.4 and 4.5 can be proved. The other assertions remains unproven, nevertheless we confirm them numerically.

Below we introduce a partial order on the state space E in by means of the shift operators S_0 and $S_i^{d_i}$. This shall be defined by

$$S_0 x \geq x, \qquad S_i^{d_i} x \geq x, \quad i \in J_0(x), \, d_i = \overline{1, m_i},$$
$$S_i^\alpha x \geq S_i^\beta x, \quad i \in J_0(x), \quad \alpha \leq \beta.$$
$$S_i^1 x \geq S_j^1 x, \quad i, j \in J_0(x), \, i \geq j.$$

Now the following statement can be formulated for the system under consideration concerning the introduced order

Theorem 4.6 *Assume the bounded, nondecreasing function v(x) has the following property*

1. $v(S_0 x) \geq v(x)$, $v(S_i^{d_i} x) \geq v(x)$, $d_i = \overline{1, m_i}$;
2. $v(S_i^{\alpha} x) \geq v(S_i^{\beta} x)$, $i \in J_0(x)$, $\alpha \leq \beta$;

Then the operator B retains this property for the value function of the model.

Proof: First we consider the behavior of the operator T_0 with respect to the introduced order on E. For the inequality 1 we have

$$
T_0 v(S_0 x) = \min_{k \in A(S_0 x)} \{v(S_0^2 x, v(S_k^1 S_0 x))\} \geq \min_{k \in A(S_0 x)} \{v(S_0 x, v(S_k^1 x))\}
$$
$$
\geq \min_{k \in A(x)} \{v(S_0 x, v(S_k x))\} = T_0 v(x),
$$

that follows from assumption on the function $v(x)$ and the relation $A(S_0 x) = A(x)$. The same argument applies for the inequality $T_0 v(S_i^{d_i} x) \geq T_0 v(x)$ taking into account that $A(S_i^{d_i} x) \subset A(x)$.

For the inequality 2 we get

$$
T_0 v(S_i^{\alpha} x) = \min_{k \in A(S_i^{\alpha} x)} \{v(S_0 S_i^{\alpha} x), v(S_k^1 S_i^{\alpha} x)\}
$$
$$
\geq \min_{k \in A(S_i^{\beta} x)} \{v(S_0 S_i^{\beta} x), v(S_k^1 S_i^{\beta} x)\} = T_0 v(S_i^{\beta} x)
$$

by virtue of the monotonicity assumption on the function $v(x)$ and the equality $A(S_i^{\alpha} x) = A(S_i^{\beta} x)$.

The same is true also for the operators T_i due to the definition (4.5). It is obvious that the operator B preserves the inequalities 1 for nondecreasing function $v(x)$ due to the properties of operators T_0 and T_j.

Without loss of generality, we assume that $\lambda + 2\mu_i + \sum_{j \in J_1(S_i^{d_i} x)} \mu_j = 1$. Further we consider the two-state service process on the server i. Then for the inequality 2 and the operator B we have

$$
Bv(S_i^{\alpha} x) - Bv(S_i^{\beta} x) = [c(S_i^{\alpha} x) - c(S_i^{\beta} x)]
$$
$$
+ \lambda [T_0 v(S_i^{\alpha} x) - T_0 v(S_i^{\beta} x)]
$$
$$
+ \sum_{j \in J_1(S_i^{d_i} x)} \mu_j (\mathbf{1}_{\{d_j < m_j\}} [v(S_i^{\alpha} x) - v(S_i^{\beta} x)] + \mathbf{1}_{\{d_j = m_j\}} [T_j v(S_i^{\alpha} x) - T_j v(S_i^{\beta} x)])
$$
$$
+ \mu_i [v(S_i^{\beta} x) + v(S_i^{\alpha} x)] - \mu_i [T_i v(S_i^{\beta} x) - v(S_i^{\beta} x)].
$$

In this expression the first three items are non-negative since the function $c(x)$ is constant upon passing from $S_i^\alpha x$ to $S_i^\beta x$ for the phases α and β. For the last item we obtain according to the definitions of the operators T_i

$$\mu_i[v(S_i^\beta x) + v(S_i^\alpha x)] - \mu_i[T_i v(S_i^\beta x) - v(S_i^\beta x)]$$
$$= \mu_i[v(S_i^\alpha x) - T_0 v(S_0^{-1} x)] = \mu_i[v(S_i^\alpha x) - v(x)] \geq 0,$$

Further, because the function $c(x)$ is nonnegative relative to the shifts from $S_i^\alpha x$ to $S_i^\beta x$, from $S_0 x$ to x and from $S_i^{d_i} x$ to x, and the value function $v = \{v(x) : x \in E\}$ is a fixed point of operator B, we obtain the inequality 1 and 2 of the theorem.
□

Taking into account the inequality 2 we can expect that as the residual service time increases the slow server will be used more often i.e.

$$v(S_0 S_i^\beta x) \leq v(S_k S_i^\beta x) \Rightarrow v(S_0 S_i^\alpha x) \leq v(S_k S_i^\alpha x), \quad i, k \in J_0(x), \alpha \leq \beta.$$

The last inequalities can be rewritten in terms of the value function in the following operators form

$$(S_0 - S_k^1)(S_i^\beta - S_i^\alpha)v(x) \leq 0, \quad i, k \in J_0(x), \alpha \leq \beta.$$

Thus, if the optimal policy is of threshold type for the service phases $\alpha \leq \beta$ there exist threshold levels q_k^* for the k-th server such that $q_k^*(\alpha) \leq q_k^*(\beta)$.

Now we investigate the question, which of the available servers should be used by the controller. For the Markovian queue the Conjecture 4.4 and 4.5 was proved at least for NJM- and the PCM–problem under the conditions (4.9) and We have not been able to analyze successfully the system $M/E_{m_j}, M/K$ or the more general model $M/E_{m_j}, E_{m_i}/K$, i.e. to show which of these two types of servers has to be switched on. In the first case the faster server j is Erlangian and another one i is exponential. In the second system, the both of servers i and j are Erlangian with arrangements (4.8) and (4.9) for any $i > j$.

In a theoretical manner we will investigate only the model $M/M, E_{m_i}/K$ where we can compare two kinds of servers, the fastest of which j are exponential with rate μ_j and the slower i are Erlangian with m_i stages and rate μ_i per stage, satisfying $\mu_j \geq \mu_i$ for the NJM–problem, and $\frac{c_j}{\mu_j} \leq \frac{c_i}{\mu_i}$ for the PCM–problem.

Theorem 4.7 *Assume the bounded, nondecreasing function v(x) has the following properties*

$$3. \quad v(S_i^1 x) \geq v(S_j^1 x), \ i,j \in J_0(x), \ i \geq j, \ \frac{c_j}{\mu_j} \leq \frac{c_i}{\mu_i}.$$

Then the operator B retains these properties for the value function of the model.

Proof: First we consider the behavior of the operator T_0 with respect to the introduced order on E. Introduce the action set $B(x)$ such that $A(S_j^1 x) = B(x) \cup \{0\} \cup \{j\}$ and $A(S_i^1 x) = B(x) \cup \{0\} \cup \{i\}$. Now for the inequality 3 we get

$$T_0 v(S_i^1 x) = \min\{v(S_j^1 S_i^1 x), \min_{k \in B(x)} \{v(S_0 S_i^1 x), v(S_k^1 S_i^1 x)\}\}$$

$$\geq \min\{v(S_i^1 S_j^1 x), \min_{k \in B(x)} \{v(S_0 S_j^1 x), v(S_k^1 S_j^1 x)\}\} = T_0 v(S_j^1 x).$$

Due to definition (4.5) of the operators T_j the property 3 is preserved, too. We only have to specify the inequality $T_j v(S_j^1 x) \geq T_j v(x)$. We note that the function $v(x)$ is defined after the decision that has been made in state x. Therefore, this function satisfies the condition $v(x) = \min_{k \in A(x)} \{v(S_0^{-1} S_k^1 x)\} = T_0 v(S_0^{-1} x)$. This implies for the state $S_i^{m_i} x$ after service completion $T_i v(S_i^{m_i} x) = T_0 v(S_0^{-1} x) = v(x) = T_i v(x)$.

Without loss of generality assume that $\lambda + \mu_i + \mu_j + \sum_{k \in J(S_i^1 S_j^1 x)} \mu_k = 1$. For the NJM– and the PCM–problem under conditions (2.29) taking into account the inequality 3 we have

$$Bv(S_i^1 x) - Bv(S_j^1 x) = [c(S_i^1 x) - c(S_j^1 x)]$$

$$+ \lambda[T_0 v(S_i^1 x) - T_0 v(S_j^1 x)] + \sum_{r \in J_1(S_i^1 S_j^1 x)} \mu_r[T_r v(S_i^1 x) - T_r v(S_j^1 x)]$$

$$+ \sum_{l \in J_1(S_i^1 S_j^1 x)} \mu_l (\mathbf{1}_{\{d_l < m_l\}}[v(S_i^1 x) - v(S_j^1 x)] + \mathbf{1}_{\{d_l = m_l\}}[T_l v(S_i^1 x) - T_l v(S_j^1 x)])$$

$$+ \mu_i \mu_j \left[\frac{v(S_i^1 x) - T_j v(S_j^1 x)}{\mu_i} - \frac{v(S_j^1 x) - v(S_i^2 x)}{\mu_j} \right].$$

In this expression the items with index r denote exponential servers and the items with index l denote the Erlangian servers.

The first three items of this expression are non-negative according to the property of the functions $c(x)$ and $v(x)$ upon passing from $S_i^1 x$ to $S_j^1 x$.

The last item is non-negative because of the following argument. If $q(x) = 0$, then

$$\mu_i \mu_j \left[\frac{v(S_i^1 x) - T_j v(S_j^1 x)}{\mu_i} - \frac{v(S_j^1 x) - v(S_i^2 x)}{\mu_j} \right] =$$

$$\mu_i \mu_j \left[\frac{v(S_i^1 x) - v(x)}{\mu_i} - \frac{v(S_j^1 x) - v(S_i^2 x)}{\mu_j} \right] \geq 0,$$

due to the monotonicity assumption on the function $v(x)$, $v(S_i^1 x) - v(x) \geq v(S_j^1 x) - v(S_i^2 x) \geq 0$ and $\mu_i \leq \mu_j$. The same we obtain for states x with $q(x) > 0$. Indeed, in this case we have $T_j v(S_j^1 x) = T_0 v(S_0^{-1} x) = v(x)$.

Now, since the operator B retains inequalities in the sense that $Bv_1(x) \geq Bv_2(x)$ for $v_1(x) \geq v_2(x)$ and the fact that the function $c(x)$ is non-negative relative to the shifts from $S_i^1 x$ to $S_j^1 x$ (according to the monotone convergence of the sequence $B^n c(x)$ w.r.t the value function of the model $v = \{v(x) : x \in E\}$), we obtain the inequality 3 of the theorem.

$\square$

A direct consequence of Theorem 4.7 is that for the system under consideration an optimal control requires to switch on the fastest available server if the system parameters satisfy the condition (2.29). In the case of inequalities (2.30) the statement of the theorem can be confirmed only by means of the numerical results. At last, the inequality 3 does not hold for all states x if the values of initial system parameters satisfy (2.31). To show this it is sufficient to consider the function $v(x)$ in the state $x = (q, 0, \ldots, 0)$ when $\lambda = 0$, that is no future arrivals occur. In this case for the value function $v(x)$ we obtain recursively

$$v(S_i^1 x) - v(S_j^1 x) = \left[\frac{m_i c_i}{\mu_i} - \frac{c_j}{\mu_j} \right] + c_0 q(x) \left[\frac{m_i}{\mu_i} - \frac{1}{\mu_j} \right].$$

The last expression is nonnegative only if $q(x) \leq \frac{1}{c_0} \left[\frac{1}{\mu_j} - \frac{m_i}{\mu_i} \right]^{-1} \left[\frac{m_i c_i}{\mu_i} - \frac{c_j}{\mu_j} \right] \geq 0$.

By virtue of the same arguments as in Theorem 2.10 for the system $M/M, E_{m_2}/2$ with two heterogeneous servers, the value function $v = \{v(x) : x \in E\}$ of the model is (S_0, S_2)-supermodular, i.e. satisfies condition (2.16)

$$(1 - S_0)(S_0 - S_2) v(x) \leq 0.$$

The last inequality means that the optimal policy for this system is of a threshold type. That means that a server in the NJM– and the PCM–problem has to be switched on only if the queue length exceeds some prespecified threshold level. For the multi-server queue numerical analysis shows that the inequality

$$(1 - S_0)(S_0 - S_k^1)v(x) \leq 0, \quad k \in J_0(x)$$

holds for any system $M/E_{m_k}/K$ that was examined, regardless which of the server, Erlangian or exponential, is the faster or with fewer mean usage cost.

In light traffic case $\lambda < \frac{\mu_k}{m_k}$, thresholds for switching on the exponential servers can be obtained by (2.21) and (2.33). For Erlangian servers the threshold levels can be obtained using the same approach as in Section 2.4.7 and 2.5.6. Recursively solving the equation

$$v(x) = \frac{c(x)}{M_1} + \sum_{j \in J_1(x)} \frac{\mathbf{1}_{\{d_j < m_j\}} v(S_j^{d_j+1} x) + \mathbf{1}_{\{d_j = m_j\}} T_j v(x)}{M_1}$$

up to $q(x) = q_2^*$ and taking into account that the first server, with parameters depending on the problem (NJM or PCM), is always used, we get for $x = (0, \ldots, 0)$ and the phase $d_1 = \overline{1, m_1}$ of the first server

$$v(S_0^{q_2^*} S_1^{d_1} x) = \frac{(m_1 - d_1 + 1)(c_1 + q_2^* c_0)}{\mu_1} + \frac{q_2^* m_1 c_1}{\mu_1} + \frac{m_1 q_2^* (q_2^* - 1) c_0}{2\mu_1}.$$

Once a queue length reaches in some state the threshold q_2^* for using the second server, the value function at this state must be less than the value function in the point where the controller does not use the second server. We omit the calculation of the value $v(S_0^{q_2^*-1} S_1^{d_1} S_2^1 x)$ and finally get

$$v(S_0^{q_2^*-1} S_1^{d_1} S_2^1 x) = \frac{m_2 c_2}{\mu_2} + v(S_0^{q_2^*-1} S_1^{d_1} x) \leq v(S_0^{q_2^*} S_1^{d_1} x),$$

$$\frac{m_2}{\mu_2} + \frac{(m_1 - d_1 + 1)(c_1 + (q_2^* - 1)c_0)}{\mu_1} + v(S_0^{q_2^*-2} S_1^1 x)$$

$$\leq \frac{(m_1 - d_1 + 1)(c_1 + q_2^* c_0)}{\mu_1} + \frac{m_1 c_1}{\mu_1} + \frac{m_1(q_2^* - 1)}{\mu_1} + v(S_0^{q_2^*-2} S_1^1 x).$$

This implies the threshold level for the second server in the state $S_1^{d_1} x$

$$q(S_1^{d_1} x) \geq q_2^*(d_1) = \frac{\mu_1}{m_1 c_0} \left[\frac{m_2 c_2}{\mu_2} - \frac{m_1 c_1}{\mu_1} \right] + \frac{d_1 - 1}{m_1}.$$

It is possible to see that with increasing of the value $d_1 = \overline{1, m_1}$, i.e. with decreasing of the residual service time, the threshold levels for the slower server increases. The threshold expressions for the third and other servers are more complicated since they depend on service phases of all servers $q_j^*(d_1, d_2, \dots, d_{j-1})$ with less indexes. For the states $S_1^1 S_2^1 \dots S_{j-1}^1 x$ the threshold level $\overline{q_j^*}$ for the j-th server in the NJM–problem can be calculated by

$$q_j^* = \frac{m_j}{\mu_j} \sum_{i=1}^{j-1} \frac{\mu_i}{m_i} - (j-1) \tag{4.13}$$

and for the PCM–problem by

$$q_j^* = \frac{1}{c_0} \left[\frac{m_j c_j}{\mu_j} \sum_{i=1}^{j-1} \frac{\mu_i}{m_i} - \sum_{i=1}^{j-1} c_i \right]. \tag{4.14}$$

We did not obtain here the threshold levels for any other states of the servers $S_1^{d_1} S_2^{d_2} \dots S_{j-1}^{d_{j-1}} x$ because they would require a quite complicated recursive solution, but the extension is possible in principle.

4.3.3   Algorithm

To analyze numerically the behavior of optimal strategies, the servers will be arranged in order given by (4.8) for the NJM–problem, and in the order (4.8) under conditions (4.10)–(4.12) for the PCM–problem.

Strategy estimation. For a given policy $f = \{f_n(x) : x = \overline{1, I}\}$ solve the equation

$$
\begin{aligned}
v_n(x) = & \frac{1}{\lambda_x}\Big(c(x) + C_1(x) + C_2(x) - g_n\Big) \\
& + \frac{1}{\lambda_x}\lambda\Big(\mathbf{1}_{\{f_n(x)=0\}} v_n(S_0 x) + \mathbf{1}_{\{f_n(x)=k\}} v_n(S_{f_n(x)}^1 x) \Big) \\
& + \frac{1}{\lambda_x} \sum_{\substack{j \in J_1(x) \\ q(x)>0 \\ d_j(x)=m_j}} \mu_j \Big(\mathbf{1}_{\{f_n(x)=0\}} v_n(S_0 S_j^{-m_j} S_0^{-1} x) \\
& \qquad\qquad + \mathbf{1}_{\{f_n(x)=k\}} v_n(S_{f_n(S_j^{-m_j} S_0^{-1} x)}^1 S_j^{-m_j} S_0^{-1} x) \Big)
\end{aligned}
$$

for all $x \in E$ under the condition $v(0) = 0$. This can be done by successive approximation up to an accuracy ε.

Strategy improvement. For a given solution $v_n = \{v_n(x) : x \in E\}$ find a new policy $f_{n+1} = \{f_{n+1}(x) : x \in E\}$, which minimizes the Bellman function (4.6) of the model:

$$f_{n+1}(x) = \operatorname*{argmin}_{k \in A(x)} \begin{cases} v_n(x + e_k), & k = \overline{1, K} \\ v_n(x + e_0), & k = 0 \end{cases}$$

The algorithm stops when two successive iterations yield the same policy.

For a description of the system states transitions at control epochs we consider the one-to-one correspondence between the multidimensional representation of the system state x and the index of such a state. Namely,

$$\#(x) = \prod_{i=1}^{K}(m_i + 1)d_0(x) + \sum_{j=1}^{K} d_j(x)\mathbf{1}_{\{j>1\}} \prod_{i=1}^{j-1}(m_i + 1) \equiv x \qquad (4.15)$$

The number of system states is $\prod_{i=1}^{K}(m_i + 1)(B - K + 1)$.

Now, if y_j is the state after possible transition from the j-th coordinate, it can be obtained with respect to introduced formula by

$$y_j = x + \frac{(d_j - d_j(x)) \prod_{i=1}^{K}(m_i + 1)}{\mathbf{1}_{\{1 \leq j \leq K\}} \prod_{i=j}^{K}(m_i + 1)}. \qquad (4.16)$$

Thus, in the one-dimensional case we have

$$S_0 x = x + \prod_{i=1}^{K}(m_i + 1), \qquad (4.17)$$

$$S_0^{-1} x = x - \prod_{i=1}^{K}(m_i + 1),$$

$$S_j^{d_j} x = x + d_j \prod_{i=1}^{j-1}(m_i + 1), \quad j \in J_0(x),$$

$$S_j^{d_j} x = x + [d_j - d_j(x)] \prod_{i=1}^{j-1}(m_i + 1), \quad j \in J_1(x),$$

$$S_j^{-d_j} x = x - d_j(x) \prod_{i=1}^{j-1}(m_i + 1), \quad j \in J_1(x).$$

4.3.4   Numerical analysis

In this section we propose numerical results of the introduced iteration algorithm. An example of the NJM–problem for the system $M/E_5/5/100$ with $m_k = 5$, $k = \overline{1,5}$, and arrival intensity $\lambda = 0.01$ is given in the control Table 4.9. The Erlangian service intensities per stage are given in Table 4.8.

Table 4.8 Values of initial system parameters for $M/E_5/5/100$ queue

i	1	2	3	4	5
μ_i	$1.90m_1$	$0.63m_2$	$0.52m_3$	$0.45m_4$	$0.30m_5$

Table 4.9 Optimal control for some system states

System State x	Queue length $q(x)$													
(d_1,d_2,d_3,d_4,d_5)	0	1	2	3	4	5	6	7	8	9	10	11	12	...
$(0,*,*,*,*)$	**1**	1	1	1	1	1	1	1	1	1	1	1	1	1
$(1,0,*,*,*)$	0	0	**2**	2	2	2	2	2	2	2	2	2	2	2
$(1,1,0,*,*)$	0	0	**3**	3	3	3	3	3	3	3	3	3	3	3
$(2,4,0,*,*)$	0	0	0	**3**	3	3	3	3	3	3	3	3	3	3
$(5,5,0,*,*)$	0	0	0	0	**3**	3	3	3	3	3	3	3	3	3
$(1,1,1,0,*)$	0	0	0	**4**	4	4	4	4	4	4	4	4	4	4
$(4,3,1,0,*)$	0	0	0	0	**4**	4	4	4	4	4	4	4	4	4
$(5,5,4,0,*)$	0	0	0	0	0	**4**	4	4	4	4	4	4	4	4
$(1,1,1,1,0)$	0	0	0	0	0	0	**5**	5	5	5	5	5	5	5
$(3,2,1,1,0)$	0	0	0	0	0	0	0	**5**	5	5	5	5	5	5
$(4,5,2,1,0)$	0	0	0	0	0	0	0	0	**5**	5	5	5	5	5

Because of the large of state space only selective states are shown in this table. Here we can see the threshold structure of optimal control policies. The fastest server is always activated and all other servers have a number of thresholds. The threshold levels for each slower server depends also on the current phases of the busy servers which are faster. In these examples, the selected threshold levels assume the values:

$$q_1^* = 0;$$
$$q_2^*(d_1) = 2, \quad d_1 = 1;$$
$$q_3^*(d_1,d_2) = 2, \quad d_1 = 1, d_2 = 1;$$
$$q_3^*(d_1,d_2) = 3, \quad d_1 = 2, d_2 = 4;$$
$$q_3^*(d_1,d_2) = 4, \quad d_1 = 5, d_2 = 5;$$

$$q_4^*(d_1, d_2, d_3) = 3, \quad d_1 = 1, \, d_2 = 1, \, d_3 = 1;$$
$$q_4^*(d_1, d_2, d_3) = 4, \quad d_1 = 4, \, d_2 = 3, \, d_3 = 1;$$
$$q_4^*(d_1, d_2, d_3) = 5, \quad d_1 = 5, \, d_2 = 5, \, d_3 = 4;$$
$$q_5^*(d_1, d_2, d_3, d_4) = 6, \quad d_1 = 1, \, d_2 = 1, \, d_3 = 1, \, d_4 = 1;$$
$$q_5^*(d_1, d_2, d_3, d_4) = 7, \quad d_1 = 3, \, d_2 = 2, \, d_3 = 1, \, d_4 = 1;$$
$$q_5^*(d_1, d_2, d_3, d_4) = 8, \quad d_1 = 4, \, d_2 = 5, \, d_3 = 2, \, d_4 = 1;$$

Thus for some fixed phases $(d_1, d_2, \ldots, d_{K-1})$ the threshold sequence looks like

$$0 = q_1^* \le q_2^*(d_1) \le q_3^*(d_1, d_2) \le \cdots \le q_K^*(d_1, d_2, \ldots, d_{K-1}).$$

Moreover, with respect to decreasing residual service times, the threshold levels satisfy the condition

$$q_2^*(1) \le q_2^*(2) \le \cdots \le q_2^*(m_1);$$
$$q_3^*(1, 1) \le q_3^*(2, 1) \le \cdots \le q_2^*(m_1, 1);$$

$$\cdots\cdots\cdots$$

$$q_K^*(1, d_2, d_3, \ldots, d_{K-1}) \le q_K^*(2, d_2, d_3, \ldots, d_{K-1}) \le \cdots$$
$$\le q_K^*(m_1, d_2, d_3, \ldots, d_{K-1})$$

and analogously, when increasing any other coordinate d_k while all others are fixed.

The results of dynamic behavior of threshold levels when the initial system parameters are varied for the system $M/E_5/3/100$ with $K = 3$ heterogeneous servers are summarized in the diagrams shown in Figures 1.1–1.6 in Appendix 4.6.1. As before, the Poisson arrival rate λ is varied over the Figures 1.1–1.3 as follows

- $\lambda=0.51$, in Figure 1.1,

- $\lambda=0.26$, in Figure 1.2,

- $\lambda=0.01$, in Figure 1.3.

In these diagrams the changing of threshold levels $q_2^*(d_1)$ for the second server (pictures labeled by letter "a") and $q_3^*(d_1, d_2)$ for the third server (pictures labeled by letter "b") represents the threshold function under variation of the first service intensity, second service intensity and Erlangian service phases. The stepped curves in these diagrams show that when the residual service time of the faster service decreases, then the incentive to make an assignment to the second slower server is greater in state $x = (\alpha_1, 0, *)$ than in state $x = (\beta_1, 0, *)$, and to the third slower server is greater in state $x = (\alpha_1, \alpha_2, 0)$ than in state $x = (\beta_1, \beta_2, 0)$ if $\alpha_k \leq \beta_k$, $k = \{1, 2\}$.

The influence of the number of phases on the threshold curves is presented in Figures 1.4–1.6, where $\lambda = 0.51$ (pictures labeled by letter "a") and $\lambda = 0.01$ (pictures labeled by letter "b"). Here we can see that the low and upper bounds always correspond to the states with the largest residual service time and the smallest residual service time, respectively. The curves for all other possible residual service times lie between these two bounds.

For the PCM–problem the control tables are given below. In the case of the servers arranged by (4.9) with condition (4.11) and with values of initial system parameters given in Table 4.10, the results of optimal policy calculation are given in control Table 4.11. Similar results were obtained for condition (4.10).

Table 4.10 Values of initial system parameters for $M/E/5/100$ queue

i	0	1	2	3	4	5
c_i	1.00	3.00	2.80	2.60	2.40	2.00
μ_i	-	1.90	0.63	0.52	0.45	0.30
γ_i	-	1.58	4.44	5.00	5.53	6.66

Table 4.11 Optimal control for some system states

System State x	Queue length $q(x)$													
$(d_1, d_2, d_3, d_4, d_5)$	0	1	2	3	4	5	6	7	8	9	10	11	12	...
(0,*,*,*,*)	**1**	1	1	1	1	1	1	1	1	1	1	1	1	1
(1,0,*,*,*)	0	0	0	0	0	**2**	2	2	2	2	2	2	2	2
(4,0,*,*,*)	0	0	0	0	0	0	**2**	2	2	2	2	2	2	2
(1,1,0,*,*)	0	0	0	0	0	0	**3**	3	3	3	3	3	3	3
(2,4,0,*,*)	0	0	0	0	0	0	0	**3**	3	3	3	3	3	3
(5,5,0,*,*)	0	0	0	0	0	0	0	0	**3**	3	3	3	3	3
(1,1,1,0,*)	0	0	0	0	0	0	0	**4**	4	4	4	4	4	4
(4,3,1,0,*)	0	0	0	0	0	0	0	0	**4**	4	4	4	4	4
(5,5,4,0,*)	0	0	0	0	0	0	0	0	0	**4**	4	4	4	4
(1,1,1,1,0)	0	0	0	0	0	0	0	0	0	0	**5**	5	5	5
(3,2,1,1,0)	0	0	0	0	0	0	0	0	0	0	0	**5**	5	5
(4,5,2,1,0)	0	0	0	0	0	0	0	0	0	0	0	0	**5**	5

Similar to the NJM–problem, in this case the optimal policy has a threshold type with one threshold for each service phase of the certain server. As above the fastest server is always switched on whenever it is idle.

Table 4.12 Values of initial system parameters for $M/E/5/200$ queue

i	0	1	2	3	4	5
c_i	0.20	1.00	1.70	2.30	3.50	7.00
μ_i	-	0.30	0.45	0.52	0.63	0.90
γ_i	-	3.33	3.78	4.42	5.56	7.78

Table 4.13 Optimal control for some system states

System State x	Service phase d_j, $j \in \overline{1,K}$				
$(d_1, d_2, d_3, d_4, d_5)$	1	2	3	4	5
(-,0,0,0,0)	-,0,22,35,49	-,0,22,35,49	-,1,22,35,49	-,1,23,36,50	-,1,23,36,50
(0,-,0,0,0)	0,-,9,35,49	0,-,9,36,50	0,-,10,36,50	0,-,10,36,50	0,-,10,36,50
(-,1,0,0,0)	-,-,2,51,70	-,-,2,51,70	-,-,3,51,71	-,-,3,51,71	-,-,3,51,71
(0,0,-,0,0)	0,4,-,30,50	0,4,-,30,50	0,5,-,31,50	0,5,-,31,50	0,5,-,31,50
(-,0,1,0,0)	-,0,-,43,70	-,0,-,43,71	-,1,-,43,71	-,1,-,44,71	-,0,-,44,72
(0,-,1,0,0)	0,-,-,24,71	0,-,-,24,71	0,-,-,24,71	0,-,-,24,72	0,-,- ,25,72
(-,1,1,0,0)	-,-,-,9,90	-,-,-,9,90	-,-,-,9,91	-,-,-,9,91	-,-,-,10,91
(0,0,0,-,0)	0,4,23,-,45	0,5,23,-,45	0,5,23,-,46	0,5,23,-,46	0,5,23,-,46
(-,0,0,1,0)	-,0,31,-,64	-,0,31,-,64	-,1,31,-,65	-,1,32,-,65	-,0,32,-,65
(0,-,0,1,0)	0,-,13,-,64	0,-,13,-,65	0,-,13,-,65	0,-,13,-,65	0,-,14,-,65
(-,1,0,1,0)	-,-,2,-,82	-,-,2,-,83	-,-,3,-,83	-,-,3,-,83	-,-,3,-,83
(0,0,-,1,0)	0,5,-,-,59	0,5,-,-,59	0,5,-,-,59	0,5,-,-,59	0,5,-,-,60
(-,0,1,1,0)	-,0,-,-,74	-,0,-,-,75	-,1,-,-,75	-,1,-,-,76	-,1,-,-,76
(0,-,1,1,0)	0,-,-,-,53	0,-,-,-,53	0,-,-,-,53	0,-,-,-,54	0,-,-,-,54
(-,1,1,1,0)	-,-,-,-,29	-,-,-,-,30	-,-,-,-,30	-,-,-,-,30	-,-,-,-,30
(0,0,0,0,-)	0,5,23,36,-	0,5,23,36,-	0,5,23,36,-	0,5,23,36,-	0,5,23,36,-
(-,0,0,0,1)	-,0,31,51,-	-,0,31,51,-	-,1,32,51,-	-,1,32,52,-	-,1,32,52,-
(0,-,0,0,1)	0,-,13,51,-	0,-,13,52,-	0,-,13,52,-	0,-,13,52,-	0,-,14,52,-
(-,1,0,0,1)	-,-,2,63,-	-,-,2,63,-	-,-,3,64,-	-,-,3,64,-	-,-,3,65,-
(0,0,-,0,1)	0,5,-,44,-	0,5,-,44,-	0,5,-,44,-	0,5,-,44,-	0,5,-,45,-
(-,0,1,0,1)	-,0,-,53,-	-,1,-,53,-	-,1,-,53,-	-,1,-,53,-	-,1,-,53,-
(0,-,1,0,1)	0,-,-,30,-	0,-,-,30,-	0,-,-,30,-	0,-,-,30,-	0,-,-,30,-
(-,1,1,0,1)	-,-,-,9,-	-,-,-,9,-	-,-,-,9,-	-,-,-,9,-	-,-,-,10,-
(0,0,0,-,1)	0,5,32,-,-	0,5,32,-,-	0,5,32,-,-	0,5,32,-,-	0,5,32,-,-
(-,0,0,1,1)	-,0,39,-,-	-,0,39,-,-	-,1,39,-,-	-,1,39,-,-	-,1,39,-,-
(0,-,0,1,1)	0,-,14,-,-	0,-,14,-,-	0,-,14,-,-	0,-,14,-,-	0,-,15,-,-
(-,1,0,1,1)	-,-,2,-,-	-,-,2,-,-	-,-,3,-,-	-,-,3,-,-	-,-,3,-,-
(0,0,-,1,1)	0,5,-,-,-	0,5,-,-,-	0,6,-,-,-	0,6,-,-,-	0,6,-,-,-
(-,0,1,1,1)	-,0,-,-,-	-,0,-,-,-	-,1,-,-,-	-,1,-,-,-	-,1,-,-,-
(0,-,1,1,1)	0,-,-,-,-	0,-,-,-,-	0,-,-,-,-	0,-,-,-,-	0,-,-,-,-

The threshold sequence is the same as for NJM–problem with the following elements

$$q_1^* = 0;$$
$$q_2^*(d_1) = 5, \quad d_1 = 1;$$
$$q_2^*(d_1) = 6, \quad d_1 = 4;$$
$$q_3^*(d_1, d_2) = 6, \quad d_1 = 1, d_2 = 1;$$

$$q_3^*(d_1, d_2) = 7, \quad d_1 = 2, \, d_2 = 4;$$
$$q_3^*(d_1, d_2) = 8, \quad d_1 = 5, \, d_2 = 5;$$
$$q_4^*(d_1, d_2, d_3) = 7, \quad d_1 = 1, \, d_2 = 1, \, d_3 = 1;$$
$$q_4^*(d_1, d_2, d_3) = 8, \quad d_1 = 4, \, d_2 = 3, \, d_3 = 1;$$
$$q_4^*(d_1, d_2, d_3) = 9, \quad d_1 = 5, \, d_2 = 5, \, d_3 = 4;$$
$$q_5^*(d_1, d_2, d_3, d_4) = 11, \quad d_1 = 1, \, d_2 = 1, \, d_3 = 1, \, d_4 = 1;$$
$$q_5^*(d_1, d_2, d_3, d_4) = 12, \quad d_1 = 3, \, d_2 = 2, \, d_3 = 1, \, d_4 = 1;$$
$$q_5^*(d_1, d_2, d_3, d_4) = 13, \quad d_1 = 4, \, d_2 = 5, \, d_3 = 2, \, d_4 = 1;$$

For the PCM–problem with the servers arranged by (4.9) and condition (4.11), the optimal control policies are presented in control Table 4.13 with initial system parameters given in Table 4.12. As before, because of the large number of system states, (e.g. 1562980 states in this example) we consider only some selected states. The optimal control policies are presented as the threshold sequences $q_1^*(x), q_2^*(x), \ldots, q_5^*(x)$, where $x = (d_1, d_2, \ldots, d_5)$, when one of the coordinates d_k is varied while all others are fixed.

This control table shows that as the residual service time of some server decreases the controller prefers more cheaper but the slower server for subsequent decision.

4.4   Controlled $M/PH/K$ queue

In this section we consider a queue $M/PH_{het}/K/B$ with phase-type service time distribution having representations (η_k, M_k). The dimension of the PH-distribution for the k-th server is denoted by m_k. The vectors $\eta_k = (\eta_k^1, \eta_k^2, \ldots, \eta_k^{m_k})$ are initial service phase distributions and the matrices $M_k = [\mu_k^{ij}]$ contain the transition intensities of the PH distribution. The service process is illustrated in Figure 4.14

Figure 4.14 Service process

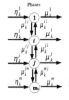

For the existence of a stationary regime when the buffer has infinite capacity the equilibrium condition is determined by

$$\lambda < \sum_{k=1}^{K} (-\eta_k^T M_k^{-1} \vec{1})^{-1}. \tag{4.18}$$

Using the shift notation, we represent the transition intensities $\lambda_{xy}(a)$ of the process $\{Z(t)\}$ by

$$\lambda_{xy}(a) = \begin{cases} \lambda[\mathbf{1}_{\{a_0=0\}} \\ +\eta_{a0}^{d_{a0}(y)}\mathbf{1}_{\{a_0\neq 0\}}], & y = S_0 x, \ a_0 = 0, \quad y = S_{a0}^{d_{a0}(y)} x, \ a_0 \neq 0, \\ \mu_j(d_j(x))[\mathbf{1}_{\{d_0(x)=0\}} \\ +\mathbf{1}_{\{d_0(x)>0,a_j=0\}}], & y = S_j^{-d_j} x, \quad j \in J_1(x), \\ \mu_j^{d_j(x)} \eta_{a_j}^{d_{a_j}(y)} \\ \mathbf{1}_{\{d_0(x)>0,a_j\neq 0\}}, & y = S_{a_j}^{d_{a_j}} S_j^{-d_j} S_0^{-1} x, \ j \in J_1(x), \\ \mu_j^{d_j(x) d_j(y)}, & y = S_j^{d_j(y)} x, \quad j \in J_1(x) \cap J_1(y), \\ -\lambda+ \\ \sum_{j\in J_1(x)} \mu_j^{d_j(x) d_j(x)}, & y = x, \\ 0, & \text{otherwise}, \end{cases}$$

where $\mu_j^{d_j(x)}$ are the components of the vector $\vec{\mu}_j = -M_j \vec{1}$. Here $a = a_0 \in A(x)$ denotes the control which has to be chosen in the case of an arrival to the state x, $a = a_j \in A(S_j^{-d_j} S_0^{-1} x)$ denotes the control in the case of a service completion on the j-th server.
In this matrix:

- the first case corresponds to an arrival of a new job in the system and sending it to the queue or to some server in accordance with the decision rule;

- the second case corresponds to a service completion with an empty queue or with control $a_j = 0$;

- the third case corresponds to a service completion and sending one of the jobs from the queue to one of available servers in accordance with the decision rule;

- the forth case corresponds to a transition of the service phases.

The diagonal elements of this matrix (the last case) equal the negative sum of all elements along the same row.

Transitions in the cases of arrivals and service completions are illustrated by the graph shown in Figure 4.15 (a) and (b), respectively

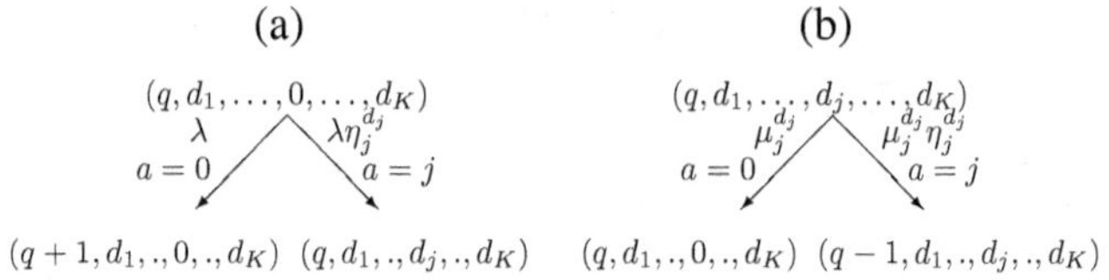

(a)   (b)

$$(q, d_1, \ldots, 0, \ldots, d_K)$$
$$\lambda \qquad \lambda \eta_j^{d_j}$$
$$a = 0 \qquad a = j$$

$$(q, d_1, \ldots, d_j, \ldots, d_K)$$
$$\mu_j^{d_j} \qquad \mu_j^{d_j} \eta_j^{d_j}$$
$$a = 0 \qquad a = j$$

$$(q+1, d_1, ., 0, ., d_K) \quad (q, d_1, ., d_j, ., d_K) \qquad (q, d_1, ., 0, ., d_K) \quad (q-1, d_1, ., d_j, ., d_K)$$

Figure 4.15

Now we obtain the optimality equation.

4.4.1 Optimality equation

For the function $V(x, t)$ and a small interval of length h we have

$$V(x, t + h)(x) = c(x)h + \left(1 - \left[\lambda - \sum_{j \in J_1(x)} \mu_j^{d_j(x)\, d_j(x)}\right] h \right) V(x, t)$$

$$+ \lambda h \min_{a_0 \in A(x)} \left\{ V(S_0 x, t), \sum_{d_{a_0}=1}^{m_{a_0}} \eta_{a_0}^{d_{a_0}} V(S_{a_0}^{d_{a_0}} x, t) \right\}$$

$$+ \sum_{\substack{j \in J_1(x) \\ q(x) > 0}} \mu_j^{d_j(x)} h \min_{a_j \in A(S_j^{-d_j} S_0^{-1} x)} \left\{ V(x, t), \sum_{d_{a_j}=1}^{m_{a_j}} \eta_{a_j}^{d_{a_j}} V(S_{a_j}^{d_{a_j}} S_0^{-1} x, t) \right\}$$

$$+ \sum_{j \in J_1(x)} \sum_{d_j \neq d_j(x)} \mu_j^{d_j(x)\, d_j} h\, V(S_j^{d_j} x, t)$$

$$+ \sum_{\substack{j \in J_1(x) \\ q(x) = 0}} \mu_j^{d_j(x)} h\, V(S_j^{-d_j} x, t).$$

In this equation, the first member of the right–hand side represents the loss of the system up to time h, the second one represents the total loss of the system during the following time t in the case that no phase changes occur in the system, the next one represents the total loss of the system during the following time t in the case that a new customer arrives before the service completion. The following member represents the loss of the system in the case of service completion with a non-empty queue before a new customer arrives, the next two members deal with the total loss of the system in the case of phase changes without arrivals or service completion, and the last one represents the total loss of the system during the following time t in the case that one of the served customers leaves the system with an empty queue before some customer arrives.

For the system under consideration, taking into account the asymptotic behavior (2.6) of the function $V(x, t)$ and passing to the limit $h \to 0$, the previous equation assumes the form

$$v(x) = \frac{1}{\lambda_x} \left[c(x) + C_1(x) + C_2(x) - g \right. \tag{4.19}$$

$$+ \left. \lambda T_0 v(x) + \sum_{j \in J_1(x)} \mu_j^{d_j(x)} T_j v(x) \right] = Bv(x)$$

where $Bv(x)$ denotes the transform operator for the function $v(x)$.

In this representation

$$\lambda_x = \left(\lambda - \sum_{j \in J_1(x)} \mu_j^{d_j(x) \, d_j(x)} \right)$$

is the total intensity of a transition from state x,

$$C_1(x) = \sum_{j \in J_1(x)} \sum_{d_j \neq d_j(x)} \mu_j^{d_j(x) \, d_j} v(S_j^{d_j} x)$$

is the loss rate due to a transition of the service phase without decision making,

$$C_2(x) = \sum_{\substack{j \in J_1(x) \\ q(x)=0}} \mu^{d_j(x)} v(S_j^{-d_j} x)$$

is the loss rate due to a service completion with an empty queue,

$$T_0 v(x) = \min \left\{ v(S_0 x), \sum_{d_k=1}^{m_k} \eta_k^{d_k} v(S_k^{d_k} x) : k = \overline{1, K} \right\} \tag{4.20}$$

is the minimal loss in case of a new job arrival,

$$T_j v(x) = T_0 v(S_j^{-d_j} S_0^{-1} x) \mathbf{1}_{\{q(x)>0\}} \tag{4.21}$$

is the minimal loss in case of a service completion and the appropriate decision making.

It is possible to see from this system of equations that the optimal policy

$$f = \{f(x) : x \in E\}$$

minimizes the function $b = \{b(x,a) : x \in E, a \in A(x)\}$ with

$$b(x,a) = \mathbf{1}_{\{a=0\}} v(x + e_0) + \sum_{1 \le k \le K} \mathbf{1}_{\{a=k\}} \sum_{1 \le d_k \le m_k} \eta_k^{d_k} v(S_k^{d_k} x) \qquad (4.22)$$

and has the form

$$f(x) = \operatorname{argmin}[b(x,a) :\ a \in A(x)]. \qquad (4.23)$$

This means that it is determined by the value function of the model

$$v = \{v(x) :\ x \in E\},$$

which is a solution of the optimality equation (4.19).

4.4.2 Monotonicity properties. Dependence on service phases

We arrange the servers for the NJM–problem in order of their mean service times increasing (or their mean service intensities decreasing), i.e.

$$0 < \overline{\mu}_1^{\ -1} \le \overline{\mu}_2^{\ -1} \le \cdots \le \overline{\mu}_K^{\ -1}$$

which is the same as

$$0 < -\eta_1^T M_1^{-1} \vec{\mathbf{1}} \le -\eta_2^T M_2^{-1} \vec{\mathbf{1}} \le \cdots \le -\eta_K^T M_K^{-1} \vec{\mathbf{1}}. \qquad (4.24)$$

For the PCM–problem let the servers be arranged in increasing order of their mean usage cost $\gamma_k = -c_k \eta_k^T M_k^{-1} \vec{\mathbf{1}}$, i.e.

$$0 < -c_1 \eta_1^T M_1^{-1} \vec{\mathbf{1}} \le -c_2 \eta_2^T M_2^{-1} \vec{\mathbf{1}} \le \cdots \le -c_K \eta_K^T M_K^{-1} \vec{\mathbf{1}} \qquad (4.25)$$

with different groups of parameters

- $$0 \le -\eta_1^T M_1^{-1} \vec{\mathbf{1}} \le -\eta_2^T M_2^{-1} \vec{\mathbf{1}} \le \cdots \le -\eta_K^T M_K^{-1} \vec{\mathbf{1}}, \qquad (4.26)$$
  $$c_1 \le c_2 \le \cdots \le c_K;$$

- $$0 \le -\eta_1^T M_1^{-1} \vec{\mathbf{1}} \le -\eta_2^T M_2^{-1} \vec{\mathbf{1}} \le \cdots \le -\eta_K^T M_K^{-1} \vec{\mathbf{1}}, \qquad (4.27)$$
  $$c_1 > c_2 > \cdots > c_K;$$

- $$0 < -\eta_K^T M_K^{-1} \vec{\mathbf{1}} < \cdots < -\eta_2^T M_2^{-1} \vec{\mathbf{1}} < -\eta_1^T M_1^{-1} \vec{\mathbf{1}}, \qquad (4.28)$$
  $$c_1 \le c_2 \le \cdots \le c_K;$$

The numerical results and our assumptions allow us to formulate the basic quantitative properties of optimal control policy for the system under study by means of the Conjectures 4.4 and 4.5, introduced for the queue with Erlangian service.

Now we introduce a partial order in E with respect to shift operators S_0 and $S_i^{d_i}$ by

$$S_0 x \geq x, \quad S_i^{d_i} x \geq x, \, i \in J_0(x), \, d_i = \overline{1, m_i};$$
$$S_i^\beta x \geq S_i^\alpha x, \, i \in J_1(x), \, \mu_i^\alpha \geq \mu_i^\beta, \, \alpha \leq \beta.$$

The states $S_i^{d_i} x$ and $S_j^{d_j} x$ for different servers $i, j \in J_0(x)$, where $d_i = \overline{1, m_i}$ and $d_j = \overline{1, m_j}$, can have different possible orders but with some condition that will be discussed later.

Similar to Theorem 4.7 of the previously analyzed queue with Erlangian service consider the following statement:

Theorem 4.16 *Assume that the bounded, nondecreasing function $v(x)$ has the following properties with respect to introduced in E partial order*

1. $v(S_0 x) \geq v(x), \, v(S_i^{d_i} x) \geq v(x), \, d_i = \overline{1, m_i};$
2. $v(S_i^\beta x) \geq v(S_i^\alpha x), \, i \in J_0(x), \, \mu_i^\alpha \geq \mu_i^\beta.$

Then the operator B introduced in (4.19) retains these properties for the value function of the model.

Proof: At first consider the operator T_0. For the inequality 1 we have

$$T_0 v(S_0 x) = \min_{k \in A_0(S_0 x)} \{ v(S_0^2 x), \sum_{d_k=1}^{m_k} \eta_k^{d_k} v(S_k^{d_k} S_0 x) \}$$

$$\geq \min_{k \in A_0(S_0 x)} \{ v(S_0 x), \sum_{d_k=1}^{m_k} \eta_k^{d_k} v(S_k^{d_k} x) \}$$

$$\geq \min_{k \in A_0(x)} \{ v(S_0 x), \sum_{d_k=1}^{m_k} \eta_k^{d_k} v(S_k^{d_k} x) \} \geq T_0 v(x),$$

where the first inequality follows from the assumption that the function $v(x)$ is nondecreasing and the second one follows from the relation $A(S_0 x) = A(x)$. The same sequence of relations is used to prove the inequality $T_0 v(S_i^{d_i} x) \geq T_0 v(x)$,

where $A(S_i^{d_i}x) \subset A(x)$.
For the inequality 2 we get

$$
\begin{aligned}
T_0 v(S_i^\beta x) &= \min_{k \in A(S_i^\beta x)} \{v(S_0 S_i^\beta x), \sum_{d_k=1}^{m_k} \eta_k^{d_k} v(S_k^{d_k} S_i^\beta x)\} \\
&\geq \min_{k \in A(S_i^\alpha x)} \{v(S_0 S_i^\alpha x), \sum_{d_k=1}^{m_k} \eta_k^{d_k} v(S_k^{d_k} S_i^\alpha x)\} = T_0 v(S_i^\alpha x),
\end{aligned}
$$

taking into account the assumptions that the function $v(x)$ is nondecreasing with respect to shift operators $S_i^\alpha x$ and $S_i^\beta x$ when $\mu_i^\alpha \geq \mu_i^\beta$, $\alpha \leq \beta$, and $A(S_i^\alpha x) = A(S_i^\beta x)$. The operators T_j preserves the mentioned properties due to the definition (4.21).
It is obvious that the operator B satisfies the inequality 1 by virtue of the properties of the function $v(x)$ and the operators T_0, T_j.
For the inequality 2 and two-state service process we have

$$
\begin{aligned}
Bv(S_i^\beta x) - Bv(S_i^\alpha x) &= [c(S_i^\beta x) - c(S_i^\alpha x)] + \lambda[T_0 v(S_i^\beta x) - T_0 v(S_i^\alpha x)] \\
&+ \sum_{j \in J_1(x)} \mu_j^{d_j} [T_j v(S_i^\beta x) - T_j v(S_i^\alpha)x] + \sum_{j \in J_1(x)} \sum_{\substack{r=1 \\ r \neq d_j(x)}}^{m_j} \mu_j^{d_j\,r} [v(S_j^r S_i^\beta x) - v(S_j^r S_i^\alpha x)] \\
&+ [\mu_i^\beta T_i v(S_i^\beta x) + \mu_i^{\beta\,\alpha} v(S_i^\alpha x) + (\mu_i^\alpha + \mu_i^{\alpha\beta}) v(S_i^\beta x)] \\
&- [\mu_i^\alpha T_i v(S_i^\alpha x) + \mu_i^{\alpha\beta} v(S_i^\beta x) + (\mu_i^\beta + \mu_i^{\beta\alpha}) v(S_i^\alpha x)].
\end{aligned}
$$

The first four items on the right–hand side of this expression are nonnegative. Indeed,

$$
c(S_i^\beta x) - c(S_i^\alpha x) = c_i + c(x) - c_i - c(x) = 0,
$$

therefore the function $c(x)$ is constant with respect to the shifts S_i^β and S_i^α.
For last two items we have

$$
\begin{aligned}
&[\mu_i^\beta T_i v(S_i^\beta x) + \mu_i^{\beta\,\alpha} v(S_i^\alpha x) + (\mu_i^\alpha + \mu_i^{\alpha\beta}) v(S_i^\beta x)] \\
&- [\mu_i^\alpha T_i v(S_i^\alpha x) + \mu_i^{\alpha\,\beta} v(S_i^\beta x) + (\mu_i^\beta + \mu_i^{\beta\,\alpha}) v(S_i^\alpha x)] \\
&= \mu_i^\beta [v(S_i^\beta x) - T_i v(S_i^\alpha x)] - \mu_i^\beta [v(S_i^\alpha x) - T_i v(S_i^\beta x)] \\
&= \mu_i^\alpha [v(S_i^\beta x) - v(x)] - \mu_i^\beta [v(S_i^\alpha x) - v(x)] \geq 0.
\end{aligned}
$$

The last expression is nonnegative by virtue of the property $T_i v(S_i^\alpha x) = T_i v(S_i^\beta x) = T_0 v(S_0^{-1} x) = v(x)$ and $\mu_i^\alpha \geq \mu_i^\beta$.

Finally, the theorem follows from the fact that the value function of the model $v = \{v(x) : x \in E\}$ is a fixed point of operator B.
□

According to condition $v(S_k^\beta x) \geq v(S_k^\alpha x)$ we expect that with decreasing service rate μ_k^β the less productive server will be used more often, since then the chance is higher that the future arrivals see a shorter queue or a smaller processing cost. Therefore we can require that

$$f(S_k^\beta x) = 0 \quad \Rightarrow \quad f(S_k^\alpha x) = 0,\ \alpha \leq \beta;$$

It is possible to rewrite the last relations in accordance with the definition of optimal policy through condition (4.23)

$$v(S_0 S_k^\beta x) \leq \sum_{d_l=1}^{m_l} \eta_l^{d_l} v(S_l^{d_l} S_k^\beta x) \quad \Rightarrow \quad v(S_0 S_k^\alpha x) \leq \sum_{d_l=1}^{m_l} \eta_l^{d_l} v(S_l^{d_l} S_k^\alpha x);$$

The last inequalities can be expressed in terms of the operators as follows

$$\left(S_0 - \sum_{d_k=1}^{m_k} \eta_k^{d_k} S_k^{d_k}\right)(S_i^\alpha - S_i^\beta)v(x) \leq 0,\ \alpha \leq \beta;\ . \tag{4.29}$$

Thus, if the optimal policy has threshold type then there exist finite thresholds for each service phase.

Now consider the property of the value function $v(x)$ with respect to an optimal decision which of the available servers should be used by the controller. We have not been able to successfully analyze even the simplified system $M/M, PH_{m_i}/K$ where the fastest server is exponential with service intensity μ_j and the slower one has a PH service time distribution with representation (η_i, M_i) of dimension m_i, nor the system $M/PH_{m_j}, M/K$ with a faster PH server, nor the somewhat more general $M/PH_{m_i}, PH_{m_j}/2$ system with the condition $(\eta_j^T M_j^{-1} \vec{\mathbf{1}})^{-1} \geq (-\eta_i^T M_i^{-1} \vec{\mathbf{1}})^{-1}$. For such queue with PH heterogeneous servers only method which can be applied to investigate the optimal policy structure is the numerical analysis (see Section 4.4.4) The numerical results allow us to expect, additionally to the inequalities in Theorem 4.16, the following property:

Conjecture 4.17 *If for some order of the points $S_i^{d_i} x$ and $S_j^{d_j} x$, where $d_i = \overline{1, m_i}$*

and $d_j = \overline{1, m_j}$, *some bounded positive function* $v(x)$ *satisfies the conditions*

3. $\displaystyle\sum_{d_i=1}^{m_i} \eta^{d_i} v(S_i^{d_i} x) \ge \sum_{d_j=1}^{m_j} \eta^{d_j} v(S_j^{d_j} x),\ i \ge j,\ d_i = \overline{1, m_i},\ d_j = \overline{1, m_j},$

$\quad - c_j \eta_j^T M_j^{-1} \vec{\mathbf{1}} \le -c_i \eta_i^T M_i^{-1} \vec{\mathbf{1}},$

then the operator B *retains this property for the value function of the model.*

Thus, we first expect and numerically confirm that the optimal control for the NJM– and the PCM–problem under conditions (4.26) and (4.27) consists in using the fastest available (NJM–problem) server with respect to arrangement (4.24) and the server with minimal mean usage cost (PCM–problem) according to arrangement (4.25). This result does not hold for the system under conditions (4.25) and (4.28). And further, an optimal policy requires to switch on the servers only if necessary, that is the optimal control is of a threshold type. Regarding the switching rule of some servers we can show that under Conjecture 4.17 the value function $v = \{v(x) : x \in E\}$ has increments $\sum_{d_i=1}^{m_i} \eta_i^{d_i} v(S_i^{d_i} x) - v(S_0 x)$ that are monotone in S_0 that assumes the inequality

$$(1 - S_0)(S_0 - \sum_{d_k=1}^{m_k} \eta_k^{d_k} S_k^{d_k}) v(x) \le 0,\ k \in J_0(x). \tag{4.30}$$

Theorem 4.18 *The value function of the model* $v = \{v(x) : x \in E\}$ *satisfies the property (4.30) under Conjecture 4.17.*

Proof: According to Conjecture 4.17, i.e. if the optimal control consists in activating the maximal mean intensity server (the NJM–problem) or the minimal mean usage cost server (the PCM–problem) if necessary, then only two solutions are possible in each state x: $f(x) = 0$ (not to service the job) or $f(x) = k$, i.e. to use the fastest server available in the state x (the NJM–problem) or the server with the lowest mean usage cost (the PCM–problem)). Here k obeys for the NJM–problem

$$\overline{\mu}_k = (-\eta_k^T M_k^{-1} \mathbf{1})^{-1} = \max\{(-\eta_l^T M_l^{-1} \mathbf{1})^{-1} : l \in J_0(x)\}$$

and for the PCM–problem

$$\frac{c_k}{\overline{\mu}_k} = -c_k \eta_k^T M_k^{-1} \mathbf{1} = \min\{-c_l \eta_l^T M_l^{-1} \mathbf{1} : l \in J_0(x)\}.$$

The set $A(x)$ of controls is independent of the shift S_0 (for the PCM–problem it is only in the cases (4.26) and (4.27)).

Below we show that the operator T_0 defined by (4.20) retains property (4.30). Therefore, it is necessary to check whether these properties are satisfied for the function $T_0 v(x) = \min\{v(S_0 x), \sum_{d_k=1}^{m_k} \eta_k(d_k) v(S_k^{d_k} x)\}$ if it is satisfied for some function $v(x)$. We have to prove the following inequality

$$(1 - S_0)(S_0 - \sum_{d_k=1}^{m_k} \eta_k^{d_k} S_k^{d_k} x) T_0 v(x) \le 0,$$

or in detail

$$\min\{v(S_0^2 x), \sum_{d_k=1}^{m_k} \eta_k^{d_k} v(S_0 S_k^{d_k} x)\} - \quad (4.31)$$

$$\sum_{d_k=1}^{m_k} \eta_k^{d_k} \min\{v(S_0 S_k^{d_k} x), \sum_{d_l=1}^{m_l} \eta_l^{d_l} v(S_l^{d_l} S_k^{d_k} x)\} -$$

$$\min\{v(S_0^3 x), \sum_{d_k=1}^{m_k} v(S_0^2 S_k^{d_k} x)\} +$$

$$\sum_{d_k=1}^{m_k} \eta_k(d_k) \min\{v(S_0^2 S_k^1 x), \sum_{d_l=1}^{m_l} \eta_l^{d_l} v(S_0 S_l^{d_l} S_k^{d_k} x)\} \le 0.$$

To prove this assertion for each point $x \in E$ we decompose it in several cases.

1. First we consider the case when the optimal control in the second and third items of (4.31) consists in sending the job to the queue, that is $f(S_k^{d_k} x) = f(S_0^2 x) = 0$, $d_k = \overline{1, m_k}$. For this case we have

$$(1 - S_0)(S_0 - \sum_{d_k=1}^{m_k} \eta_k^{d_k} S_k^{d_k}) T_0 v(x)$$

$$= T_0 v(S_0 x) - \sum_{d_k=1}^{m_k} \eta_k^{d_k} v(S_0 S_k^{d_k} x) - v(S_0^3 x) + \sum_{d_k=1}^{m_k} \eta_k^{d_k} v(S_0^2 S_k^{d_k} x)$$

$$= (1 - S_0)(S_0 - \sum_{d_k=1}^{m_k} \eta_k^{d_k} S_k^{d_k}) v(S_0 x) \le 0.$$

2. Now consider the case when the optimal control for the second and third items of (4.31) coincide and consists in sending the job to some idle server, that is $f(S_k^{d_k}x) = f(S_0^2 x) = f \neq 0$, $d_k = \overline{1, m_k}$. In this case we have

$$
(1 - S_0)(S_0 - \sum_{d_k=1}^{m_k} \eta_k^{d_k} S_k^{d_k}) T_0 v(x)
$$

$$
= T_0 v(S_0 x) - \sum_{d_k=1}^{m_k} \sum_{d_f=1}^{m_f} \eta_k^{d_k} \eta_f^{d_f} v(S_k^{d_k} S_f^{d_f} x)
$$

$$
- \sum_{d_k=1}^{m_k} \eta_f^{d_f} v(S_0^2 S_f^{d_f} x) + \sum_{d_k=1}^{m_k} \eta_k^{d_k} T_0 v(S_0 S_k^{d_k} x)
$$

$$
\leq \sum_{d_f=1}^{m_f} \eta_f^{d_f} v(S_0 S_f^{d_f} x) - \sum_{d_k=1}^{m_k} \sum_{d_f=1}^{m_f} \eta_k^{d_k} \eta_f^{d_f} v(S_k^{d_k} S_f^{d_f} x)
$$

$$
- \sum_{d_k=1}^{m_k} \eta_f^{d_f} v(S_0^2 S_f^{d_f} x) + \sum_{d_k=1}^{m_k} \sum_{d_f=1}^{m_f} \eta_k^{d_k} \eta_f^{d_f} v(S_0 S_k^{d_k} S_f^{d_f} x)
$$

$$
= \sum_{d_f=1}^{m_f} \eta_f^{d_f} (1 - S_0)(S_0 - \sum_{d_k=1}^{m_k} \eta_k^{d_k} S_k^{d_k}) v(S_f^{d_f} x) \leq 0
$$

by virtue of inequalities

$$
(1 - S_0)(S_0 - \sum_{d_k=1}^{m_k} \eta_k^{d_k} S_k^{d_k}) v(S_f^{d_f} x) \leq 0,
$$

which form the sum of negative values.

3. Let the optimal control in third item be $f(S_0^2 x) = 0$ and in second item be $f(S_k^{d_k}x) = l \neq 0$, $d_k = \overline{1, m_k}$.
By summing inequalities (4.30) for the function $v(x)$ at the points $S_k^{d_k}$, $d_k = \overline{1, m_k}$ and $S_0 x$, respectively, i.e.

$$
\sum_{d_k=1}^{m_k} \eta_k^{d_k} v(S_0 S_k^{d_k} x) - \sum_{d_k=1}^{m_k} \sum_{d_l=1}^{m_l} \eta_k^{d_k} \eta_l^{d_l} v(S_k^{d_k} S_l^{d_l} x)
$$

$$
- \sum_{d_k=1}^{m_k} \eta_k^{d_k} v(S_0^2 S_k^{d_k} x) + \sum_{d_k=1}^{m_k} \sum_{d_l=1}^{m_l} \eta_k^{d_k} \eta_l^{d_l} v(S_0 S_k^{d_k} S_l^{d_l} x) \leq 0,
$$

and

$$v(S_0^2 x) - \sum_{d_k=1}^{m_k} \eta_k^{d_k} v(S_0 S_k^{d_k} x) - v(S_0^3 x) + \sum_{d_k=1}^{m_k} \eta_k^{d_k} v(S_0^2 S_k^{d_k} x) \leq 0$$

we get the inequality

$$v(S_0^2 x) - \sum_{d_k=1}^{m_k} \sum_{d_l=1}^{m_l} \eta_k^{d_k} \eta_l^{d_l} v(S_k^{d_k} S_l^{d_l} x) - v(S_0^3 x) + \sum_{d_k=1}^{m_k} \sum_{d_l=1}^{m_l} \eta_k^{d_k} \eta_l^{d_l} v(S_0 S_k^{d_k} S_l^{d_l} x) \leq 0.$$

Finally we obtain

$$(1 - S_0)(S_0 - \sum_{d_k=1}^{m_k} \eta_k^{d_k} S_k^{d_k}) T_0 v(x)$$

$$= T_0 v(S_0 x) - \sum_{d_k=1}^{m_k} \sum_{d_l=1}^{m_l} \eta_k^{d_k} \eta_l^{d_l} v(S_k^{d_k} S_l^{d_l} x) - v(S_0^3 x) + \sum_{d_k=1}^{m_k} \eta_k^{d_k} T_0 v(S_0 S_k^{d_k} x)$$

$$\leq v(S_0^2 x) - \sum_{d_k=1}^{m_k} \sum_{d_l=1}^{m_l} \eta_k^{d_k} \eta_l^{d_l} v(S_k^{d_k} S_l^{d_l} x) - v(S_0^3 x) + \sum_{d_k=1}^{m_k} \sum_{d_l=1}^{m_l} \eta_k^{d_k} \eta_l^{d_l} v(S_0 S_k^{d_k} S_l^{d_l} x) \leq 0.$$

4. Now consider the second item of inequality (4.31)

$$\sum_{d_k=1}^{m_k} \eta_k^{d_k} \min\{v(S_0 S_k^{d_k} x), \sum_{d_l=1}^{m_l} \eta_l^{d_l} v(S_l^{d_l} S_k^{d_k} x)\}.$$

Taking into account the inequalities (4.29) we have

$$v(S_0 S_k^{\beta} x) \leq \sum_{d_l=1}^{m_l} \eta_l^{d_l} v(S_l^{d_l} S_k^{\beta} x) \Rightarrow v(S_0 S_k^{\alpha} x) \leq \sum_{d_l=1}^{m_l} \eta_l^{d_l} v(S_l^{d_l} S_k^{\alpha} x),$$

$$v(S_0 S_k^{\alpha} x) \geq \sum_{d_l=1}^{m_l} \eta_l^{d_l} v(S_l^{d_l} S_k^{\alpha} x) \Rightarrow v(S_0 S_k^{\beta} x) \geq \sum_{d_l=1}^{m_l} \eta_l^{d_l} v(S_l^{d_l} S_k^{\beta} x)$$

if $\mu_k^{\alpha} \geq \mu_k^{\beta}$.

Therefore, we have to consider two more cases, namely when for the second item of (4.31) it is optimal to use the queue as the optimal decision for a phase in α on the k-th server and to use the idle server if the phases is in β, taking into account

that $\mu_k^\alpha \geq \mu_k^\beta$, $\alpha \cup \beta = \overline{1,m_k}$
In this case we have

$$\sum_{d_k=1}^{m_k} \eta_k^{d_k} \min\{v(S_0 S_k^{d_k} x), \sum_{d_l=1}^{m_l} \eta_l^{d_l} v(S_l^{d_l} S_k^{d_k} x)\}$$

$$= \sum_\alpha \sum_{d_l=1}^{m_l} \eta_k^\alpha v(S_k^\alpha S_l^{d_l} x) + \sum_\beta v(S_0 S_k^\beta x).$$

For the third item of (4.31) there exist two subcases, namely $f(S_0^2 x) = k$ and $f(S_0^2 x) = 0$. Therefore, in the first subcase for the inequality (4.31) we have

$$(1 - S_0)(S_0 - \sum_{d_k=1}^{m_k} \eta_k^{d_k} S_k^{d_k}) T_0 v(x)$$

$$= T_0 v(S_0 x) - \sum_\alpha \sum_{d_l=1}^{m_l} \eta_k^\alpha \eta_l^{d_l} v(S_k^\alpha S_l^{d_l} x) - \sum_\beta \eta_k^\beta v(S_0 S_k^\beta x)$$

$$- \sum_{d_k=1}^{m_k} \eta_k^{d_k} v(S_0^2 S_k^{d_k} x) + \sum_{d_k=1}^{m_k} \eta_k^{d_k} T_0 v(S_0 S_k^{d_k} x)$$

$$\leq \sum_\alpha \eta_k^\alpha v(S_0 S_k^\alpha x) - \sum_\alpha \sum_{d_l=1}^{m_l} \eta_k^\alpha \eta_l^{d_l} v(S_k^\alpha S_l^{d_l} x)$$

$$- \sum_\alpha \eta_k^\alpha v(S_0^2 S_k^\alpha x) + \sum_\alpha \sum_{d_l=1}^{m_l} \eta_k^\alpha \eta_l^{d_l} v(S_0 S_k^\alpha S_l^{d_l} x)$$

$$= \sum_\alpha \eta_k^\alpha (1 - S_0)(S_0 - \sum_{d_l=1}^{m_l} \eta_l^{d_l} S_l^{d_l}) v(S_k^{d_k} x) \leq 0,$$

by virtue of the inequality (4.30).
In the second subcase, when $f(S_0^2 x) = 0$, we consider the sum of inequalities

$$\sum_\alpha \eta_k^\alpha v(S_0 S_k^\alpha x) - \sum_\alpha \sum_{d_l=1}^{m_l} \eta_k^\alpha \eta_l^{d_l} v(S_k^\alpha S_l^{d_l} x)$$

$$- \sum_\alpha \eta_k^\alpha v(S_0^2 S_k^\alpha x) + \sum_\alpha \sum_{d_l=1}^{m_l} \eta_k^\alpha \eta_l^{d_l} v(S_0 S_k^\alpha S_l^{d_l} x) \leq 0$$

and

$$v(S_0^2 x) - \sum_{d_k=1}^{m_k} \eta_k^{d_k} v(S_0 S_k^{d_k} x) - v(S_0^3 x) + \sum_{d_k=1}^{m_k} \eta_k^{d_k} v(S_0^2 S_k^{d_k} x) \leq 0.$$

As a result of the sum we obtain the following inequality

$$v(S_0^2 x) - \sum_\alpha \sum_{d_l=1}^{m_l} \eta_k^\alpha \eta_l^{d_l} - \sum_\beta \eta_k^\beta v(S_0 S_k^\alpha x)$$

$$- v(S_0^3 x) + \sum_\alpha \sum_{d_l=1}^{m_l} \eta_k^\alpha \eta_l^{d_l} v(S_0 S_k^\alpha S_l^{d_l} x) + \sum_\beta \eta_k^\beta v(S_0^2 S_k^\beta x) \leq 0.$$

Using the last expression we get

$$(1 - S_0)(S_0 - \sum_{d_k=1}^{m_k} \eta_k^{d_k} S_k^{d_k}) T_0 v(x)$$

$$= T_0 v(S_0 x) - \sum_\alpha \sum_{d_l=1}^{m_l} \eta_k^\alpha \eta_l^{d_l} v(S_k^\alpha S_l^{d_l} x) - \sum_\beta \eta_k^\beta v(S_0 S_k^\beta x)$$

$$- v(S_0^3 x) + \sum_{d_k=1}^{m_k} \eta_k^{d_k} T_0 v(S_0 S_k^{d_k} x)$$

$$\leq v(S_0^2 x) - \sum_\alpha \sum_{d_l=1}^{m_l} \eta_k^\alpha \eta_l^{d_l} - \sum_\beta \eta_k^\beta v(S_0 S_k^\alpha x)$$

$$- v(S_0^3 x) + \sum_\alpha \sum_{d_l=1}^{m_l} \eta_k^\alpha \eta_l^{d_l} v(S_0 S_k^\alpha S_l^{d_l} x) + \sum_\beta \eta_k^\beta v(S_0^2 S_k^\beta x) \leq 0,$$

taking into account that $\alpha \cup \beta = \overline{1, m_k}$.
For the boundary points $q(x) = B$, $J_0(x) = \emptyset$, the inequality (4.31) is also satisfied since the shift operators are defined by (4.1). Finally, the operators T_j retain the property (4.30) by virtue of the definition (4.21).

Now, we can prove that under Conjecture (4.17) the value function of the model $v = \{v(x) : x \in E\}$ satisfies the property (4.30). This assertion follows from the fact that the property (4.30) is retained for linear operations defining the operator B given by (4.19). The function $c(x)$ satisfies the condition (4.30)

$$(1 - S_0)(S_0 - \sum_{d_k=1}^{m_k} \eta_k^{d_k} S_k^{d_k})c(x)$$

$$= c(S_0 x) - \sum_{d_k=1}^{m_k} \eta_k^{d_k} c(S_k^{d_k} x) - c(S_0^2) + \sum_{d_k=1}^{m_k} \eta_k^{d_k} c(S_0 S_k^{d_k} x)$$

$$= c_0 + c(x) - [c_k + c(x)] \sum_{d_k=1}^{m_k} \eta_k^{d_k} - 2c_0 - c(x) + [c_0 + c_k + c(x)] \sum_{d_k=1}^{m_k} \eta_k^{d_k} = 0.$$

From monotone convergence

$$\sum_{d_k=1}^{m_k} \eta_k^{d_k} \lim_{n \to \infty} B^n c(S_k^{d_k} x) = \sum_{d_k=1}^{m_k} \eta_k^{d_k} v(S_k^{d_k} x)$$

we obtain necessary result.
□

We note that this result can be proved analogously for the PCM–problem under condition (4.28) but only if the number of servers $K = 2$. Otherwise we use numerical analysis which confirmed the assertion for multi-server queue.

By virtue of Theorem 4.18 under Conjecture 4.17 in the case of light traffic $\lambda < \overline{\mu}_K$ using iteratively the optimality equation (4.19) for the second server if the state $x = (0, 0, \ldots, 0)$ we get

$$\begin{pmatrix} v(S_0^{q_2^*-1} S_1^1 x) \\ v(S_0^{q_2^*-1} S_1^2 x) \\ \cdot \\ \cdot \\ \cdot \\ v(S_0^{q_2^*-1} S_1^{m_1} x) \end{pmatrix} = -M_1^{-1} \vec{1}(c_1 + (q_2^* - 1)c_0)$$

$$+ \vec{1} \left[\frac{(q_2^* - 1)c_1}{\overline{\mu}_1} + \frac{c_0(q_2^* - 2)(q_2^* - 1)}{2\overline{\mu}_1} \right].$$

If q_2^* is a threshold for using the second server the following inequality holds

$$\sum_{d_2=1}^{m_2} \eta_2^{d_2} v(S_0^{q_2^*-1} S_1^{d_1} S_2^{d_2} x) \leq v(S_0^{q_2^*} S_1^{d_1} x)$$

For the last inequality we have

$$\sum_{d_2=1}^{m_2} \eta_2^{d_2} v(S_0^{q_2^*-1} S_1^{d_1} S_2^{d_2} x) = \vec{1}\frac{c_2}{\bar{\mu}_2} + v(S_0^{q_2^*-1} S_1^{d_1} x) \leq v(S_0^{q_2^*} S_1^{d_1} x)$$

and now we obtain the vector of thresholds for the second server for each service phase

$$\begin{pmatrix} q_2(1) \\ q_2(2) \\ \cdot \\ \cdot \\ \cdot \\ q_2(m_1) \end{pmatrix} \leq \begin{pmatrix} q_2^*(1) \\ q_2^*(2) \\ \cdot \\ \cdot \\ \cdot \\ q_2^*(m_1) \end{pmatrix} = \vec{1}\frac{\bar{\mu}_1}{c_0}\left[\frac{c_2}{\bar{\mu}_2} - \frac{c_1}{\bar{\mu}_1}\right] + M_1^{-1}\vec{1}\bar{\mu}_1 + \vec{1}.$$

For the value of "mean" threshold we have

$$\sum_{d_1=1}^{m_1} \eta_1^{d_1} q_2^*(d_1) = \overline{q_2^*} = \frac{\bar{\mu}_1}{c_0}\left[\frac{c_2}{\bar{\mu}_2} - \frac{c_1}{\bar{\mu}_1}\right].$$

In general case $q_j^* = q^*(d_1, d_2, \ldots, d_{j-1})$ and the "mean" threshold formula has the following form

$$\overline{q_j^*} = \frac{1}{c_0}\left[c_j \eta_j^T M_j^{-1} \vec{1} \sum_{i=1}^{j-1} (\eta_i^T M_i^{-1} \vec{1})^{-1} - \sum_{i=1}^{j-1} c_i\right],$$

4.4.3 Algorithm

To analyze the behavior of optimal strategies for the NJM–problem the servers will be arranged in order (4.24) and for the PCM–problem in order (4.25) under conditions (4.26)–(4.28).

Strategy estimation. For a given policy $f = \{f_n(x) : x = \overline{1, I}\}$ solve the equation

$$v_n(x) = \frac{1}{\lambda_x}\left(c(x) + C_1(x) + C_2(x) - g_n\right)$$

$$+ \frac{1}{\lambda_x}\lambda\left(\mathbf{1}_{\{f_n(x)=0\}}v_n(S_0x) + \mathbf{1}_{\{f_n(x)=k\}}\sum_{d_k=1}^{m_k}\eta_k^{d_k}v_n(S_k^{d_k}x)\right) +$$

$$+ \frac{1}{\lambda_x}\sum_{\substack{j\in J_1(x)\\q(x)>0}}\mu_j^{d_j(x)}$$

$$\left(\mathbf{1}_{\{f_n(S_0^{-1}S_j^{-d_j}x)=0\}}v_n(S_j^{-d_j}x) + \mathbf{1}_{\{f_n(S_0^{-1}S_j^{-d_j}x)=k\}}\sum_{d_k=1}^{m_k}\eta_k^{d_k}v_n(S_k^{d_k}S_j^{-d_j}S_0^{-1})\right)$$

for all $x \in E$ under the condition $v(0) = 0$. This can be done up to an accuracy ε by successive approximation.

Strategy improvement. For a given solution $v_n = \{v_n(x) : x \in E\}$ find a new policy $f_{n+1} = \{f_{n+1}(x) : x \in E\}$, which minimizes the Bellman function (4.22) of the model:

$$f_{n+1}(x) = \underset{k\in A(x)}{\mathrm{argmin}}\begin{cases}\sum_{d_k=1}^{m_k}\eta_k^{d_k}v_n(x + d_ke_k), & k = \overline{1,K}\\ v_n(x + e_0), & k = 0\end{cases}$$

The algorithm stops when two successive iterations yield the same policy.

For a description of system state transitions by virtue of a one-dimensional representation we use the formulas (4.15)-(4.17).

4.4.4 Numerical analysis

Consider the system $M/PH_{het}/5/100$ with five states for each PH server. The control table for an arrival intensity $\lambda = 0.01$ is presented in Table 4.20. The matrices $M_k = [\mu_k^{ij}]$ as well as service intensities from the phases μ_k^i and the initial service phase distributions η_k, $k = \overline{1,5}$ are given below. We note that for all servers we keep the elements μ_k^{ij}, $i \neq j$ of matrices M_k and $\eta_k^{d_i}$ of vectors η_k constant. We change only the service intensities μ_k^i. Therefore, a detailed representation of the matrix M_k is given only for the first server. For the other servers we present only the service intensities μ_k^i.

$$
M_1 = \begin{pmatrix}
-2.14 & 0.01 & 0.05 & 0.03 & 0.04 \\
0.05 & -2.09 & 0.01 & 0.02 & 0.03 \\
0.04 & 0.02 & -1.96 & 0.02 & 0.01 \\
0.03 & 0.01 & 0.01 & -1.85 & 0.02 \\
0.02 & 0.02 & 0.02 & -0.01 & -1.80
\end{pmatrix}, \; \eta_1 = \begin{pmatrix} 0.30 \\ 0.25 \\ 0.20 \\ 0.15 \\ 0.10 \end{pmatrix}
$$

$$
\mu_1 = \begin{pmatrix} 2.01 \\ 1.98 \\ 1.87 \\ 1.78 \\ 1.73 \end{pmatrix}, \; \mu_2 = \begin{pmatrix} 0.75 \\ 0.72 \\ 0.61 \\ 0.52 \\ 0.47 \end{pmatrix}, \; \mu_3 = \begin{pmatrix} 0.65 \\ 0.62 \\ 0.51 \\ 0.42 \\ 0.37 \end{pmatrix}, \; \mu_4 = \begin{pmatrix} 0.58 \\ 0.55 \\ 0.44 \\ 0.35 \\ 0.30 \end{pmatrix}, \; \mu_5 = \begin{pmatrix} 0.44 \\ 0.41 \\ 0.30 \\ 0.21 \\ 0.16 \end{pmatrix} .
$$

The mean service intensities of the PH-type servers are given in Table 4.19. In this control table only selected states are given because of the large number of system states. One can see that similar to the previous model the optimal control is of a threshold type and depends on the service phases and the fastest available server, in the sense of the largest mean service intensity, has to be switched on if necessary.

Table 4.19 Values of initial system parameters for $M/PH/5/100$ queue

i	1	2	3	4	5
$\overline{\mu_i}$	1.90	0.63	0.52	0.45	0.30

Table 4.20 Optimal control for some system states

System State x $(d_1, d_2, d_3, d_4, d_5)$	Queue length $q(x)$													
	0	1	2	3	4	5	6	7	8	9	10	11	12	...
$(0,*,*,*,*)$	**1**	1	1	1	1	1	1	1	1	1	1	1	1	
$(1,0,*,*,*)$	0	0	**2**	2	2	2	2	2	2	2	2	2	2	
$(5,0,*,*,*)$	0	**2**	2	2	2	2	2	2	2	2	2	2	2	
$(1,1,0,*,*)$	0	0	**3**	3	3	3	3	3	3	3	3	3	3	
$(2,4,0,*,*)$	0	0	**3**	3	3	3	3	3	3	3	3	3	3	
$(5,5,0,*,*)$	0	0	**3**	3	3	3	3	3	3	3	3	3	3	
$(1,1,1,0,*)$	0	0	0	**4**	4	4	4	4	4	4	4	4	4	
$(4,3,1,0,*)$	0	0	0	**4**	4	4	4	4	4	4	4	4	4	
$(5,5,4,0,*)$	0	0	0	**4**	4	4	4	4	4	4	4	4	4	
$(1,1,1,1,0)$	0	0	0	0	0	0	0	0	**5**	5	5	5	5	
$(3,2,1,1,0)$	0	0	0	0	0	0	0	**5**	5	5	5	5	5	
$(4,5,2,1,0)$	0	0	0	0	0	0	0	**5**	5	5	5	5	5	

The fastest server is always activated. All other servers have different thresholds for different service phases. Thus, now the threshold levels for using a slower server depends also on the service phases of the busy servers with lower indexes. We note that in this example we chose such service intensities that the larger intensity corresponds to a smaller service phase, that is

$$\mu_k^1 \geq \mu_k^2 \geq \cdots \geq \mu_k^5.$$

From the table the selective threshold levels take their values as

$$q_1^* = 0;$$
$$q_2^*(d_1) = 2, \quad d_1 = 1;$$
$$q_2^*(d_1) = 1, \quad d_1 = 1;$$
$$q_3^*(d_1, d_2) = 2, \quad d_1 = 1, d_2 = 1;$$
$$q_3^*(d_1, d_2) = 2, \quad d_1 = 2, d_2 = 4;$$
$$q_3^*(d_1, d_2) = 2, \quad d_1 = 5, d_2 = 5;$$
$$q_4^*(d_1, d_2, d_3) = 3, \quad d_1 = 1, d_2 = 1, d_3 = 1;$$
$$q_4^*(d_1, d_2, d_3) = 3, \quad d_1 = 4, d_2 = 3, d_3 = 1;$$
$$q_4^*(d_1, d_2, d_3) = 3, \quad d_1 = 5, d_2 = 5, d_3 = 4;$$
$$q_5^*(d_1, d_2, d_3, d_4) = 8, \quad d_1 = 1, d_2 = 1, d_3 = 1, d_4 = 1;$$
$$q_5^*(d_1, d_2, d_3, d_4) = 7, \quad d_1 = 3, d_2 = 2, d_3 = 1, d_4 = 1;$$
$$q_5^*(d_1, d_2, d_3, d_4) = 7, \quad d_1 = 4, d_2 = 5, d_3 = 2, d_4 = 1;$$

Therefore, for some fixed phases $(d_1, d_2, \ldots, d_{K-1})$ threshold sequence looks like

$$0 = q_1^* \leq q_2^*(d_1) \leq q_3^*(d_1, d_2) \leq \cdots \leq q_K^*(d_1, d_2, \ldots, d_{K-1}).$$

Moreover, with respect to increasing of service phase indices, threshold levels satisfy the condition

$$q_2^*(m_1) \leq q_2^*(4) \leq \cdots \leq q_2^*(1);$$
$$q_3^*(m_1, 1) \leq q_3^*(m_1 - 1, 1) \leq \cdots \leq q_2^*(1, 1);$$
$$\cdots\cdots\cdots$$
$$q_K^*(m_1, d_2, d_3, \ldots, d_{K-1}) \leq q_K^*(m_1 - 1, d_2, d_3, \ldots, d_{K-1}) \leq \cdots$$
$$\leq q_K^*(1, d_2, d_3, \ldots, d_{K-1}).$$

The analogous condition shall hold when the value of any other coordinate d_k decreases.

The results of dynamic behavior of threshold levels when initial system paremeters are varied for the system $M/PH_{het}/3/100$ with $K = 3$ heterogeneous servers
are summarized in the diagrams shown in Figures 2.1–2.3. in Appendix 4.6.2. As
before, the Poisson arrival rate λ is varied over the Figures 2.1–2.3 as follows

- λ=0.51, in Figure 2.1,

- λ=0.26, in Figure 2.2,

- λ=0.01, in Figure 2.3.

In these diagrams the changing of threshold levels $q_2^*(d_1)$ for the second server
(pictures labeled by letter "a") and $q_3^*(d_1, d_2)$ for the third server (pictures labeled
by letter "b") represents the threshold function under variation of the first average
service intensity, second average service intensity and service phases.
The results show that the incentive to make an assignment to the second server
is greater in state $x = (\beta_1, 0, *)$ than in state $x = (\alpha_1, 0, *)$, and to the third
server is greater in state $x = (\beta_1, \beta_2, 0)$ than in state $x = (\alpha_1, \alpha_2, 0)$ if $\mu_{\alpha_k} \geq$
μ_{β_k}, $k = \{1, 2\}$. The stepped curves in these diagrams show that the low bound
of each curve family corresponds to the states of faster server where it has the
smallest service intensity from this phase, i.e. $d_k = 5$ and vice versa, for the upper
bound when $d_k = 1$. Even in the case of different values of initial service phase
distributions, the main criterion which is used by controller to make a decision
with respect to different service phases of the same server is the value of service
intensity from this phase.
For the PCM–problem with the servers arranged by (2.28) and condition (2.30),
and with initial parameters given in Table 4.21, the optimal control policies are
given in control Table 4.22.

Table 4.21 Values of initial system parameters for $M/PH/5/100$ **queue**

i	0	1	2	3	4	5
c_i	1.00	3.00	2.80	2.60	2.40	2.00
$\overline{\mu_i}$	-	1.90	0.63	0.52	0.45	0.30
γ_i	-	1.58	4.44	5.00	5.53	6.66

Table 4.22 Optimal control for some system states

System State x	Queue length $q(x)$													
(d_1,d_2,d_3,d_4,d_5)	0	1	2	3	4	5	6	7	8	9	10	11	12	...
$(0,*,*,*,*)$	**1**	1	1	1	1	1	1	1	1	1	1	1	1	1
$(1,0,*,*,*)$	0	0	0	0	0	**2**	2	2	2	2	2	2	2	2
$(4,0,*,*,*)$	0	0	0	0	0	**2**	2	2	2	2	2	2	2	2
$(1,1,0,*,*)$	0	0	0	0	0	0	**3**	3	3	3	3	3	3	3
$(2,4,0,*,*)$	0	0	0	0	0	0	**3**	3	3	3	3	3	3	3
$(5,5,0,*,*)$	0	0	0	0	0	0	**3**	3	3	3	3	3	3	3
$(1,1,1,0,*)$	0	0	0	0	0	0	0	0	**4**	4	4	4	4	4
$(4,3,1,0,*)$	0	0	0	0	0	0	0	**4**	4	4	4	4	4	4
$(2,2,2,0,*)$	0	0	0	0	0	0	0	**4**	4	4	4	4	4	4
$(1,1,1,1,0)$	0	0	0	0	0	0	0	0	0	0	0	0	0	**5**
$(3,2,1,1,0)$	0	0	0	0	0	0	0	0	0	0	0	0	**5**	5
$(4,5,2,1,0)$	0	0	0	0	0	0	0	0	0	0	0	0	**5**	5

Similar to the NJM–problem, in this case the optima policy is of threshold type and taking into account that

$$\mu_k^1 \geq \mu_k^2 \geq \cdots \geq \mu_k^5,$$

the elements of control sequence are

$$q_1^* = 0;$$
$$q_2^*(d_1) = 5, \quad d_1 = 1;$$
$$q_2^*(d_1) = 5, \quad d_1 = 1;$$
$$q_3^*(d_1,d_2) = 6, \quad d_1 = 1,\, d_2 = 1;$$
$$q_3^*(d_1,d_2) = 6, \quad d_1 = 2,\, d_2 = 4;$$
$$q_3^*(d_1,d_2) = 6 \quad d_1 = 5,\, d_2 = 5;$$
$$q_4^*(d_1,d_2,d_3) = 8, \quad d_1 = 1,\, d_2 = 1,\, d_3 = 1;$$
$$q_4^*(d_1,d_2,d_3) = 7, \quad d_1 = 4,\, d_2 = 3,\, d_3 = 1;$$
$$q_4^*(d_1,d_2,d_3) = 7, \quad d_1 = 5,\, d_2 = 5,\, d_3 = 4;$$
$$q_5^*(d_1,d_2,d_3,d_4) = 13, \quad d_1 = 1,\, d_2 = 1,\, d_3 = 1,\, d_4 = 1;$$
$$q_5^*(d_1,d_2,d_3,d_4) = 12, \quad d_1 = 3,\, d_2 = 2,\, d_3 = 1,\, d_4 = 1;$$
$$q_5^*(d_1,d_2,d_3,d_4) = 12, \quad d_1 = 4,\, d_2 = 5,\, d_3 = 2,\, d_4 = 1;$$

For condition (2.29) we have the same results, that is each server has several thresholds depending on the service phases but independent on the states of servers with greater mean usage costs.

Table 4.23 Values of initial system parameters for $M/PH/5/100$ **queue**

i	0	1	2	3	4	5
c_i	0.20	1.00	1.70	2.30	3.50	7.00
$\overline{\mu}_i$	-	0.30	0.45	0.52	0.63	0.90
γ_i	-	3.33	3.78	4.42	5.56	7.78

Table 4.24 Optimal control for some system states

System State x	Service phase d_j, $j \in \overline{1,K}$				
$(d_1, d_2, d_3, d_4, d_5)$	1	2	3	4	5
(-,0,0,0,0)	-,0,20,39,47	-,0,20,39,47	-,0,20,39,47	-,0,20,38,46	-,0,19,38,46
(0,-,0,0,0)	0,-,10,40,48	0,-,10,40,48	0,-,10,40,47	0,-,9,39,47	0,-,9,39,47
(-,1,0,0,0)	-,-,3,57,68	-,-,3,57,68	-,-,3,57,68	-,-,2,56,67	-,-,2,56,66
(0,0,-,0,0)	0,5,-,32,48	0,5,-,32,48	0,5,-,32,48	0,4,-,32,47	0,4,-,32,47
(-,0,1,0,0)	-,0,-,45,68	-,0,-,45,68	-,0,-,45,68	-,0,-,44,67	-,0,-,44,66
(0,-,1,0,0)	0,-,-,26,69	0,-,-,26,69	0,-,-,26,68	0,-,-,26,68	0,-,-,26,68
(-,1,1,0,0)	-,-,-,10,88	-,-,-,10,88	-,-,-,10,87	-,-,-,10,87	-,-,-,10,86
(0,0,0,-,0)	0,5,21,-,46	0,5,21,-,46	0,5,21,-,46	0,5,21,-,46	0,5,21,-,46
(-,0,0,1,0)	-,0,28,-,65	-,0,28,-,65	-,0,28,-,65	-,0,28,-,64	-,0,28,-,64
(0,-,0,1,0)	0,-,13,-,66	0,-,13,-,66	0,-,13,-,65	0,-,13,-,65	0,-,13,-,65
(-,1,0,1,0)	-,-,3,-,84	-,-,3,-,84	-,-,3,-,84	-,-,2,-,83	-,-,2,-,82
(0,0,-,1,0)	0,6,-,-,60	0,6,-,-,60	0,5,-,-,60	0,5,-,-,59	0,5,-,-,59
(-,0,1,1,0)	-,0,-,-,75	-,0,-,-,75	-,0,-,-,75	-,0,-,-,74	-,0,-,-,73
(0,-,1,1,0)	0,-,-,-,55	0,-,-,-,55	0,-,-,-,55	0,-,-,-,54	0,-,-,-,54
(-,1,1,1,0)	-,-,-,-,31	-,-,-,-,31	-,-,-,-,31	-,-,-,-,31	-,-,-,-,30
(0,0,0,0,-)	0,5,21,41,-	0,5,21,41,-	0,5,21,40,-	0,5,21,40,-	0,5,21,40,-
(-,0,0,0,1)	-,0,29,57,-	-,0,29,57,-	-,0,28,57,-	-,0,28,57,-	-,0,28,56,-
(0,-,0,0,1)	0,-,13,58,-	0,-,13,58,-	0,-,13,58,-	0,-,13,57,-	0,-,13,57,-
(-,1,0,0,1)	-,-,3,73,-	-,-,3,73,-	-,-,3,72,-	-,-,2,72,-	-,-,2,71,-
(0,0,-,0,1)	0,6,-,46,-	0,6,-,46,-	0,6,-,46,-	0,6,-,46,-	0,6,-,46,-
(-,0,1,0,1)	-,0,-,56,-	-,0,-,56,-	-,0,-,56,-	-,0,-,55,-	-,0,-,55,-
(0,-,1,0,1)	0,-,-,32,-	0,-,-,32,-	0,-,-,31,-	0,-,-,31,-	0,-,-,31,-
(-,1,1,0,1)	-,-,-,11,-	-,-,-,11,-	-,-,-,10,-	-,-,-,10,-	-,-,-,10,-
(0,0,0,-,1)	0,6,29,-,-	0,6,29,-,-	0,6,29,-,-	0,6,29,-,-	0,6,29,-,-
(-,0,0,1,1)	-,0,36,-,-	-,0,36,-,-	-,0,36,-,-	-,0,36,-,-	-,0,35,-,-
(0,-,0,1,1)	0,-,14,-,-	0,-,14,-,-	0,-,14,-,-	0,-,14,-,-	0,-,14,-,-
(-,1,0,1,1)	-,-,3,-,-	-,-,3,-,-	-,-,3,-,-	-,-,2,-,-	-,-,2,-,-
(0,0,-,1,1)	0,6,-,-,-	0,6,-,-,-	0,6,-,-,-	0,6,-,-,-	0,6,-,-,-
(-,0,1,1,1)	-,0,-,-,-	-,0,-,-,-	-,0,-,-,-	-,0,-,-,-	-,0,-,-,-
(0,-,1,1,1)	0,-,-,-,-	0,-,-,-,-	0,-,-,-,-	0,-,-,-,-	0,-,-,-,-

For the PCM–problem under condition (2.31) the optimal control policies are calculated in control Table 4.24 with initial system parameters given in Table 4.23

and by

$$
M_1 = \begin{pmatrix} -0.57 & 0.01 & 0.05 & 0.03 & 0.04 \\ 0.05 & -0.52 & 0.01 & 0.02 & 0.03 \\ 0.04 & 0.02 & -0.39 & 0.02 & 0.01 \\ 0.03 & 0.01 & 0.01 & -0.28 & 0.02 \\ 0.02 & 0.02 & 0.02 & -0.01 & -0.23 \end{pmatrix}, \eta_1 = \begin{pmatrix} 0.30 \\ 0.25 \\ 0.20 \\ 0.15 \\ 0.10 \end{pmatrix}
$$

$$
\mu_1 = \begin{pmatrix} 0.44 \\ 0.41 \\ 0.30 \\ 0.21 \\ 0.16 \end{pmatrix}, \mu_2 = \begin{pmatrix} 0.58 \\ 0.55 \\ 0.44 \\ 0.35 \\ 0.30 \end{pmatrix}, \mu_3 = \begin{pmatrix} 0.65 \\ 0.62 \\ 0.51 \\ 0.42 \\ 0.37 \end{pmatrix},
$$

$$
\mu_4 = \begin{pmatrix} 0.75 \\ 0.72 \\ 0.61 \\ 0.52 \\ 0.47 \end{pmatrix}, \mu_5 = \begin{pmatrix} 1.02 \\ 0.99 \\ 0.88 \\ 0.79 \\ 0.74 \end{pmatrix}.
$$

In this table the optimal control sequences $q_1^*(x), q_2^*(x), \ldots, q_5^*(x)$ are given for some selective states x, where one of the coordinates d_k is varied while all other are fixed. For this case of the PCM–problem, the thresholds depend on all elements of the system state and while the service intensity $\mu_k^{d_k}$ of some slower but cheaper server decreases, the incentive to use more expensive and faster server becomes larger.

4.5   Conclusions

In this chapter we discussed controlled queueing systems with heterogeneous servers and service phases. We have proposed some quantitative properties of optimal policies for this type of queues. But while the systems become more complex, theoretical results are difficult to obtain. Therefore, a numerical analysis has been used in order to obtain the qualitative properties of optimal control that in turn allow to estimate possible theoretical results. We have proposed an algorithm for computing the average cost control rule for this type of systems.
We have shown that an optimal policy of job allocation for such systems is of threshold type and the service phases are the arguments of the threshold function.

With respect to the NJM–problem the decision maker or controller has to activate the server with the largest mean service rate $\overline{\mu_k}$ and each server has several thresholds, one for each service phase, which are independent of the slower slower servers. In the case of Erlangian service time distributions the threshold function is increasing with decreasing residual service time of the faster server. In the case of PH service, this threshold function is increasing in service rate from the phase.

The same picture we observed in the PCM–problem under service arrangement (2.28) and initial system parameters conditions (2.29) and (2.30). In this case it is optimal to switch on the available server with lowest mean usage cost and each server has a group of thresholds independing on the states of servers with larger mean usage cost. The behavior of threshold function according to different service phases is the same as for the NJM–problem.

For the PCM–problem under the same servers arrangement (2.28) and condition (2.31), the optimal policy is also of threshold type but with a more complex structure. Namely, for each state there exists an own threshold sequence, thus in some states the controller can use different available servers, depending on the queue length. Moreover, while the queue length increases, the use of faster but more expensive servers becomes more preferable for the controller. For the system with Erlangian service, the controller prefers more cheaper servers for decreasing residual service times. In case of PH service, the incentive to use more expensive and faster server becomes larger when the service intensity from some slower but cheaper server decreases.

4.6   Appendices

4.6.1 $M/E_{m_k}/K$

Figure 1.1   **(a)**   **(b)**

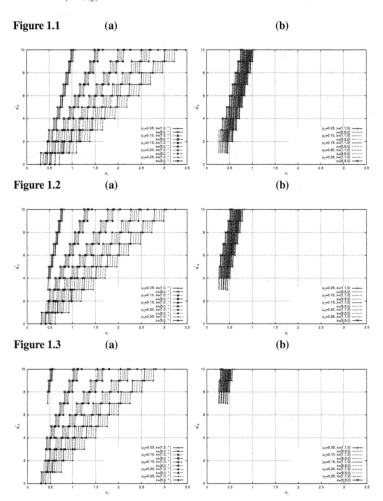

Figure 1.2   **(a)**   **(b)**

Figure 1.3   **(a)**   **(b)**

Figure 1.4 (a) (b)

Figure 1.5 (a) (b)

Figure 1.6 (a) (b)

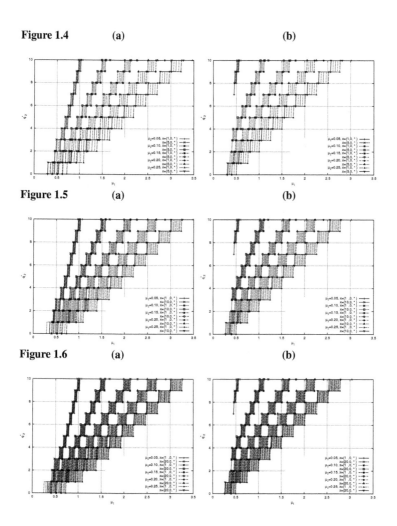

4.6.2 $M/PH_{het}/K$

Figure 2.1   (a)   (b)

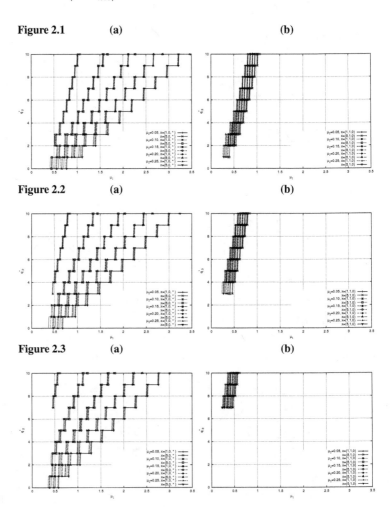

Figure 2.2   (a)   (b)

Figure 2.3   (a)   (b)

Chapter 5

Controlled $MAP/PH/K$ queue

In this chapter an optimal control of queueing system $MAP/PH_{het}/K$ with Markovian arrival process, phase–type service time distribution is considered. This type of queue represents the general case for all previous queues. To provide the numerical analysis an optimal control algorithm will be derived. It was implemented similar to the previous chapters by application of the Markov decision theory and dynamic programming to the present queueing system. In this chapter we consider two optimality criteria introduced in the Chapter 2, i.e. the mean number of jobs in the system minimization (the NJM–problem) and the mean total processing cost minimization (the PCM–problem). We will show that the optimal control policy for this system is of a threshold type and the threshold levels depend now on the arrival modulating and the service phases.

5.1 Introduction.

The development of matrix–analytical methods in queueing theory have led to substantial improvements in the field of stochastic modeling. Phase–type distributions (PH, see [52]) and Markovian arrival processes (MAPs, see [47]and [51]) have greatly enhanced the classes of tractable service time distributions and arrival processes for queueing systems. While they still allow a Markovian analysis of their respective queueing processes (see [52, 53]), they can approach any general service time distribution and arrival process with arbitrarily small error (see [69], pp.30ff, and [4]). Examinations of $MAP/PH/K$ queues are readily available (e.g. [11, 13, 50]), as well as some steady state characteristics for the system with homogeneous and heterogeneous servers (e.g. [6]) and statistical model fitting for MAPs and PH distributions (see [5] and [12]). In further research on the continuity of queues (cf. [29]) it will be seen how good an approximation can be expected from Markovian queues.

While the first steps in the analysis of a stochastic model are statistical model fitting (yielding parameters from the real world) and a descriptive examination of the system (expressing the relevant distributions in terms of initial parameters) have been done for $MAP/PH/K$ queues, a missing link to an applicability of these models is the examination of optimal control procedures.

As a topic of the present chapter we consider the Markov sequential decision model introduced in Chapter 2 which can be applied to the controlled queueing systems under consideration.

5.2   Problem description

Consider a $MAP/PH_{het}/K/B$ queuing system with K heterogeneous servers (in the sense of their different mean service times) represented in Figure 5.1.

Figure 5.1 Queueing system

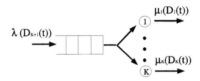

The arrival process is described by a Markov process on the phase space $\{1, \dots, m_0\}$ with intensity matrix $\Lambda + N$ where as before Λ contains the intensities for state changes without arrivals and the elements of N are intensities for state changes accompanied by an arrival. The diagonal elements of N yield intensities for arrivals without phase change. The service time distributions are of phase-type with representations (η_k, M_k) where η_k is an m_k-dimensional vector of initial service phase distribution and M_k is an $(m_k \times m_k)$-transition intensity matrix. The arrival and service distributions were discussed in Sections 3 and 4.

The equilibrium condition when $B = \infty$ is determined by

$$\lambda = \sum_{i=1}^{m}\sum_{j=1}^{m} \pi_{D_{K+1}}(i)\nu_{ij} < \sum_{k=1}^{K} \bar{\mu}_k = \sum_{k=1}^{K} -\eta_k^T M_k^{-1}\vec{1}^{-1}, \tag{5.1}$$

where $\pi_{D_{K+1}}$ is the equilibrium distribution of the process $D_{K+1}(t)$.

The definitions and notations of the optimization problem are exactly the same as before. We only mention that now we consider the observed vector process $\{X(t)\}$ with state space $E = \mathbf{N} \times \prod_{k=1}^{K}\{0,\ldots,m_k\} \times \{1,\ldots,m_0\}$. Its components $\{D_0(t), D_1(t),\ldots,D_K(t), D_{K+1}(t)\}$ have the same meanings as for the systems with MAP and PH service, discussed in previous chapters.

The transition intensities $\lambda_{xy}(a)$ of the process $\{Z(t)\}$ have the following form

$$\lambda_{xy}(a) = \begin{cases}
\lambda_{d_{K+1}(x)d_{K+1}(y)}, & y = S_{K+1}^{d_{K+1}(y)}x, \\[2mm]
\nu_{d_{K+1}(x)d_{K+1}(y)}[\mathbf{1}_{\{a_0=0\}} \\
+\eta_{a_0}^{d_{a_0}(y)}\mathbf{1}_{\{a_0\neq 0\}}], & y = S_{a_0}^{d_{a_0}} S_{K+1}^{d_{K+1}(y)}x, \\[2mm]
\mu_j^{d_j(x)}[\mathbf{1}_{\{q(x)=0\}} \\
+\mathbf{1}_{\{q(x)>0,a_j=0\}}], & y = S_j^{-d_j}x, & j \in J_1(x), \\[2mm]
\mu_j^{d_j(x)}\eta_{a_j}^{d_{a_j}(y)} \\
\mathbf{1}_{\{q(x)>0,a_j\neq 0\}}, & y = S_{a_j}^{d_{a_j}} S_j^{-d_j} S_0^{-1}x, & j \in J_1(x), \\
\mu_j^{d_j(x)d_j(y)}, & y = S_j^{d_j(y)}x, \\
& & j \in J_1(x)\cap J_1(y), \\[2mm]
\lambda_{d_{K+1}(x)d_{K+1}(x)} \\
+\sum_{j\in J_1(x)}\mu_j^{d_j(x)d_j(x)}, & y = x, \\[2mm]
0, & \text{otherwise,}
\end{cases}$$

where $\mu_j^{d_j(x)}$ are the components of the vector $\bar{\mu}_j = -M_j\bar{1}$. Here $a = a_0 \in A(x)$ denotes the control which has to be chosen in the case of an arrival to the state x, $a = a_j \in A(S_j^{-d_j}S_0^{-1}x)$ denotes the control in the case of a service completion on the j-th server.

In this matrix:

- the first case corresponds to a transition of an arrival phase without a new job arrival;

- the second case corresponds to an arrival of a new job in the system and sending it to the queue or to some server in accordance with the decision rule;

- the third case corresponds to the service completion with empty queue or with control $a_j = 0$;

- the forth case corresponds to the service completion and sending one of the jobs from the queue to one of the available servers in accordance with decision rule;

- the fifth case corresponds to a transition of the service phases.

The diagonal elements of this matrix (the last case) equal the negative sum of all elements along the same row.

For this system the arrival and service completion transitions are illustrated by the graph shown in Figure 5.2 (a) and (b), respectively

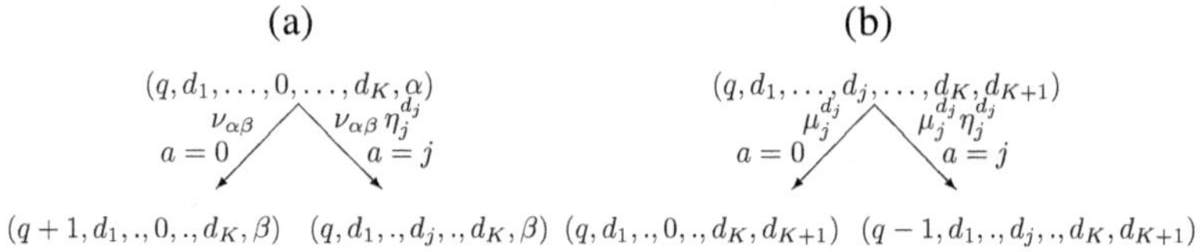

Figure 5.2

5.3 Optimality equation

For the function $V(x, t)$, which represents the minimal total loss in the system up to time t, and a small time interval of length h, the following equation can be obtained by a Markov process argument:

$$V(x, t+h) = c(x)h + \left(1 + \left[\lambda_{d_{K+1}(x)d_{K+1}(x)} + \sum_{j \in J_1(x)} \mu_j^{d_j(x)\,d_j(x)}\right]h\right)V(x, t)$$

$$+ sum_{d_{K+1}}\nu_{d_{K+1}(x)d_{K+1}}h \min_{a_0 \in A(x)} \left\{V(S_0 S_{K+1}^{d_{K+1}}x, t), \sum_{d_{a_0}=1}^{m_{a_0}} \eta_{a_0}^{d_{a_0}} V(S_{a_0}^{d_{a_0}} S_{K+1}^{d_{K+1}}x, t)\right\} +$$

$$\sum_{\substack{j\in J_1(x)\\q(x)>0}} \mu_j^{d_j(x)}h, \quad \min_{a_j\in A(S_k^{-d_k}S_0^{-1}x)} \left\{V(x,t), \sum_{d_{a_j}=1}^{m_{a_j}} \eta_{a_j}^{d_{a_j}}V(S_{a_j}^{d_{a_j}}S_0^{-1}x,t)\right\}$$

$$+ \sum_{\substack{d_{K+1}\neq\\d_{K+1}(x)}} \lambda_{d_{K+1}(x)d_{K+1}}h\,V(S_{K+1}^{d_{K+1}}x,t) + \sum_{j\in J_1(x)}\sum_{d_j\neq d_j(x)} \mu_j^{d_j(x)\,d_j}h\,V(S_j^{d_j}x,t)$$

$$+ \sum_{\substack{j\in J_1(x)\\q(x)=0}} \mu_j^{d_j(x)}h\,V(S_j^{-d_j}x,t).$$

In this equation, the first member of the right–hand side represents the loss of the system up to time h, the second one represents the total loss of the system during the following time t in the case that no phase changes occur in the system, the next one represents the total loss of the system during the following time t in the case that a new customer arrives before the service completion. The following member represents the loss of the system in the case of service completion with non-empty queue before new customer arrival, the next two members deal with the total loss of the system in the case of phase changes without arrivals or service completion, and the last one represents the total loss of the system during the following time t in the case that one of the served customers leaves the system with empty queue before some customer arrives.

For the system under consideration after some transformations, taking into account the asymptotic behavior (2.6) of the function $V(x,t)$ and passing to the limit $h\to 0$, the previous equation assumes the form

$$v(x) = \frac{1}{\lambda_x}\left[c(x)+C_1(x)+C_2(x)-g+\right. \tag{5.2}$$

$$+ \left.\sum_{d_{K+1}=1}^{m_0} \nu_{d_{K+1}(x)d_{K+1}}T_0 v(S_{K+1}^{d_{K+1}}x) + \sum_{j\in J_1(x)} \mu_j^{d_j(x)}T_j v(x)\right] = Bv(x),$$

where $Bv(x)$ denotes the transform operator for the function $v(x)$. In this representation

$$\lambda_x = -\left(\lambda_{d_{K+1}(x)d_{K+1}(x)} + \sum_{j\in J_1(x)} \mu_j^{d_j(x)\,d_j(x)}\right)$$

is the total intensity of a transition from state x,

$$C_1(x) = \sum_{d_{K+1}\neq d_{K+1}(x)} \lambda_{d_{K+1}(x)d_{K+1}}v(S_{K+1}^{d_{K+1}}x) + \sum_{j\in J_1(x)}\sum_{d_j\neq d_j(x)} \mu_j^{d_j(x)\,d_j}v(S_j^{d_j}x)$$

is the loss rate due to a transition of the MAP or the service phase without decision making,

$$C_2(x) = \sum_{\substack{j \in J_1(x) \\ q(x)=0}} \mu^{d_j(x)} v(S_j^{-d_j} x)$$

is the loss rate due to a service completion with an empty queue,

$$T_0 v(x) = \min\left\{ v(S_0 x), \sum_{d_k=1}^{m_k} \eta_k^{d_k} v(S_k^{d_k} x) : \ k = \overline{1, K} \right\}$$

is the minimal loss in case of a new job arrival,

$$T_j v(x) = T_0 v(S_0^{-1} S_j^{d_j} x) \mathbf{1}_{\{q(x)>0\}}$$

is the minimal loss in case of service completion and appropriate decision making. The optimal policy

$$f = \{f(x) : x \in E\}$$

minimizes the function $b = \{b(x, a) : x \in E, a \in A(x)\}$ determined by (4.22).

5.4   Monotonicity properties

For the PH-type heterogeneous servers in the case of the NJM–problem the arrangement is determined by the inequality (4.24) and for the PCM–problem by the inequality (4.25) with conditions (4.26)–(4.28). All the systems which have been already discussed in previous chapters are the particular cases of this system with MAP and PH-type service time distribution. And all the results obtained above also hold for this system. Below we formulate the general statements for this queue based on obtained theoretical and numerical results. But by the reason of the fact that these assertions can only be partially proved, they are formulated as conjectures.

Conjecture 5.3 *The value function of the model* $v = \{v(x) : \ x \in E\}$ *has the* *following properties*

1. $v(S_0 x) \geq v(x), \; \sum_{d_i=1}^{m_i} \eta_i^{d_i} v(S_i^{d_i} x) \geq v(x), \; i \in J_0(x);$

2. $\sum_{d_j=1}^{m_j} \eta_j^{d_j} v(S_j^{d_j} x) \leq \sum_{d_i=1}^{m_i} \eta_i^{d_i} v(S_i^{d_i} x), \; i, j \in J_0(x), \; j \leq i;$

3. $\sum_{d_1=1}^{m_1} \eta_1^{d_1} v(S_1^{d_1} x) \leq v(S_0 x);$

4. $v(S_{K+1}^{\alpha} x) \leq v(S_{K+1}^{\beta} x), \; \nu_{\alpha} \leq \nu_{\beta};$

5. $v(S_i^{\alpha} x) \leq v(S_i^{\beta} x), \; \mu_i^{\alpha} \geq \mu_i^{\beta}, \; i \in J_0(x).$

Based on the properties of the value function $v(x)$ the following strengthened conjecture can be formulated

Conjecture 5.4 *Under conditions of Conjecture 5.3 the value function* $v = \{v(x) : x \in E\}$ *of the model satisfy monotonicity properties which can be expressed in the operators form as follows*

1. $(1 - S_0)(S_0 - \sum_{d_k=1}^{m_k} \eta_k^{d_k} S_k^{d_k}) v(S_i^{\alpha} x) \leq 0, \; k \in J_0(x), \; i = \overline{1, K+1};$

2. $(1 - S_0)(S_0 - \sum_{d_k=1}^{m_k} \eta_k^{d_k} S_k^{d_k}) v(S_i^{\beta} x) \leq 0, \; k \in J_0(x), \; i = \overline{1, K+1};$

3. $(S_0 - \sum_{d_k=1}^{m_k} \eta_k^{d_k} S_k^{d_k})(S_{K+1}^{\alpha} - S_{K+1}^{\beta}) v(x) \leq 0, \; \nu_{\alpha} \leq \nu_{\beta}, \; k \in J_0(x);$

4. $(S_0 - \sum_{d_k=1}^{m_k} \eta_k^{d_k} S_k^{d_k})(S_i^{\alpha} - S_i^{\beta}) v(x) \leq 0, \; \mu_i^{\alpha} \geq \mu_i^{\beta}, \; k \in J_0(x).$

Thus we expect that that the optimal policy is of threshold type, as stated below

Corollary 5.5 *The optimal policy for the system* $MAP/PH_{het}/K$ *is of threshold type with finite thresholds for each arrival and service phase, i.e. for the NJM–problem and the PCM–problem for each server j there exist* $\prod_{i=\{0\} \cup J_1(x)}^{j-1} m_i$

levels of the queue length $q_j^*(d_1, d_2, \ldots, d_{j-1}, d_{K+1})$ which depends both on arrival and service phases of servers with smaller index with respect to arrangements (4.24) and (4.25) and it is necessary to switch on some server only if $q(x) \geq q_j^*(d_1(x), d_2(x), \ldots, d_{j-1}(x), d_{K+1}(x))$. In the case of the NJM–problem the decision maker has to use the fastest available server, for the PCM–problem under conditions (4.26) and (4.27) the optimal is the server with fewest mean usage cost. In the case of the PCM–problem under condition (4.28) in each state x for each idle server there exist two-level threshold policy with levels $q_j^*(x)$ and $q_{j+1}^*(x)$ which depend on the system state, i.e. the controller may use some available in the state x server, if $q_j^*(x) \leq q(x) < q_{j+1}^*(x)$.

5.5 Algorithm

To analyze the behavior of optimal strategies the servers for the NJM–problem will be arranged in order (4.24) and for the PCM–problem in order (4.25) with conditions (4.26)–(4.28).

Strategy estimation. For a given policy $f = \{f_n(x) : x = \overline{1, I}\}$ solve the equation

$$v_n(x) = \frac{1}{\lambda_x}\left(c(x) + C_1(x) + C_2(x) - g_n\right)$$

$$+ \frac{1}{\lambda_x}\sum_{d_{K+1}=1}^{m_0} \nu_{d_{K+1}(x)d_{K+1}}$$

$$\left(\mathbf{1}_{\{f_n(S_{K+1}^{d_{K+1}}x)=0\}} v_n(S_0 S_{K+1}^{d_{K+1}}x) + \mathbf{1}_{\{f_n(S_{K+1}^{d_{K+1}}x)=k\}}\sum_{d_k=1}^{m_k} \eta_k^{d_k} v_n(S_k^{d_k} S_{K+1}^{d_{K+1}}x)\right) +$$

$$\frac{1}{\lambda_x}\sum_{\substack{j \in J_1(x) \\ q(x)>0}} \mu_j^{d_j(x)}$$

$$\left(\mathbf{1}_{\{f_n(S_0^{-1}S_j^{-d_j}x)=0\}} v_n(S_j^{-d_j}x) + \mathbf{1}_{\{f_n(S_0^{-1}S_j^{-d_j}x)=k\}}\sum_{d_k=1}^{m_k} \eta_k^{d_k} v_n(S_k^{d_k} S_j^{-d_j} S_0^{-1}x)\right)$$

for all $x \in E$ under the condition $v(0) = 0$. This can be done up to an accuracy ε by successive approximation.

Strategy improvement. For a given solution $v_n = \{v_n(x) : x \in E\}$ find a new policy $f_{n+1} = \{f_{n+1}(x) : x \in E\}$, which minimizes the Bellman function (4.22) of the model:

$$f_{n+1}(x) = \underset{k \in A(x)}{\operatorname{argmin}} \begin{cases} \sum_{d_k=1}^{m_k} \eta_k^{d_k} v_n(x + d_k e_k), & k = \overline{1, K} \\ v_n(x + e_0), & k = 0 \end{cases}$$

The algorithm stops when two successive iterations yield the same policy.

For description of the system states changing we use one-dimensional representation of the system states, namely

$$\#(x) = \prod_{i=1}^{K}(m_i+1)(d_0(x)m_0 + d_{K+1}(x) - 1) + \sum_{j=1}^{K} d_j(x)\mathbf{1}_{\{j>1\}} \prod_{i=1}^{j-1}(m_i+1) \equiv x$$

and the number of states is $\prod_{i=1}^{K}(m_i+1)m_{K+1}(B - K + 1)$.

Now, if y_j is the state after possible transition from the j-th coordinate it can be obtained with respect to introduced formula

$$y_j = x + \frac{(d_j - d_j(x)) \prod_{i=1}^{K}(m_i+1)\mathbf{1}_{\{j=0\}} m_0}{\mathbf{1}_{\{1 \leq j \leq K\}} \prod_{i=j}^{K}(m_i+1)}.$$

Now for the shift operators the formulas (3.6)-(3.6) and (4.15)-(4.17) can be used for algorithm realization.

5.6 Numerical analysis.

Since the dynamic behavior for the PCM–problem requires to vary a large number of system parameters we omit the examples of control-diagrams. Also we omit presentation of control-tables because the structure of optimal control policies for this model is a combination of results obtained for the systems $MAP/M/K$ and $M/PH/K$.

In this section we investigate the threshold levels behaviour for the NJM–problem in the following systems

- $E_{m_0}/E_{m_k}/K$,   Section 5.6.1

- $MAP/E_{m_k}/K$,   Section 5.6.2

- $PH/PH_{het}/K$,   Section 5.6.3

- $MAP/PH_{het}/K$,   Section 5.6.4

by virtue of control diagrams presented in appendices in Section 5.8.

5.6.1 $E_{m_0}/E_{m_k}/K$ queue.

For the system $E_5/E_5/3/100$ with $K = 3$ servers and $m_k = 5$ number of arrival and service phases (stages), $k = \overline{0, K}$, the numerical results of the optimal threshold calculation are summarized in the control diagrams shown in Figures 1.1–1.6 in Appendix 5.8.1. The arrival rate per stage λ is varied over the figures 1.1–1.3 as follows

- $\lambda = 2.55$, $\overline{\lambda} = \frac{\lambda}{m_0} = 0.51$,   in Figure 1.1,

- $\lambda = 1.30$, $\overline{\lambda} = \frac{\lambda}{m_0} = 0.26$,   in Figure 1.2,

- $\lambda = 0.05$, $\overline{\lambda} = \frac{\lambda}{m_0} = 0.01$,   in Figure 1.3.

In these diagrams the changing of threshold levels $q_2^*(d_1, d_4)$ for the second server (pictures labeled by letter "a") and $q_3^*(d_1, d_2, d_4)$ for the third server (pictures labeled by letter "b") represents the threshold function with under the variation of the first mean service intensity, second mean service intensity as well as Erlangian arrival and service phases.

The stepped curves in these diagrams show that when the residual interarrival time decreases and the residual service time increases the incentive to make an assignment to the second server is greater in state $x = (\alpha_1, 0, *, \alpha_4)$ than in state $x = (\beta_1, 0, *, \beta_4)$, and for the third server is greater in state $x = (\alpha_1, \alpha_2, 0, \alpha_4)$ than in state $x = (\beta_1, \beta_2, 0, \beta_4)$ if $\alpha_k \leq \beta_k$, $k = \{1, 2\}$ and $\alpha_4 \geq \beta_4$.

The influence of the number of phases on the threshold curves is presented in control diagrams shown in Figures 1.4–1.6 where $\overline{\lambda} = 0.51$ (pictures labeled by letter "a") and $\overline{\lambda} = 0.01$ (pictures labeled by letter "b") and the number of arrival phases is varied over the figures

- $m_0{=}5$,   Figure 1.4,

- $m_0=10$, Figure 1.5,

- $m_0=20$, Figure 1.6.

From these pictures one can see that the low bounds of each curves family corresponds to the state with smallest residual interarrival time and largest residual service time. The upper bound represents the state with largest residual interarrival time and smallest residual service time. The curves for all other possible residual interarrival and service times lie between these two bounds.

5.6.2 $MAP/E_{m_k}/K$ queue.

In this section we investigate the system $MAP/E_{m_k}/3/100$ with $K = 3$ servers, $m_k = 5$ Erlangian service phases, $k = \overline{1,K}$ and MAP is characterized by matrices Λ and N of dimension $m_0 \times m_0$, $m_0 = 2$. The results of threshold levels dynamic behavior for this system are summarized in control diagrams shown in Figures 2.1–2.6 in Appendix 5.8.2. Parameters for arrivals with average $\overline{\lambda} = \{0.51, 0.26, 0.01\}$ take the following values

- $N = \begin{pmatrix} 0.500 & 0.400 \\ 0.100 & 0.240 \end{pmatrix}$, $\Lambda = \begin{pmatrix} -1.900 & 1.000 \\ 0.500 & -0.840 \end{pmatrix}$ in Figure 2.1,

- $N = \begin{pmatrix} 0.350 & 0.180 \\ 0.100 & 0.010 \end{pmatrix}$, $\Lambda = \begin{pmatrix} -1.430 & 0.900 \\ 0.500 & -0.610 \end{pmatrix}$ in Figure 2.2,

- $N = \begin{pmatrix} 0.030 & 0.010 \\ 0.010 & 0.001 \end{pmatrix}$, $\Lambda = \begin{pmatrix} -1.040 & 1.000 \\ 0.010 & -0.021 \end{pmatrix}$ in Figure 2.3.

These control diagrams shows threshold functions $q_2^*(d_1, d_4)$ for the second server (pictures labeled by letter "a") and $q_3^*(d_1, d_2, d_4)$ for the third server (pictures labeled by letter "b") depending on first and second mean service intensities as well as on arrival and service phases. The pictures show that the incentive to make an assignment to the second server is greater in state $x = (\alpha_1, 0, *, \alpha_4)$ than in state $x = (\beta_1, 0, *, \beta_4)$, and to the third is greater in state $x = (\alpha_1, \alpha_2, 0, \alpha_4)$ than in state $x = (\beta_1, \beta_2, 0, \beta_4)$ if $\alpha_k \le \beta_k$, $k = \{1, 2\}$ and $\nu_{\alpha_4} \ge \nu_{\beta_4}$, that is in the case of residual service time and arrival intensity increasing.
The control diagrams on the Figures 2.4–2.6

- $N = \begin{pmatrix} 0.000 & 0.200 \\ 1.000 & 0.000 \end{pmatrix}$, $\Lambda = \begin{pmatrix} -0.630 & 0.430 \\ 0.000 & -1.000 \end{pmatrix}$ pictures labeled by letter "a",

- $N = \begin{pmatrix} 0.030 & 0.010 \\ 0.010 & 0.001 \end{pmatrix}$, $\Lambda = \begin{pmatrix} -1.040 & 1.000 \\ 0.010 & -0.021 \end{pmatrix}$ pictures labeled by letter "b"

represent the dependence on the number of service phases which are varied over the figures

- $m_1=5$,   in Figure 2.4,

- $m_1=10$, in Figure 2.5,

- $m_1=20$, in Figure 2.6.

The low bound of the curves family represents the state with largest residual service time on the first server and arrival intensity from the phase. Otherwise there is an upper bound. All other threshold curves are located between these two bounds.

5.6.3 $PH/PH_{het}/K$ queue.

For the system with PH arrivals having representation (η_0, Λ) of dimension $m_0=5$ and heterogeneous PH service time distributions (η_k, M_k), of dimensions $m_k=5$, $k = \overline{1,K}$ and $K = 3$ servers the behavior of optimal control policies is presented in control-diagrams shown in Figures 3.1–3.3 in Appendix 5.8.3. As usual, the mean arrival rate $\overline{\lambda} = (-\eta_0^T \Lambda^{-1} \vec{1})^{-1}$ is varied over the figures as $\overline{\lambda} = \{0.51, 0.26, 0.01\}$ and for Λ, η_0 and $\lambda^{d_{K+1}}$ we have the following values, respectively

$$
\bullet \quad \begin{pmatrix}
-2.27 & 0.10 & 0.20 & 0.30 & 0.40 \\
0.10 & -1.27 & 0.20 & 0.10 & 0.10 \\
0.10 & 0.15 & -0.97 & 0.05 & 0.10 \\
0.01 & 0.05 & 0.10 & -0.87 & 0.20 \\
0.01 & 0.01 & 0.02 & 0.05 & -0.57
\end{pmatrix},
\begin{pmatrix}
0.01 \\ 0.02 \\ 0.05 \\ 0.17 \\ 0.75
\end{pmatrix},
\begin{pmatrix}
1.27 \\ 0.77 \\ 0.57 \\ 0.51 \\ 0.48
\end{pmatrix},
$$

in Figure 3.1,

- $$\begin{pmatrix} -2.02 & 0.10 & 0.20 & 0.30 & 0.40 \\ 0.10 & -1.02 & 0.20 & 0.10 & 0.10 \\ 0.10 & 0.15 & -0.72 & 0.05 & 0.10 \\ 0.01 & 0.05 & 0.10 & -0.62 & 0.20 \\ 0.01 & 0.01 & 0.02 & 0.05 & -0.32 \end{pmatrix}, \begin{pmatrix} 0.01 \\ 0.02 \\ 0.05 \\ 0.17 \\ 0.75 \end{pmatrix}, \begin{pmatrix} 1.02 \\ 0.52 \\ 0.32 \\ 0.26 \\ 0.23 \end{pmatrix},$$

in Figure 3.2,

- $$\begin{pmatrix} -0.13 & 0.01 & 0.02 & 0.03 & 0.04 \\ 0.04 & -0.12 & 0.03 & 0.02 & 0.01 \\ 0.02 & 0.03 & -0.11 & 0.04 & 0.01 \\ 0.03 & 0.04 & 0.01 & -0.105 & 0.02 \\ 0.01 & 0.03 & 0.04 & 0.02 & -0.101 \end{pmatrix}, \begin{pmatrix} 0.01 \\ 0.02 \\ 0.05 \\ 0.17 \\ 0.75 \end{pmatrix}, \begin{pmatrix} 0.03 \\ 0.02 \\ 0.01 \\ 0.005 \\ 0.001 \end{pmatrix},$$

in Figure 3.3.

In these diagrams the changing of threshold levels $q_2^*(d_1, d_4)$ for the second server (pictures labeled by letter "a") and $q_3^*(d_1, d_2, d_4)$ for the third server (pictures labeled by letter "b") represents the threshold function with under the variation of the first mean service intensity, second mean service intensity as well as arrival and service phases.

Because of a large number of values for representations (η_k, M_k), $k = \overline{1, K}$ we omit them only giving in the diagrams the mean values of service intensities $\bar{\mu}_k = (-\eta^T M_k \vec{1})^{-1}$. These values are calculated using the inverse matrix program. We note that for all servers the values of service intensity from the phase $\mu_k^{d_k}$ satisfy $\mu_k^\alpha \geq \mu_k^\beta$ when $\alpha \leq \beta$, $k = \overline{1, K}$.

As we can see from proposed control diagrams the incentive to make an assignment to the second server is greater in state $x = (\alpha_1, 0, *, \alpha_4)$ than in state $x = (\beta_1, 0, *, \beta_4)$, and to the third server is greater in state $x = (\alpha_1, \alpha_2, 0, \alpha_4)$ than in state $x = (\beta_1, \beta_2, 0, \beta)$ if $\lambda_{\alpha_4} \geq \lambda_{\beta_4}$ and $\mu_k^{\alpha_k} \leq \mu_k^{\beta_k}$, $k = \{1, 2\}$.

5.6.4 $MAP/PH_{het}/K$ queue.

In this section we investigate the system $MAP/PH_{het}/3/100$ with $K = 3$ servers, PH-type service distribution with representations (η_k, M_k) of dimension $m_k = 5$, $k = \overline{1, K}$ and MAP is characterized by matrices Λ and N of dimension $m_0 \times m_0$, $m_0 = 2$. The results of threshold levels dynamic behavior for this system are summarized in control diagrams shown in Figures 4.1–4.3 in Appendix 5.8.4. As before, the parameters for arrivals with average $\overline{\lambda} = \{0.51, 0.26, 0.01\}$ take the following values

- $N = \begin{pmatrix} 0.000 & 0.200 \\ 1.000 & 0.000 \end{pmatrix}$, $\Lambda = \begin{pmatrix} -0.630 & 0.430 \\ 0.000 & -1.000 \end{pmatrix}$ in Figure 4.1,

- $N = \begin{pmatrix} 0.350 & 0.180 \\ 0.100 & 0.010 \end{pmatrix}$, $\Lambda = \begin{pmatrix} -1.430 & 0.900 \\ 0.500 & -0.610 \end{pmatrix}$ in Figure 4.2,

- $N = \begin{pmatrix} 0.030 & 0.010 \\ 0.010 & 0.001 \end{pmatrix}$, $\Lambda = \begin{pmatrix} -1.040 & 1.000 \\ 0.010 & -0.021 \end{pmatrix}$ in Figure 4.3.

As before, in these diagrams the changing of threshold levels $q_2^*(d_1, d_4)$ for the second server (pictures labeled by letter "a") and $q_3^*(d_1, d_2, d_4)$ for the third server (pictures labeled by letter "b") represents the threshold function with under the variation of the first mean service intensity, second mean service intensity as well as Erlangian arrival and service phases.

These pictures confirm the results that the incentive to make an assignment to the second server is greater in the state state $x = (\alpha_1, 0, *, \alpha_4)$ than in state $x = (\beta_1, 0, *, \beta_4)$, and to the third server is greater in state $x = (\alpha_1, \alpha_2, 0, \alpha_4)$ than in state $x = (\beta_1, \beta_2, 0, \beta)$ if $\nu_{\alpha_4} \geq \nu_{\beta_4}$ and $\mu_k^{\alpha_k} \leq \mu_k^{\beta_k}$, $k = \{1, 2\}$.

5.7 Conclusions

In this chapter we investigate the queue with arrival modulating and service phases, i.e. the general case of all previous systems and accumulate together all previous results. The optimal control policy for such a system obeys the low of threshold nature and threshold function has arrival and service phases as arguments. Threshold function has the same monotone properties as in previous systems with Markovian arrival process and PH-type service time distribution.

Obtained optimality equation and proposed algorithm represent the general description of the family of queues which are the particular case of this one. Numerical analysis permits successfully investigate an optimal control nature, since the value of the optimal threshold is very difficult to compute explicitly. The numerical results for each queueing system investigated in this book show that the threshold level for using the server in the NJM–problem and the PCM–problem has a weak dependence on the condition of the slower servers. And the optimal control may vary by at most 1 when conditions of these servers change. It was shown as well that the optimal threshold level depends on the arrival and service phases. Moreover, the threshold curves lie along the threshold curve for Markovian queue with mean iterarrival and service time characteristics of the system with phases. And again the optimal thresholds for different arrival or service phases varied by at most 1. Therefore, we suspect that in practice the threshold levels for Markovian queues with mean arrival and service rates of the systems with phases can be quite a good approximation for optimal thresholds of such systems.

The investigation of the optimal policy structure and threshold properties can facilitate implementation of these policies. For each new arriving job, a decision maker only has to maintain the information about the queue length to use the optimal server. The decision to perform a switching to another server can be made via a table lookup.

5.8 Appendices

5.8.1 $E_{m_0}/E_{m_k}/K$

Figure 1.1   **(a)**   **(b)**

Figure 1.2   **(a)**   **(b)**

Figure 1.3   **(a)**   **(b)**

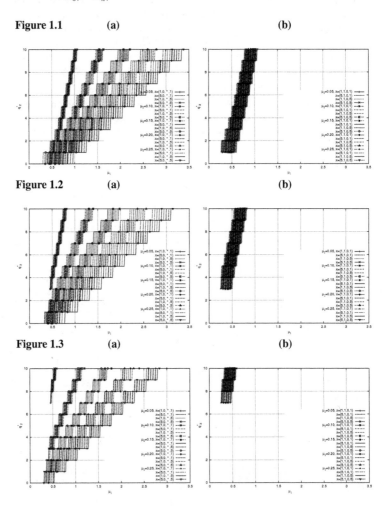

Figure 1.4   **(a)**   **(b)**

Figure 1.5   **(a)**   **(b)**

Figure 1.6   **(a)**   **(b)**

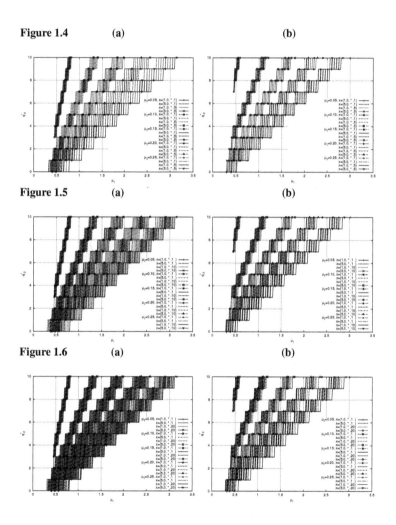

5.8.2 $MAP/E_{m_k}/K$

Figure 2.1   **(a)**   **(b)**

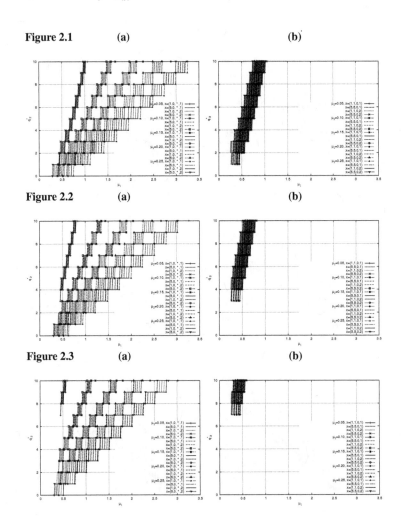

Figure 2.2   **(a)**   **(b)**

Figure 2.3   **(a)**   **(b)**

Figure 2.4   (a)   (b)

Figure 2.5   (a)   (b)

Figure 2.6   (a)   (b)

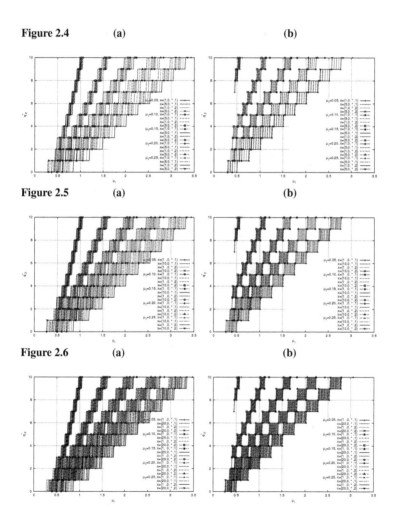

5.8.3 $PH/PH_{het}/K$

Figure 3.1   **(a)**   **(b)**

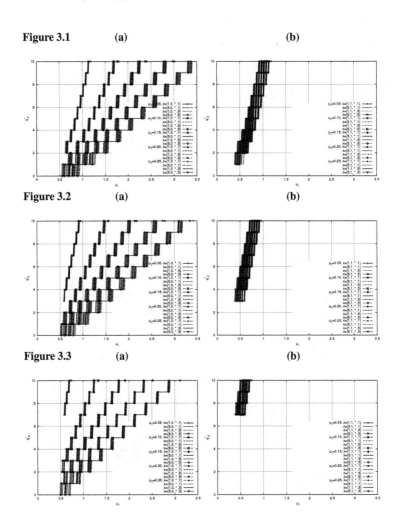

Figure 3.2   **(a)**   **(b)**

Figure 3.3   **(a)**   **(b)**

5.8.4 $MAP/PH_{het}/K$

Figure 4.1   **(a)**   **(b)**

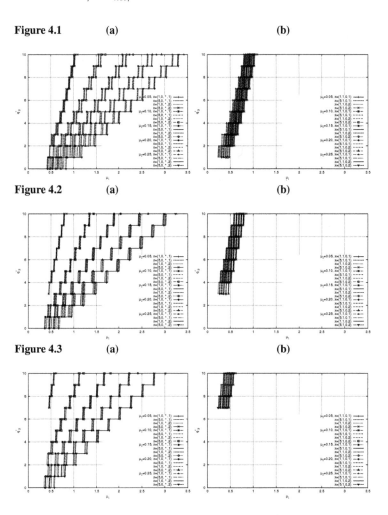

Figure 4.2   **(a)**   **(b)**

Figure 4.3   **(a)**   **(b)**

Bibliography

[1] A. K. Agravala, E. G. Goffman, M. R. Garey, S. K. Tripathi. A stochastic optimization algorithm minimizing expected flow times on uniform processors. *IEEE Transactions on Computers*, **33**: 351-356, 1984.

[2] E. Altman, G. Koole. On submodular functions of dynamic programming. *Technical Report 2658*, INRIA Sophia Antipolis, 1995.

[3] E. Altman, T. Jimenez, G. Koole. On optimal call admission control in a resource-sharing system. *Vrije University, Amsterdam*, 2000.

[4] S. Asmussen and G. Koole. Marked point processes as limits of Markovian arrival streams. *Journal of Applied Probability*, **30**(2): 365–372, 1993.

[5] S. Asmussen, O. Nerman, and M. Olsson. Fitting phase-type distributions via the EM algorithm. *Scandinavian Journal of Statistics*, **23**(4): 419–441, 1996.

[6] S. Asmussen, J.R. Mueller. Calculation of steady state waiting time distribution in $GI/PH/c$ and $MAP/PH/c$ queues. *Queueing systems*, **37**: 9–29, 2001.

[7] D. Baum. Convolution algorithms for $BMAP/G/1$-Queues. *Forschungsbericht, Universität Trier, Abteilung Mathematik und Informatik*, **96**(22).

[8] D. Baum. The infinite server queue with Markov additive arrivals in space. *Forschungsbericht, Universität Trier, Abteilung Mathematik und Informatik*, **98**(31).

[9] P. P. Bocharov, A. V. Pechinkin, Theory of queueing systems (in Russian). *Russian Peoples' Friendship University, Moscow*, 1995.

217

[10] R. K. Boel, N. K. Talat. Performance analysis and optimal threshold policies for queueing systems with several heterogeneous servers and Markov modulated arrivals. *Katholik University, Belgium*, 1997.

[11] L. Breuer. The Periodic BMAP/PH/c Queue. *Queueing Systems*, **38**(1): 67–76, 2001.

[12] L. Breuer. An EM Algorithm for Batch Markovian Arrival Processes and its Comparison to a Simpler Estimation Procedure. *Annals of Operations Research*, **112**, 2002.

[13] L. Breuer, A. Dudin, and V. Klimenok. A Retrial BMAP/PH/N System. *Queueing Systems*, **40**(4): 431–455, 2002.

[14] G. Brouns Optimal control of routing to two parallel finite capacity queues or two parallel Erlang loss systems with dedicated and flexible arrivals. *University of Amsterdam*, 2002.

[15] D. Y. Burman, D. R. Smith. An asymptotic analysis of a queueing system with Markov modulated arrivals. *Operations Research*, **34**: 105–119, 1986.

[16] T. Crabill, D. Gross, M. J. Magazine. A classified bibliography of research on optimal design and control of queues. *Operation Research*, **25**: 219–232, 1977.

[17] D. Driankov, H. Hellendoorn, M. Reinfrank. An introduction to fuzzy control. *Springer-Verlag, Berlin, New York*, 1993.

[18] A. N. Dudin, V. I. Klimenok. Optimal admission control in a queueing system with heterogeneous traffic. *Operations Research Letters*, **31**: 108–118, 2003.

[19] A.N. Dudin, B.D. Choi, Y.H. Chung. The $BMAP/SM/1$ retrial queue with controllable operation modes. *European Journal of Operational Research*, **131**: 16–30, 2001.

[20] D. V. Efrosinin, V. V. Rykov. Numerical analysis of optimal control policies for queueing systems with heterogeneous servers. *Information processes*, **2**(2): 252–256, 2002.

[21] D. V. Efrosinin, L. Breuer. Threshold behavior of optimal policies in controlled queueing systems. *DCCN'03 workshop in Moscow*, 2003.

[22] D. V. Efrosinin. Threshold phenomenon in controlled retrial $MAP/PH/K$ queue with heterogeneous servers. *Trier University*, 2003.

[23] M. C. Fu, S. I. Marcus, I-J. Wang. Monotone optimal policies for a transient queueing staffing problem. *Institute for Systems Research*, 1998.

[24] P. Glasserman, D. D. Yao. Monotone structure in discrete event systems. *Wiley Series*, 1994.

[25] Y. He, M. Fu, S. Marcus. Simulation-based algorithms for average cost Markov decision Processes. *Technical report, University of Maryland*, 1999.

[26] S. K. Hipp, U. D. Holzbaur. Decision processes with monotone hysteretic policies. *Operations Research*, **36**(4) ,1988.

[27] R. A. Howard. Dynamic programming and Markov processes. *Wiley Series*, 1960.

[28] W. S. Jewell. Controllable semi-Markov Processes. *Cybernetics*, **4**: 97–137, 1967.

[29] V. V. Kalashnikov. Mathematical methods in queuing theory. *Kluwer*, 1994.

[30] F. P. Kelly. Routing in circuit switched networks: optimization, shadow prices and decentralization. *Applied Mathematics*, 1987.

[31] M. Yu. Kitaev, V. V. Rykov. Controlled queueing systems. *CRC Press, New York*, 1995.

[32] L. Kleinrock. Queueing Systems. Volume I: Theory. *New York, Wiley*, 1975.

[33] G. Koole. A simple proof of the optimality of a threshold policy in a two-server queueing system. *Systems Control Letters*, **26**: 301–303, 1995.

[34] K. R. Krishnan, T. J. Ott. State dependent routing for telephone traffic: theory and results. *Proceedings of the IEEE Conference on Decision and Control*, 1986.

[35] P. Langrock, W. W. Rykow. Methoden und Modelle zur Steurung von.Bedienungssystemen. *Handbuch der Bedienungs theorie, Berlin, Akademie-Verlag* **2**: 422–486, 1984.

[36] R. L. Larsen. Control of multiple exponential servers with application to computer systems. *Ph.D. thesis, University of MD*, 1981.

[37] R. L. Larsen, A. K. Agrawala. Control of a heterogeneous two-server exponential queueing system. *IEEE Transactions on Software Engineering*, **9**(4): 522–526, 1983.

[38] L.-M. Le Ny, B. Tuffin. A simple analysis of heterogeneous multi-server threshold queues with hysteresis. *Institut National de Recherche en Informatique, France*, 2000.

[39] O. H. Lerma, J. B. Lassere. Discrete-Time Markov Control Processes. *Applications of Mathematics, New-York*, 1996.

[40] O. H. Lerma, J. B. Lassere. Further topics on discrete-time Markov control processes. *Application of Mathematics, New-York*, 1999.

[41] W. Lin, P. R. Kumar. Optimal control of a queueing system with two heterogeneous servers. *IEEE Transactions on Automatic Control*, **29**: 696–703, 1984.

[42] S. Lippman. Applying a new device in the optimization of exponential queueing systems. *Operations Research*, **23**: 687–710, 1975.

[43] S. Lippman. Semi-Markov decision processes with unbounded rewards. *The Mathematical Scientist*, **19**(7): 717–731, 1973.

[44] F. V. Lu, R. F. Serfozo. $M/M/1$ Queueing decision processes with monotone hysteretic optimal policies. *Operations Research*, **32**: 1116–1132, 1984.

[45] H. P. Luh, I. Viniotis. Optimality of threshold policies for heterogeneous server systems. *Raleign, North Carolina State University*, 1990.

[46] H.P. Luh, I. Viniotis. Threshold control policies for heterogeneous server systems, *Mathematical Methods of Operations Research*, **55**: 121–142, 2002.

[47] D. M. Lucantoni. New results on the single server queue with a batch Markovian arrival process. *Communications in Statistics, Stochastic Models*, **7**(1): 1–46, 1991.

[48] D. M. Lucantoni, K. S. Hellstern, M. F. Neuts. A single-server queue with server vacations and a class of non-Renewal arrival processes. *Advantage of Applied Probability*, **22**: 676–705, 1990.

[49] H. Mine, S. Osaki. Markovian Decision Processes. *Elsevier*, **XI**: 142, 1970.

[50] V. Naoumov, U. R. Krieger, and D. Wagner. Analysis of a multi-server delay-loss system with a general Markovian arrival process. *Matrix-analytic methods in stochastic models, Flint, MI, Dekker, New York*, 43–66, 1997.

[51] M. F. Neuts. Markov chains with applications in queueing theory, which have a matrix-geometric invariant probability vector. *Advanced Applied Probability*, **10**: 185–212, 1978.

[52] M. F. Neuts. Matrix-geometric solutions in stochastic models. *The Johns Hopkins University Press, Baltimore, London*, 1981.

[53] M. F. Neuts. Structured stochastic matrices of M/G/1 type and their applications. *New York etc.: Marcel Dekker*, 1989.

[54] R. Nobel. Hysteretic and heuristic control of queueing systems. *Vrije University, Phd dissertation*, 1998.

[55] R. Nobel, H. C. Tijms. Optimal control of a queueing system with heterogeneous servers. *IEEE Transactions on Autom. Control*, **45**(4), 2000.

[56] R. Nobel. Optimal control of an $M^X/G/1$ queue with varying arrival rate and service mode. *Motable Publications, Inc., Vrije University, Amsterdam*, 1995.

[57] A. B. Piunovskiy. Optimal control of random sequences in problems with constraints. *Kluwer Academic Publishers*, 360, 1997.

[58] M. L. Puterman. Markov Decision Process. *Wiley series in Probability and Mathematical Statistics*, 1994.

[59] M.I. Reiman. Optimal control of a heterogeneous two server queue in light traffic. *AT&T Bell Labs., Murray Hill, NJ*, 1989.

[60] M.I. Reiman, B. Simon. Open queueing systems in light traffic. *Mathematical Operations Research*, **14**: 26–59, 1989.

[61] Sh. Ross. Applied probability models with optimization applications. *Holden Day, San Francisco*, 1970.

[62] Z. Rosberg, A.M. Makowski. Optimal routing to parallel heterogeneous servers - small arrival rates. *Transactions on automatic control*, **35**(7): 789–796, 1990.

[63] Z. Rosberg, P. Varaiya, J. Walrand. Optimal control of service in tandem queues. *IEEE Transactions on Automatic Control*, **27**: 600–610, 1982.

[64] V. V. Rykov. Markov decision processes with finite state and decision spaces. *Probability Theory and its Applications*, **11**(2): 302–311, 1966.

[65] V. V. Rykov. Controllable queueing systems (In Russian). *Itogi nauki i techniki. Teoria verojatnostey i Matematicheskoy Statistiki. Teoreticheskaia Kibernetika*, **12**: 45-152, 1975. There is English translation in Journal of Soviet Mathematics.

[66] V. V. Rykov. On monotonicity conditions for optimal policies for controlling queueing systems. *Autom. and Remote Control*, **60**(9): 1290–1301, 1999.

[67] V. V. Rykov. Monotone Control of Queueing Systems with Heterogeneous Servers. *QUESTA*, **37**: 391–403, 2001.

[68] B. Sandjai, G. Koole. On the structure of value functions for threshold policies in queueing models. *University of Amsterdam*, 2002.

[69] R. Schassberger. Warteschlagen. *Wien-New York, Springer-Verlag*, 1973.

[70] L. Sennott. Stochastic dynamic programming and control of queueing systems. *New York, Wiley*, 328, 1999.

[71] R. F. Serfozo. An equivalence between continuous and discrete time Markov decision processes. *Operations Research*, **27**: 616–620, 1979.

[72] S. Shenker, A. Weinrib. Asymptotic analysis of large heterogeneous queueing systems. *Bell Communication Research*, 1988.

[73] Sh. Stidham Jr. Optimal control of admission to a queueing system. *IEEE Transactions on Automatic Control*, **30**: 705–713, 1985.

[74] Sh. Stidham Jr., R. Weber, A survey of Markov decision models for control of networks of queues. *QUESTA*, **13**: 291–314, 1993.

[75] H. C. Tijms. Stochastic models. An algorithmic approach. *John Wiley and Sons*, 1994.

[76] H. C. Tijms. Stochastic modeling and analysis. A computational approach. *John Wiley and Sons*, 1986.

[77] D. Topkis. Minimizing a submodular function on a lattice. *Operations Research*, **26**(2): 305–321, 1978.

[78] R. Weber. On a conjecture about assigning jobs to processors of different speeds. *IEEE Transactions on Automatic Control*, **38**: 166–170, 1993.

[79] F. Wolf, G. Danzig. Markov chains and linear programming. *Cybernetics*, **4**: 86–96, 1967.

[80] J. Walrand. A note on 'Optimal control of a queueing system with two heterogeneous servers'. *Systems Control Letters*, **4**: 131-134, 1984.

[81] I. Viniotis, A. Ephremides. Extension of the optimality of a threshold policy in heterogeneous multi-server queueing systems. *IEEE Transactions on Automatic Control*, **33**: 104-109, 1988.

[82] C. Zhang, J. S. Baras. A new adaptive aggregation algorithm for infinite horizon dynamic programming. *Technical research report, the Center for Satellite and Hybrid Communication Networks*, 2001.

[83] R. Zhang, Y. A. Phillis. Fuzzy routing of queueing systems with heterogeneous servers. *IEEE Robotics and Automation*, **3**: 2340–2345, 1997.

Acknowledgements

The fundamental idea for the elaboration of new analysis technique in the field of the controlled queueing systems goes back to Prof. Vladimir Rykov, whose basic idea motivates for further investigation in this area of mathematics. During the process of development he continued helpful scientific discussions and in every way support this work. I would like to express my sincere gratitude and appreciation.

Many thanks go to Prof. Dieter Baum for refereeing this book and his important remarks about the structure and scientific accuracy. Also I would like to express him my hearty thanks that he gave me a chance to work in the area of mathematical research and complete my thesis in Trier University.

Also I would like to express my sincere appreciation to Dr. Lothar Breuer for his helpful comments and discussions that led to a significant improvement in the present research.

Further, I would like to thank Prof. Wolfgang Sendler for refereeing this book.

Separately I thank Dr. Norbert Müller for his helpful advises how to handle the Linux software, and system administrator Oleg Gaier for his professional and quick help in case of software fallback and hardware failure.

Finally, I would like to thank my wife Natasha that she has shown interest in my work, and she not only countenanced me during the process of thesis development but also she helped me greatly with a translation into English and German.

www.ingramcontent.com/pod-product-compliance
Lightning Source LLC
LaVergne TN
LVHW022308060326
832902LV00020B/3342